T0329548

"I think we're too comfortable in our assumption that it has been mended. Rather, I think the conditions are setting us up for another very real crisis somewhere."
Richard Meddings

"Arguments are even being made that banks should be allowed to regulate themselves. Imagine."
Adrian Blundell-Wignall

"Look, being a … risk compliance guy means you are sitting there and you are watching all the kids in the pool and you know somebody is doing something they shouldn't be doing in the pool but you don't know who the hell it is."
Michael Hintze

"For me it was more about who's making money, and why is he is making money, and can he explain to me in an intuitive way how he is making it?"
John Breit

"But whether we really need a regulatory rulebook with more than 10,000 pages (Dodd-Frank), I wonder."
Hugo Bänziger

"I don't know how many pages of forms would give you the information that you get from meeting somebody face to face and asking some pertinent questions."
Paul Bostok

CRISIS WASTED?

Leading Risk Managers on Risk Culture

Frances Cowell
Matthew Levins

WILEY

This edition first published 2016
© 2016 John Wiley & Sons, Ltd

Registered office
John Wiley & Sons Ltd, The Atrium, Southern Gate, Chichester, West Sussex, PO19 8SQ, United Kingdom

For details of our global editorial offices, for customer services and for information about how to apply for permission to reuse the copyright material in this book please see our website at www.wiley.com.

All rights reserved. No part of this publication may be reproduced, stored in a retrieval system, or transmitted, in any form or by any means, electronic, mechanical, photocopying, recording or otherwise, except as permitted by the UK Copyright, Designs and Patents Act 1988, without the prior permission of the publisher.

Wiley publishes in a variety of print and electronic formats and by print-on-demand. Some material included with standard print versions of this book may not be included in e-books or in print-on-demand. If this book refers to media such as a CD or DVD that is not included in the version you purchased, you may download this material at http://booksupport.wiley.com. For more information about Wiley products, visit www.wiley.com.

Designations used by companies to distinguish their products are often claimed as trademarks. All brand names and product names used in this book are trade names, service marks, trademarks or registered trademarks of their respective owners. The publisher is not associated with any product or vendor mentioned in this book.

Limit of Liability/Disclaimer of Warranty: While the publisher and author have used their best efforts in preparing this book, they make no representations or warranties with respect to the accuracy or completeness of the contents of this book and specifically disclaim any implied warranties of merchantability or fitness for a particular purpose. It is sold on the understanding that the publisher is not engaged in rendering professional services and neither the publisher nor the author shall be liable for damages arising herefrom. If professional advice or other expert assistance is required, the services of a competent professional should be sought.

Library of Congress Cataloging-in-Publication Data

Cowell, Frances, author.
  Crisis wasted? : leading risk managers on risk culture / Frances Cowell, Matthew Levins.
    pages cm
  Includes bibliographical references and index.
  ISBN 978-1-119-11585-4 (cloth)
  1. Financial services industry–Risk management.   2. Financial institutions–Risk management.   3. Financial risk.   4. Investment advisors.   I. Levins, Matthew, author.   II. Title.
  HG173.C69 2016
  332.1068′1dc23   2015025690

A catalogue record for this book is available from the British Library.

ISBN 978-1-119-11585-4 (hardback)   ISBN 978-1-119-11587-8 (ebk)
ISBN 978-1-119-11586-1 (ebk)   ISBN 978-1-119-11588-5 (obk)

Cover design: Wiley
Cover image: (c) andrey_l/Shutterstock

Set in 13.5/15pt BemboLtStd by Aptara, New Delhi, India
Printed in Great Britain by TJ International Ltd, Padstow, Cornwall, UK

Frances dedicates the work to Josie.
Matthew dedicates the work to Sonia.

Contents

Preface

In a Paris café in April 2013, the conversation turned to how the financial services industry was shaping up following the global financial crisis. We – Frances and Matthew – shared an uneasy intuition that some developments, especially in regulations – despite the best intentions to the contrary – could have the result of actually making the financial system more fragile. Risk management and governance failures, such as the 2012 London Whale, where JP Morgan incurred massive losses in CDS contracts, and similarly massive losses in 2008 at Société Générale caused by a rogue trader in stock index derivatives, continue to happen, suggesting that the professional risk management put in place by large, sophisticated organisations was not working as it should.

There was a sense that an opportunity was being wasted and the debate about what was needed to reinforce financial stability was somehow being hijacked by a combination of popular mis-information, political short-sightedness and special interests. But was this merely a perception stemming from our common perspective? What did others think?

From casual conversations, it was evident that many friends and colleagues shared our views, prompting questions about how widely they were shared outside our circles. In particular, what other factors were operating that we were perhaps unaware of? What extra insights could be had from the best informed market participants and observers?

Matthew proposed a formal exercise: to ask those who were most caught up in it as it all happened. The transcripts of the conversations would result in a readable and substantial book to make available to decision-makers, in the financial services industry and elsewhere, insights from the inside point of view, thereby leading to a more

constructive and informed debate and perhaps even influencing decisions in favour of sensible regulation that would reinforce stability not
undermine it.

Both having been risk takers turned risk managers, in banking and
investment management respectively, since the early 1980s, we had
therefore lived through a number of financial crises. This experience
allowed us to select and engage an interesting and impressive faculty
of interviewees, and to pose good, pointy questions that would fuel
debate.

We reasoned that, like us, our readers would want to know why
some developments since the crisis have been so disappointing. Like
us, they would like better to understand the sub-agendas that operate on decision-making in financial organisations, their regulators and
supervisors; to leverage the perspectives and insights of insiders and to
understand what is really going on.

Constructive debate necessarily entails a forward-looking orienta-
tion. That said, given that the aim is to mitigate the effects of a future
financial crisis, reflection on past events is inevitable and can be instruc-
tive. But the past must be kept in perspective, since the conditions that
prevailed then will not be repeated exactly in the future. To paraphrase
the ubiquitous risk warnings in prospectuses, the past is not necessarily
a guide to what will happen in the future. Learn from the past, but
don't extrapolate from it.

Our first steps were to gather initial feedback and ideas – for practical execution as well as to crystallise our thinking about issues we
should address and that would emerge during our inquiry. In doing
this, we were struck by the general enthusiasm for the project (only
one person was not whole-heartedly supportive). This was of course
due partly to its likely commercial appeal, but more important was that
so many people saw it as a project that needed to happen. It seemed
that even more people than we had imagined agreed that a new level
of debate was called for.

Themes and questions

The next challenge was to decide how structured or otherwise the
conversations should be. Certainly, readers would benefit from some

comparability between the views of each interviewee, which suggests some structure; but interviews that are too constrained or structured would risk limiting the potential for unique insights. What people choose to talk about is as important as what they say.

This led to the idea of common themes, or threads, which would connect the conversations while allowing scope for each interviewee to address the issue closest to his or her heart. The themes were thus conceived as parameters rather than boundaries.

In developing the themes, we were keen to leap-frog arguments that are already well aired, such as conflicts inherent in the way many investment bankers are rewarded. But where we found that we could add a new perspective to an existing debate, we have done so, and so we include themes such as the complexity of models for valuation and risk, contradictions in regulatory regimes and possible unintended consequences.

Lots of "brainstorming" and plenty of war stories later, about 20 somewhat inter-connected themes emerged. These in turn boiled down to three macro themes: behaviour, models and regulation.

Within each theme, the challenge in framing the questions was to be specific enough to give the interviewees something to get their teeth into, but open enough to be relevant to more general issues.

Behaviour, the first theme, covers organisations and the people who work in them – what is increasingly referred to as organisations' risk culture: how it regards risk. A good indication of an organisation's attitude to risk is the status it accords risk management. This seemed to us a good place to start our questions too. Our experience of working in different organisations told us that this is about more than the organisational hierarchy, it is also about the relationship between the risk manager and risk takers – at all levels of the organisation, from the dealer and the risk analyst to the CEO and the CRO. For example, how equal are they in the event of a dispute? How equal *can they be*? What mix of personalities works best? What organisational structure works best? Which day-to-day practices work best?

The next bloc of questions is about how well equipped the risk manager is. How much has the organisation invested in the tools, and the skills needed to deploy them effectively, both to measure and report risk, and also to manage it? Aware that many readers are unfamiliar with how risk models work, we have done our best to present these questions in a way that does not demand any technical knowledge. (Technical explanations, for those interested, can be found in the appendices.) We have therefore aimed for questions that steer clear of the arcane details of risk measurement and focus instead on what their users think of them. How useful are the risk reports that inform supervisors, regulators and investors? The world is complex, should the models be too? Should everyone use the same one, or does this lead to herding that exacerbates systemic risk?

The last and most extensive theme concerns regulations. What is likely to work and what is not likely to work? Why? What might be the unintended consequences? Might there be a better way of doing it?

Another challenge was to avoid imposing our views on the interviews. This is easier said than done, since we draw heavily on our own experience to formulate questions. We therefore were at pains to couch questions in as even handed a way as possible, to avoid leading the witnesses. Nevertheless, we acknowledge that the very choice of questions can affect the course of conversations. Even so, as each conversation developed, our views are sometimes, unavoidably, drawn out.

Research

Reading around our themes and talking with friendly experts was an adventure in itself. It uncovered a number of rich veins of research, including valuable early and ongoing work on the theory of regulation, original approaches to understanding and estimating risk appetite and of calibrating market instability, as well as very thoughtful pieces on the pros and cons of analytical versus behavioural ways of managing risk: detailed VaR reports versus an hour in the pub with some traders.

Perhaps the most rewarding was that we learned about a number of innovations that promise to address some tricky problems that came up during our conversations. Because these innovations are concrete evidence that some good has indeed come from the crisis, they seem valuable enough to merit their own chapter. They are a stimulating challenge to the book's title.

For a selection of other books and articles that stood out, interested readers are directed to the Further Reading section.

Engaging the faculty of interviewees

Clearly the interviewees are selected to achieve the right complement of perspectives, without regard for the views that they might hold. They span banking, investment banking and investment management, which together can be thought of as capital formation, capital transfer and capital warehousing. Or, put another way, risk formation, risk transfer and risk warehousing. We regard the three functions as inseparable and co-dependent in a capitalist system in the same way that respiration and photosynthesis are mutually dependent in a world of carbon-based life forms. The views from academia, regulators and supervisors complement practitioners' perspectives.

Cliché it may be, but modern capital markets do operate within a single, global ecosystem. So we sought geographical diversification – though in reality the debate is dominated by North America and Europe, since that is where, for the most part, the crisis happened.

In an important sense, engaging faculty members was the easiest part of the project. Our invitations almost all met with enthusiastic acceptance, including two participants to whom we were unknown before the interviews and to whom we had no formal introduction – cold emails, in effect. This we received as an endorsement: people really believed that the project was needed; we were genuinely flattered that people of such calibre were so supportive! Nevertheless, two were obliged to decline to be interviewed. Unfortunately they were from the same geographical and professional group, which is therefore less represented than we would have liked it to be. Otherwise, the faculty of interviewees is a good illustrative sample of the financial industry.

Execution

Conducting the interviews was always going to be the fun bit of this project, but it was much more fun than either of us anticipated. We were genuinely delighted by how generous our faculty were with their time and the frankness with which they expressed themselves. Their initial enthusiasm did not wane throughout the interviews – if anything, the opposite is true, and we hope this is conveyed in the transcripts you are about to read.

A number of things stand out from the interviews themselves. The first is that nearly all our faculty attribute the success of their careers to close contact with very thoughtful (and often now famous) people. Many had the good fortune to be mentored or otherwise supported by thought leaders in economic and investment theory. But in pondering this luck we remind ourselves of the old adage that one makes one's own luck. If luck was involved, then it was, in each case, at least matched by talent, discipline and hard work. Working with our faculty was correspondingly stimulating and enjoyable.

Another thing that stands out is both the divergence and the commonality of views expressed in the interviews. We sought debate and we got it! It was tempting at times to raise an argument that had been put forward by a previous interviewee, but this impulse had to be contained in the interests of giving approximately equal air time to each point of view, and of not favouring subsequent interviewees over earlier ones. This is more important than it might seem: due to the practicalities of travel schedules, an unfortunate side-effect would have been that it would have favoured some continents over others, and any bias so introduced might therefore have been systematic.

Some observers of the book's gestation wondered aloud about the "tricky" task of deciding in what order interviews should appear: first, last and in the middle. Anyone who has organised, addressed or merely attended a conference or seminar knows how sensitive this can be. Exercising a mix of impartiality and judgement, we took the view that each interviewee, or at least most, would give more emphasis to some themes than to others, and that this would implicitly determine where in the book their interview should sit, once the themes' order in the book had been decided.

For the order of the themes themselves, it seemed logical to apply the order in which questions had been arranged, beginning with behavioural themes, such as the relationship of risk management to the rest of the organisation, followed by what we need to understand about risk tools and risk reports, and what it all means for regulation and policy and how we approach the possibility (or certainty, depending on your point of view) of another financial meltdown. Risk culture features both at the start, with the place of risk management within individual organisations; and at the end, with regulators' increasing interest in risk culture within organisations.

It turned out that each interviewee did tend to favour some themes over others, which is serendipitous, as it means that we were able to avoid that delicate decision and let participants place themselves.

To complete the book, we needed to decide how much and what kind of material we, as "authors", should add. We believe that readers are perfectly capable of deriving their own inferences and conclusions from each interview, so we butted out, keeping our contribution to each interview chapter to a bare minimum. At the same time, each question and each answer derived from a narrative, or specific risk management issue, to which many, if not most, readers would not be privy. The Background chapter aims to provide a sort of primer on the themes, and the issues concerned, so that readers from any background can engage in and follow the conversations with a minimum of footnotes. Some of the background material supposes familiarity with some technical detail that, if included in the text, most readers would find an arcane disruption to the narrative, but cannot be left out entirely. We compromise by giving an intuitive explanation in the appendices.

Setting the Scene opens the book with a reminder of what set off the wave of regulation and reform of financial organisations, and why a new level of informed debate is now needed. Our other contributions are the Innovations chapter and Further Reading section already mentioned, and a final, Interpretation chapter, in which we bring the various themes together and suggest some conclusions.

In Crisis Wasted?, we believe we have succeeded in our aim of drawing out informed opinions. Readers will agree with some of the views expressed and disagree with others. We invite you to express your view on www.riskculture.today. We look forward to hearing from you.

Acknowledgements

The genesis of this book is due to a combination of the global financial crisis of 2007–08 and two collections of conversations with interesting people: *The Super Analysts*[1] by Andrew Leeming, an erstwhile colleague, and Arjo Klamer's *Conversations with Economists*.[2]

As we developed our ideas and worked out the practicalities of preparing and writing the book, we were cheered on by nearly everyone we spoke to. We are particularly grateful to a number of friends and colleagues, past and present, for their encouragement and support.

Apart from giving us the idea for the book, Andrew also gave very generously of his time, encouraging us to benefit from his experience, helping us to avoid plenty of pitfalls and make the most of our resources. Our faculty of interviewees don't know it, but they have Andrew to thank too: he cut the questions that we asked them to think about before the interview down from 20 to five pages!

Andrew, together with John Beggs, Ron Bewley, Jillian Broadbent, Craig Davis, Mike Katz, Mark Lawrence, Rodney Maddock, Kevin Nixon and Peter Warne, all helped crystallise our thinking about the themes and questions, and directed us to useful background material. Ophelia Cowell came up with some helpful suggestions about how to prepare and present our questions to the interviewees. Mark Kritzman treated us to a very stimulating and absorbing hour and a half on topical innovations that have occurred as direct responses to the financial crisis. Gerald Ashley contributed an interesting and very informative conversation about the nature of systemic complexity and how to model it.

Andrew, Angela Campbell, Mike Katz, Mark Lawrence, Jason MacQueen, Rosemary Thorne and Peter Warne suggested and helped arrange contact with our faculty.

Eugenie White, Tom Wheelwright, Malcolm McIvor, Heather Loewenthal and Alberto Arabia all read the work in progress and gave generous, enthusiastic and constructive feedback.

Sonia and Brigitte Levins took on the critical task of transcribing the interviews from their audio format.

Sonia and Alberto held our respective hands.

Thomas Hyrkiel and Werner Coetzee of Wiley made us feel very special throughout the project with their enthusiasm, responsiveness and support. Jeremy Chia, also of Wiley, has been a constructive and very responsive editor.

Most of all, the people who gave their time and not a trivial amount of thought and effort, first to make themselves available to be interviewed and then to help with the hard work of editing the raw transcripts into a form that people will enjoy reading.

We owe a big thank you to each of them. Thank you!

Notes

1 Leeming, A., *The Super Analysts – Conversations with The World's Leading Stock Market Investors and Analysts* (Singapore, Wiley, 2000).
2 Klamer, A., *Conversations with Economists* (Maryland, Rowman & Littlefield, 1988).

About the Authors

Frances Cowell is a specialist investment risk consultant working with R-Squared Risk Management in Paris and London. She is a founding director of the London Quant Group, a not-for-profit that provides a forum for discussion of practical issues in quantitative investment techniques for the investment management industry. She previously worked as an investment manager at NatWest Investment Management in Australia, having helped pioneer risk-controlled trading in the nascent market for financial derivatives in Australia. Following her move to London, she was Head of Investment Risk at Morley Fund Management (now Aviva Investors) and CRO for CCLA Fund Management.

Matthew Levins is a risk consultant with a practice that spans banks in China, Asia and Australia. Previously, he directed trading, broking, capital market and risk practices in Australia, working for leading firms such as the Commonwealth Bank of Australia and Bankers Trust Australia. In the early 1980s, he took a leading role in the nascent market for financial derivatives in Australia. This entailed developing and refining robust decision rules to support underwriting and trading in fixed income swaps and options, as well as equity, soft commodity and foreign exchange options. He effectively helped pioneer much of the work that informs current hedging and risk control in modern banking.

1

Setting the Scene

Between 12 and 21 December 2006 the data for asset-backed securities index futures (ABX 2006-1 AAA spread) showed a small but significant departure from its normal daily pattern of price fluctuations. This coincided with rumours that a trading division of a major US investment bank had expertly quit its collateralised debt obligation (CDO) portfolio. Over the ensuing months, analyst reports began to circulate that led some banks to delve into their loan portfolios to see if they had exposures to these securities. What sparked this activity? The US housing prices had begun to trend down, many "low start" loans were approaching anniversaries when their interest payments would "step up". In February 2007, HSBC recognised the problem in its New York branch with a $10.5 billion charge. Market makers reacted by forcing a 350% increase in volatility.

Hitherto, the originating banks had bundled up these higher interest loans and securitised them. The resulting pools of securitised debt were re-packaged into CDOs, where equity and debt investors could participate in a preferred tranche and trade off a levered return against reduced exposure to losses on default relative to the overall pool of loans. New products were dreamt up, such as funds that borrowed to lever further the promised returns that would rid the originating

1

investment banks of the inventories of higher risk equity tranches that were accumulating in their books.

Underpinning the market were assumptions about average rates of default that these loans would see. The US government had encouraged products like low-start loans as a means of providing home finance to borrowers who had until then been excluded from home ownership. With little credit history to draw on, analysts had to strike an educated guess as to the likely number of defaults. From the beginning of rapid growth in "no-document" loans in 2004, it took until early 2007, when low interest payment inducements were due to expire, for the divergent trend of high defaults to emerge.

Possibly dismissed as "too soon to call", the "low-doc" CDO machine continued to revolve at a breakneck pace. Documentation processes for these instruments, and indeed many other credit derivative contracts, fell way behind. The NY Fed called several round table meetings to gauge the depth of the problem and set an agreed remediation path. Yet new tickets[1] continued, seemingly unabated, to be written.

Re-engineering the higher expected default frequency into securitisation and CDO models showed that these structures were over-promising returns. Higher frequency of defaults, like peeling away the layers of an onion, meant for CDO structures not only that regular interest payments to the investors were jeopardised, but that the expected loss of all capital increased. Curiously to some, the valuation effect was often most damaging in the so-called "super senior" tranches, rated "AAA".

By mid-2007, the approaching savage repricing had yet to occur but the market place seemed to have reached saturation, and the new issues market showed signs of imminent closure. Some structured credit funds managed by the US investment house Bear Stearns imploded. As if to preserve capital, banks began to enforce tighter underwriting standards across their businesses. There was little they could do for loans already "baked into their book", so the emphasis turned to re-financings and holdings of traded securities.

This hardening of underwriting standards saw hitherto high-quality securitisations or revolving finance facilities supported by even low-risk assets, such as portfolios of shopping centres, falter (and borrowers forced to liquidation). Banks also withdrew their support for loan notes issued by securitised vehicles.

Little did they at first realise, but to get the securitised assets off their balance sheets in the first place, the banks were required to provide a standby line of liquidity that would purchase the loan notes should a market buyer not be found. These requirements were, for the most part, an unplanned call on their balance sheets. Liquidity started to become scarcer.

Organisations such as Northern Rock, whose liability management was reliant on an "open" securitisation market, fell to a run by its retail depositors. A Canadian money market fund broke the buck. A CDO fund had to close. Around this time, with sponsorship by the Fed, Bank of America purchased Countrywide, a major West Coast provider of "low doc" loans. Credit markets generally began to sell off in an orderly way, while most other markets adjusted, with a lag, to tightening credit spreads. It was not until the northern winter before equity markets began to reverse their positive trend.

The manufacturers of CDOs to varying degrees financed their warehouses and production lines using repurchase agreements[2] (repos). Again, these contracts took assets and liabilities off balance sheet. But, as with the standby lines in securitisation structures, to maintain contracts off balance sheet the borrower was obliged to top up collateral as its value deteriorated. Liquidity tightened further. Parcels of CDOs were being sold off as repos struggled to be rolled over or renewed. The increased supply of paper for sale saw lower and lower prices register, while waning confidence in the value of CDOs aggravated the liquidity effect. Liquidity became unobtainable for some borrowers.

The pressure to liquidate a difficult-to-value balance sheet became too much for Bear Stearns. In February 2008, it was sold to JP Morgan after the NY Fed established a company to buy $30 billion worth of assets at just 7% of their price immediately before trading in Bear Stearns stock was suspended.

CDOs continued to lose value. Statutory profits and reporting fell hostage to the accounting classification for warehoused stock. With each reporting period, waves of securities became categorised "level 3", automatically requiring greater capital to be assigned to them. As it reeled from these effects, it became increasingly obvious that the banking system in the US was systemically undercapitalised. The Fed and US Treasury stepped in to restore order, but it was not until the decision to allow Lehman Brothers to file for bankruptcy that it became clear that the regulators had overestimated the effectiveness of their regulations.

In 2008 Comptroller Dugan reflected that while "investors should never rely exclusively on credit ratings in making investment decisions, the plain fact is that triple A credit ratings are a powerful green light for conservative investors all over the world".[3] And so it had been that in the preceding period re-packaging of these securities had not only spread throughout the US banks and money market funds, but to US agencies and beyond its shores to the balance sheets of financial institutions in other countries.

Write-downs and illiquidity combined to take down banks that had aggressively made loans to property developers. Icelandic banks failed, with the assets of the three banks taken over by its supervisor equal to more than 11 times the country's GDP – an early indication of the effective limits of financial globalisation. German Landesbanks in time announced their losses and needed to be re-capitalised. In the UK, banks were crippled, partly due to write-downs to goodwill and loan impairment on the balance sheets of recently purchased Dutch banking assets. And so it played out across most of the northern hemisphere and parts of Asia.

From initial insouciance about the prospect of Lehman Brothers filing for Chapter 11 following its death spiral of the preceding months, the act itself led to something of an avalanche throughout the US – investors in money market funds that held now worthless Lehman Brothers debt were unable to redeem shares for their $1 face value. A run on money market funds ensued, clogging the repo market that broker dealers depended on, and obliging the US Treasury to step in to guarantee money market funds. The global insurer AIG also needed volumes of support, as it had been the dominant provider of credit derivatives through its London branch.

Money market funds sought to liquidate assets to meet redemptions and fund the additional collateral now needed to secure financing. At the same time, the margins required in the repo market continued to increase, and it became impossible to use some assets as collateral for loans. Organisations that could, called funds from their foreign affiliates in order to meet the obligations of their US operations. US affiliates, mostly branches, of foreign banks were under even greater liquidity pressure than were local banks, partly because their access to deposits from US citizens and residents was limited. This forced them to raise funds from outside the US, further contributing to international contagion of the liquidity squeeze, with the effect felt most acutely in London.

As valuation of financial assets became more an art than a science, asset markets such as equities were sold down around the world, as agents sought to raise liquidity wherever they could. Major exchanges generally behaved well, but the continued downtrend was further fuelled by investors withdrawing commitments to managed money, leading to the closure of many funds.

Part of the problem in funding liquidity was that some assets pledged as security had been re-hypothecated by holders of the collateral. When collateral was recalled, often the specific paper was unavailable, obliging investors to sell other assets to meet their own margin calls and redemptions.

One consequence of the turmoil was that collateral requirements could not be calculated in the usual way. This is because margins and collateral requirements are calculated using statistical processes that draw on recent asset price return history. The turbulence now prevailing meant that these processes broke down, particularly for non-traded and over-the-counter instruments. Futures exchanges and prime brokers were thus obliged, in effect, to guess the amount of collateral required. This meant that "Chinese walls", intended to avoid conflicts of interests within organisations, were tested, as prime brokers set collateral levels at capitulation points for "clients" who were in some cases part of the same organisation.

Shortly after the failure of Lehman Brothers the system became unmanageable in private hands. Governments, advised by their regulators, stepped in.

All will remember the steps taken by governments to traverse the crisis with the Troubled Asset Relief Program, and ultimately quantitative easing by the Fed in the US, the recapitalisation of British banks with public money, the decision of the Irish government to guarantee all bank deposits (which later led to its call for help from the European Union) and the need for the Swiss authorities to save UBS.

After throwing a TARP-o-line over impaired assets and entities and providing extraordinary amounts of public support, regulators set about digesting the outcomes. The "live laboratory test" of failure presented them with many avenues to follow as they set about re-calibrating regulation and supervisory procedures.

Notes

1 Transactions.
2 An arrangement whereby a bond is sold with a contract to repurchase it at a given date and price in the future. In effect, short-term borrowing.
3 Comptroller Dugan Outlines Steps In Response to Losses by Banks and Investors Holding Tranches of Securities Considered Safe, 27 February 2008, Press Release 2008-22.

2 | Background

I think we're too comfortable in our assumption that it has been mended. Rather, I think the conditions are setting us up for another very real crisis somewhere.

Richard Meddings

Spurred on by bank failures and government rescues in the northern hemisphere, regulators at the global and sovereign state level have embarked upon a decade's work to overhaul the governance of financial institutions. The scope of this enterprise has been immense following the prodigal global financial crisis and its aftermath. Banking regulation has seen new capital measures proposed, new risks identified with derivatives and collateral markets, more conservative balance sheet treatments for "special investment vehicles", efforts to align remuneration with outcomes, and renewed emphasis on the role and culture necessary to support risk activities. Efforts have also entailed forcing products onto exchanges in the name of transparency, but little appears to have been done to invite more cautious trading. Regulators and organisations are, however, focusing on behaviour, culture and risk appetite.

In periods of moderate market stress, complementary risk appetites of different organisations reinforce the relative resilience of the system because of the co-existence of long versus short risk horizons and risk appetites that range from very low to very high. For example, long-term investors are able to stand in as buyers of even the most distressed assets that would add to liquidity pressures for short-term investors. But resilience can, in extreme circumstances, give way to contagion, whereby failure in one part of the system can cause distress in a seemingly unrelated corner.

How and why this happens are questions that many people believe remain open – it may be that the product set of long-term investors is narrower than those in the domain of traders. How to prevent it happening is another; as is to what extent the regulations now coming into force help to improve the stability of the financial system – and protect the wider economy from the worst consequences of instability. These and other questions are the subject of dialogues that make up the next ten chapters.

Conversations with market participants sometimes turn to subjects that are hard for an outsider to follow without some important background. This chapter aims to fill in the background to issues, or themes, that are missing from the conversations themselves.

Each faculty member represents a different point of view from the others, so articulating a unique set of themes. As expected, themes overlap with each other and a number of them recur, which serves to highlight areas of common concern or controversy. To provide context and to juxtapose, as closely as possible, overlapping and related themes, we identify three macro-themes, which we call:

- Behaviour
- Risk modelling and measurement
- Regulation.

Readers will also find in the Appendices more background information about some of the issues and mechanics of risk management within organisations and a basic guide to how some complex products work. Individual terms are given in the Glossary.

Behaviour

Themes that reflect the culture within financial organisations are:

- The role of the risk manager
- Asymmetries of the risk management role
- Professional risk managers
- Independence
- Judgement versus analysis
- Why become a risk manager?
- Risk silos
- Crisis management.

The role of the risk manager

Regulators and investors expect risk management to be pivotal to the operations of financial firms. This requirement is partly due to the leverage the firms are allowed to employ and the rapid and multi-faceted way financial market volatility impacts on the firm. One initiative has been to give more prominence and authority within organisations to the Chief Risk Officer (CRO) than they previously enjoyed. The aim is to enhance the influence of the risk management function, and therefore its presumed effectiveness, as a means of, among other things, containing the organisation's susceptibility to extreme events.

Yet an easy way for organisations to satisfy demands for more focus on risk management can sometimes be to hide behind accepted wisdom, such as "industry best practice", or more generally, the "reasonable person test". An example might be elevating the remuneration of the CRO while containing his real influence by selecting an individual lacking the necessary personal qualities – or simply of not the right calibre – to balance the influence of risk takers. Kaplan and Mikes note in their 2012 article: "For all the rhetoric about its importance and the money invested in it, risk management is too often treated as a compliance issue."[1]

So despite the value now generally accorded risk management, manifest in typically well-resourced and influential risk management functions, we still hear reports of outspoken risk managers being shown the door or simply ignored, for example because they voice disagreement with the firm's strategy.

Asymmetries in the risk management role

One argument is that the occasional over-riding of risk managers is an inevitable consequence of the asymmetries inherent in the risk manager's role: asymmetries of status, information and incentives.

First, it is clear that the risk manager should have equal status with risk takers so that neither is in a position to override the decisions of the other. Some believe that the CRO therefore must be a board-level appointment. Others would go further and say that even this does not guarantee that the CRO will not be over-ridden by the Chief Executive Officer (CEO) or a coalition of other board members.

Second, information about risk-taking activities that is available to the risk manager vis-à-vis the risk taker is inevitably incomplete and delayed. This happens because the risk manager does not receive the same stream of market information and signals that the risk taker does, and as a result he is necessarily at a disadvantage when a position or concentration of risk needs to be challenged.

Third is that the risk manager must command superior or a broader spectrum of skills when compared with specialist divisional heads. For a start, he must be adept in the profit-generating, risk-taking activities he oversees in order to manage the risks they embed. Without a full understanding of the investment manager's or banking divisional head's techniques and strategies and their inter-play with market conditions, the risk manager cannot hope to spot potential areas of weakness and recommend pre-emptive or remedial actions.

Yet even with enhanced status within the organisation, it is not clear why individuals of this calibre would choose to become a risk manager rather than a – usually better paid – trader or portfolio manager. This is especially so, given that the risk manager's job is also more risky: while dealers' and portfolios managers' remuneration profiles combine potentially large gains that are often linked directly to successful risk taking, with losses mostly limited to the loss of the individual's job; the risk manager's job has limited and less visible upside potential (crises averted, losses contained), but plenty of downside risk (being held accountable for all failures of risk management, real and perceived).

Elevation of risk managers' remuneration and alignment of revenue generators' remuneration to longer-termed revenue outcomes can partly address this asymmetry, but by necessity cannot redress it completely.

Professional risk managers

Many very talented people still choose this career. Their career paths have, in the past, tended to start by gaining experience in the operations function of the organisation (where things like settlements, valuations, reconciliations and accounting take place) through performance measurement and analysis, then to risk management – often with the aim of a front office, risk-taking role such as portfolio analyst, manager or trader. The result is that some risk takers have a background in, and therefore sympathy with, risk management priorities. Risk managers, in their turn, understand issues that can cause problems in diverse parts of the organisation.

As more resources are directed to managing risk, we see the emergence of career risk professionals who benefit from specialist technical training, but have little experience of other areas of the organisation, and in some cases see their ultimate career goal in the senior ranks of risk management rather than in risk-taking roles. While some organisations recognise the value of "cross-fertilisation" and take active steps to ensure that risk takers and risk managers gain experience of both, for example, in the course of training of graduate hires, not all do. In the absence of active cross-fertilisation, trust and empathy between risk takers and risk managers can suffer, often to the detriment of the risk manager's influence and utility.

Risk manager independence

It is generally accepted that the risk manager should be independent of the risk-taking activities he oversees. This means that, at a minimum, the risk manager's remuneration must be unrelated to the profit generated by those risk-taking activities. But there are different degrees of independence.

Some organisations see risk management as a sort of collaboration between risk taker and risk manager, whereby the risk manager gives an informed second opinion of risk-taking decisions. Achieving this collabaration entails fairly close and frequent contact between the two, so that the risk manager is constantly aware of what risks are being put in place. In this scenario, the risk manager often relies on the risk taker volunteering information about his activities; while the risk taker has enough confidence in the risk manager to share information freely and to see value in the risk manager's opinions.

Many argue that such close collaboration dulls the risk manager's independence and so could lead to some risks not being scrutinised as closely as they deserve. They argue that risk management should be quite removed from risk-taking activities in order to maintain its objectivity.

The counter-argument is that if the risk manager is too independent he can miss signals, aggravating the asymmetry of information between risk taker and risk manager and eventually reducing the role to that of risk control, depending heavily on risk models and reports rather than a thorough knowledge of the business.

This in turn can foster a "policing" approach to risk management, which at its worst can deteriorate into a game of cat and mouse. Distance between risk managers and risk-taking teams can also deter some talented potential risk managers, who otherwise might have seen it as a step toward a career in investment management or trading.

Judgement v analysis

Regardless of how independent it is, risk oversight clearly needs to be objective. But as with independence, there are degrees of objectivity.

Intuition and objective analysis clearly are both valuable, and most people believe that the ideal is some mix of the two. Yet most risk managers lean toward one or the other, relying mostly on either quantitative risk analyses or judgement. Annette Mikes describes this in her 2011 paper,[2] in which she identifies cultures of "quantitative enthusiasm", dedicated to risk measurement and reporting, and "quantitative scepticism". The latter is oriented primarily to judgement, where risk managers interpret alternative intuitive future economic scenarios and emerging risk issues. Each approach has its adherents and detractors.

Quantitative risk management is characterised by a disciplined process that demands risk managers with excellent technical skills who function within it. It is easy to report, since reports consist mainly of statistics that can be compared over time and across parts of the organisation. Quantitative reports are scalable in that risk measures and portfolios can be added at any time. They are also easily aggregated to the level of the whole organisation, so that it can be represented in terms of its risk exposures. On the other hand, risks that emerge ad hoc are easily missed if the manager is too reliant on pre-specified risk statistics. Being primarily process driven, quantitative risk processes accommodate smoothly the arrival of new risk managers and departure of existing ones. They also tend to encourage a very specialist risk manager career path with less cross-fertilisation with other parts of the organisation.

Judgement-based risk management relies more on key individuals and their experience working with risk takers, drawing from their experience and intuition in order to spot ad hoc risks that may not be captured by pre-defined risk analyses. A feel for the sorts of unanticipated risks that help the organisation to respond quickly and effectively to unanticipated risks is at least as important as advanced technical skills. The ability to communicate clearly both the nature of the risk and how it is managed is critical.

Risk silos

Most people believe that risk is best managed holistically – at the highest level possible so that it takes account of all relevant covariances, inter-dependencies and the causation that amplifies downside risk. But this can be impractical in a very large organisation where the natural response is to "compartmentalise" risk management, for example into silos specialising in things like investment risk (market and credit risk, asset allocation and stock selection risk), liquidity risk, counterparty risk and operations risk. This can introduce the danger that unanticipated sources of risk "fall between the cracks", in that they fail to be captured by any designated risk function. Adding to this, the separation of

accountability into silos for profit centres, budgets and bonus calculations discourages collaboration and risk sharing across departments.

Enterprise-level risk management that links investment, counterparty, operations, legal and compliance, reputational risks and more
is sometimes proposed as a means of ensuring that all risk is "captured" even when it does not fit easily into a defined risk category. But
this may be difficult to implement in practice, for example, because it
demands exceptional skills and complex system support.

Crisis management

Each crisis is different and so by definition is hard to plan for. This
is made even harder because people can behave out of character in a
time of crisis. One of the main tools for estimating exposure to crises
is scenario analyses that simulate the effects of a market event. These
usually draw on data sampled from the past (and so implicitly the aggregate impacts of people's behaviour), but may not take account of how
individuals within the organisation respond.

Human responses to crises can conform to patterns; for example,
with the stress of a major market disruption, managers understandably can lose confidence in the risk information they have to hand: its
completeness can be questioned and information can be regarded as
stale. Extreme caution can take over within individual firms, which,
when aggregated across many actors, exacerbates market illiquidity and
even volatility. As staff move between organisations, often across continents, they bring with them skills and practices, which, together with
the complexity of financial products and models, can contribute to
industry-wide group-think, which can add to contagion.[3] Andrew
Haldane notes in a 2011 speech that "risk perceptions are as important as reality. Behavioural economics tells us that financial crashes can
leave lasting psychological scars on risk-taking."

Modelling and measurement

The faculty identifies five aspects of models and an important measurement issue.

Risk management:

- Subjectivity
- Complexity
- Calibration
- Standardisation
- Mark-to-market valuation.

Risk models – subjectivity

Even the most objective and rigorous models embed some subjectivity. Indeed, the very choice of modelling methodology is necessarily a subjective one, relying on the judgement of a single individual or a small group of individuals. Selection of data sampling, choice of risk metrics, design of stress tests, too, are all products of human judgement. For example, the specification of parameters and data sample for simulation analyses and risk measurement is normally a human input. René Stultz[4] identifies six subjective inputs to risk models that contributed to their apparent failure during the crisis, the second of which is selection of inappropriate risk measures. The result is that objective risk models can actually amplify subjectivity by concentrating judgement-based decisions on the part of a relatively small number of people.

Michael Power, in his 2004 article,[5] writes that "[m]odels and measures would be part of broader organisational narratives of uncertainty" and "[risk management] would depend essentially on human capacities to imagine alternative futures to the present, rather than quantitative ambitions to predict the future". But he qualifies this: "To the extent that process represents the codification of accumulated wisdom, it should be sustained subject to the possibility of constant challenge."

Risk models – complexity

The very complexity of sophisticated models for asset valuation and for risk modelling can be a source of uncertainty and risk if the models are not well-enough understood by those who use them.

Advanced models add value by facilitating asset pricing and risk measurement for sophisticated products that allow organisations to target and manage risk and to improve returns. Analysts with good technical skills can encourage the use of increasingly complex asset and portfolio modelling techniques. The danger is that, as applications and variants of a complex model expand to accommodate "new" or "one-off" transactions, the model can become stretched beyond the scope of its original purpose, which in combination with often inadequate review of the assumptions embedded in it,[6] can lead to mis-estimation of actual exposures, mis-allocation of risk and inefficient hedging. An example is the use of copula[7] analysis in CDO modelling, chronicled by Mackenzie and Spears in their 2012 paper.[8]

Less complex models avoid this problem, but at the possible cost of over-simplifying the nature of risk exposures and thereby failing to capture material sources of risk, often understating it.

Risk models – calibration

It has become clear that many apparent risk model failures were in fact due not to shortcomings in the models themselves, but rather in how they were used. The most obvious misuse was unquestioning reliance on historical data aggravated by selection of inappropriate data intervals. In using historical data samples, risk models in effect extrapolate from the past and so assume that it is a good indication of what the future will be like. René Stultz identifies over-reliance on historical data as the first of his six items.

For example, bankers and investment bankers estimate short-term risks by sampling data from the most recent one or two years using daily observations. Meanwhile, investment managers, with longer investment horizons, usually sample data from the most recent two to five years, using weekly or monthly return observations. This means that, at the onset of the crisis in 2007, the maximum look-back period extended only to 2002, a period of exceptional calm in financial markets, while many look-back periods were much shorter. An obvious remedy to the problem of unrepresentative data samples is to sample data from earlier intervals or from periods that include significant volatility and market stress; but there are two reasons why this is not always satisfactory.

The first is that, even when suitable data going back far enough are available, they may embed (worse) problems of data quality and reliability, especially in less mature markets. For example, to capture, in 2007, the 1987 stock market crash, which is in some respects the last major event in global markets, would have entailed sampling at least 20 years of data.

The second reason is that long data sampling intervals can confound market conditions, such as different currency and interest rate regimes and stock market structures, introducing data that are irrelevant to the future in those markets. For example, a feature of several developed markets in the 1990s was the large-scale privatisation and listing of telecoms and other hitherto publicly owned utilities that changed market structures in important ways. Similarly, European currency and interest rate alignment has changed fundamentally since the late 1980s. In effect, data from 1987 were not necessarily relevant to market conditions prevailing at the onset of the global financial crisis.

Risk models – standardisation

There is an argument that comparable institutions should conform to agreed modelling principles and methodologies. This already happens to an extent: Merton's model for credit risk is considered to be standard by many, if not most, participants; Black-Scholes is generally accepted for option pricing, as are cross-sectional risk factors within variance-covariance models of equity risk. All have achieved the status of accepted wisdom (despite recognised flaws in some).

But organisations still tend to apply their own variations, which can amount to material differences of methodologies. And, just as different risk model methodologies can give different risk measures, even using the same input data, the answer a risk model delivers depends on the data fed into it. So variation of output from one organisation to another can be significant, and indeed, there are valid reasons why they sample from different sets of past data.

But different model variants can cause problems of comparability. Jon Danielsson of the LSE notes in the abstract to a 2014 paper[9]

that "… the potential for different models to provide inconsistent outcomes, is shown to be increasing with and caused by market uncertainty. During calm periods, the underlying risk forecast models produce similar risk readings; hence, model risk is typically negligible.
However, the disagreement between the various candidate models
increases significantly during market distress …"

Some regulators, such as UCITS,[10] demand some degree of standardisation. Others favour limiting the freedom of participants to adjust
inputs to their risk models, for example, by using prescribed data samples spanning 90 days rather than 120 days, or six months versus five
years.

Standardised risk models can certainly simplify compliance and the
regulatory burden of proof for banks; and, for the purposes of comparing bank risk reports, standard models with common settings are
desirable or even imperative.

A counter-argument is that diversity of models and data sampling
methods can add resilience to the system by reducing the tendency of
all organisations to react to a shock in the same way and at the same
time – which exacerbates market volatility.

There is also the danger that, when a majority of participants
use the same or very similar risk measurement methodology, a
flaw or simplifying assumption in the methodology has market-
wide implications, potentially leading to system-wide misallocation of
risk.

Others point out that risk model "standardisation" can stifle innovation in modelling techniques that otherwise might lead to more accurate and valid risk estimation, with the result that design flaws become
entrenched and accepted without question, resulting in a kind of scle-
rosis of risk methodology.

Mark-to-market valuation

Since the crisis, many advocate strict mark-to-market valuation. The
reasoning is that this implicitly recognises unrealised profits and losses
as they occur with market fluctuations. In theory, any liquidation of
a position will simply transform an unrealised profit or loss into a
realised one, with little or no impact on the valuation of the fund or

entity. Mark-to-market valuation is also considered objective and hard to manipulate. But there are some limitations.

The first is that it assumes liquid markets, whereby the most recent traded price on an exchange is never very different from the price at which a position can be traded in practice. The assumption of liquidity can be violated in at least two circumstances. The first is when a position is large relative to the traded volume in the instrument. The second is when the instrument to be traded is itself neither liquid nor can its market price be modelled, or derived, from the prices of other, liquid instruments.

Another issue is that mark-to-market is not appropriate to all types of investments. Just as it implicitly recognises profits and losses as they occur, at the same frequency it recognises the volatility of the instrument or investment – and hence the volatility of the overall portfolio, which can be mis-stated if mark-to-market valuation is carried out too frequently. For example mark-to-market carried out for a position or portfolio daily, weekly or monthly gives quite different measures of volatility, not all of which are relevant to the type of investment in question.

Pension funds with long-term and known liability structures, for example, need not respond to daily fluctuations in market prices, so daily volatility is irrelevant to their risk profiles. Neither do bank loan books, so long as loans are being repaid according to their prescribed schedules. The argument is that frequent marking-to-market can be counter-productive because daily interest rate measures cause a bank's loan portfolio to embed volatility that is irrelevant to its economic value and can give risk to unnecessary trading.

Regulation

The natural response of regulators and policy-makers to the global financial crisis has been to protect both investors and the stability of the financial system by imposing more regulation. Many believe that tighter regulation will be one of the main drivers of the future of the banking and financial services industry. The consequences for financial organisations and products, the financial system and the real economy can be far-reaching and perhaps surprising.

Many believe that some regulations are better conceived than others, and that tighter is not necessarily better. Markus Brunnermeier, in the Executive Summary of his 2009 article,[11] observes: "At the heart of the crisis were highly regulated institutions in regulated jurisdictions. The crisis has involved a regulatory failure as much as anything else. Our solution is not more regulation per se, though that may well be required in some areas, but better and different regulation."

Others see the expansion of regulation as endemic in a system that has become too complex and therefore unmanageable. Greater regulation, with its attendant compliance costs, forces the re-appraisal of business models, which may over time see less complex organisations evolve. For example, organisations with well-developed retail and business banking brands that limit their activities to utilitarian products and shun investment banking and complex trading operations may emerge. As fewer and fewer undertake investment banking or market making, the supply of capital directed to such activities will diminish, reducing the capacity of the market place to be influenced by speculation.

Conversations about regulation raise a wide range of themes about how the regulation is crafted, the direct effects of regulations on organisations, their likely implications for systemic stability, alternatives to the current approach and a number of questions that faculty believe remain open.

- Principles of regulation
  - Rules v principles
  - Complexity of regulation
  - Transparency of institutions and products
- Effects on organisations
  - Burden of compliance – risk managers
  - Burden of compliance – boards of directors
- Risk issues
  - Structured products
  - Caveat emptor
  - Risk horizon
  - Risk transfer
  - Pro-cyclicality
  - Stress tests

- Systemic issues
  - Fragmentation of the global financial system
  - Model harmonisation
  - Moral hazard
  - Too big to fail – break up the banks?
  - Assets and liabilities
  - Regulators and politicians
  - Shadow banking
  - Risk appetite
  - Risk culture.

Rules v principles

Regulation can rely primarily either on pre-defined rules or on principles and judgement.

Rules-based regulation is conceptually simple, but has some drawbacks. Its critics argue that, first, it generally does not adapt well to market evolution. Second, it is prone to complexity and contradiction, as new rules are added and obsolete rules remain in force. Third, fixed rules can be open to gaming, as in the practice of regulatory arbitrage, or circumvention, whereby participants conform to the letter but not the spirit of the regulation.

Some believe it can also introduce a sort of "compliance mindset" on the part of organisations that is characterised by excessive risk aversion, a tendency toward rules-based risk management, where the incentive can be to avoid breaches of rules rather than actively to manage risk, and a reduction in the reward for healthy risk-taking: a sort of "too scared to fail" syndrome.

Principles-based or judgement-based regulation works by defining the spirit of the regulation, imposing the responsibility of practical interpretation on organisations themselves. Disputes about whether an organisation has complied with the intention of the regulation are decided case by case. This can introduce uncertainty for organisations. But its advantage is that it is harder to circumvent. And because its ultimate application is specific to individual cases, it is by definition adaptable to changing conditions.

Complexity

The task of devising individual regulations that are at once simple enough to be widely communicated while still addressing effectively the complexities of modern financial markets and organisations is not straightforward.

Many people favour simple rules, such as limits on bank leverage ratios, that are easy to communicate and comply with and, some argue, hard to circumvent. Others believe that this approach is too simplistic and can give a misleading, often understated, indication of the true risk of banks and investment products, potentially masking critical sources of risk.

Transparency

Many believe that transparency – providing information about organisations and financial products to the market at large – is a better and more robust way of ensuring that financial institutions are properly accountable than by imposing ever more intrusive, and often arbitrary, rules and regulations. The reasoning is that the collective wisdom of a large number of market participants with access to the information they need will exert more effective pressure through market mechanisms, either as shareholders or potential clients, than even very well-crafted regulation.

The counter-argument is that this approach has shown itself to be unreliable, for example shareholders apparently failed to exert a moderating influence on risk taking in banks in the lead-up to the crisis.

So far, the main focus has been on controlling risk and protecting investors through regulation, while the question of transparency receives much less attention. An example of how this can fall short is the information that is available to investors about the risks inherent in investment products, such as funds, trusts and Exchange Traded Funds (ETFs) that they may invest in. Usually this consists of bland and largely substance-free statements about the possibility of the price going either up or down, and exhorting investors to seek professional advice, when information about sensitivities to things like currencies, interest rates, equities and commodity markets would be more useful. Prospectuses have become so long and full of detail that they are effectively inaccessible to most people, with the result that they serve mainly to protect the issuer rather than the investor.

Transparency has also been lacking in the annual reports of the financial organisations themselves: "… the dangers of all this debt grew more ominous because transparency was not required or desired … Massive short-term borrowing, combined with the liabilities unseen by others in the market, heighten the chances that the system could rapidly unravel."[12]

Burden of compliance – risk managers

As regulation becomes more complex and more abundant – and sometimes contradictory – practitioners may struggle to understand or keep up with their compliance obligations. This can reach the point where so much of a firm's resources are concerned with measuring and reporting risk, that interpreting, understanding and managing it necessarily suffer.

A survey conducted by IFI Global[13] of investment and risk professionals in asset management firms, consultants, service providers and banks[14] to gauge the likely effect of the AIFMD[15] found that many participants think that the Directive could actually detract from the efficacy of risk management. Small firms, in particular, who cannot muster the resources for a dedicated in-house risk function, will seek to contain the costs of compliance by reducing the task to a box-ticking exercise and/or by delegating it to the Chief Operating Officer (COO) or the compliance team – thereby complying with the letter but not the spirit of risk management requirements.

Douglas Flint of HSBC in August 2014 remarked that "unprecedented" demands on banks increase red tape and deter managers from pursuing the risks necessary to carry out their main business.

Many fear that one consequence of increasing complexity and costs to organisations caused by the number of regulatory requirements is likely to be an increase in bank charges, which will disproportionately affect small investors and retail bank customers potentially increasing the number of "unbanked" individuals.

Burden of compliance – boards of directors

Tightened regulation will sharply increase the demands on, and work-load of, members of bank boards, who may well currently lack the ability to fulfil them competently. For example, in addition to existing responsibilities, boards are expected to command a good understanding of a range of operations-level practices, some of which – such as risk estimation techniques, pricing and valuation methodologies – demand advanced technical expertise.

At the same time, members of bank risk committees are expected to oversee ongoing improvement in risk culture throughout the organisa-tion. Yet for an individual board member in a large global organisation to know how the risk culture operates in the context of local customs and mores in all corners of the organisation is herculean, and may well be unrealistic. Together with responsibility for details that, arguably, are best attended to by managers, the burden can become a deterrent to recruiting the most talented directors.

Surveys commissioned by the Institute of International Finance (IIF) of responses to the AIFMD, among others, have remarked on the relative lack of risk management expertise within the boards of invest-ment funds. One reported consequence is that it impedes the capacity of the board to pose informed questions. Another is that information communicated to boards is often inadequate and not timely enough to support conclusions about what risks are being taken.

Structured products

Structured products have received considerable attention since the cri-sis of 2007–08, becoming associated with complexity, opacity and in some cases, regulatory or ratings arbitrage. One issue has been the prac-tice of bundling investments of varying quality within multi-tranched products, with the aim of reducing the risk of the whole through the diversification so achieved. A result is that the true risk to investors is sometimes understated. This can happen when risk is estimated using flawed assumptions of correlations, for example by estimating them from unrepresentative data samples and assuming uniform correlations for all possible market conditions.

Another issue has been that the salesmen and financial advisers who sell investment products often are not fully aware of the risks to the investor, further increasing the likelihood of their unsuitability.

Caveat emptor

While banks are – with reason – frequently accused of mis-selling financial products to consumers, it can be argued that they were mainly responding to market demand. For example, the challenge of delivering suitable high yield products with low risk in low interest rate environments led to some very complex products being sold to relatively unsophisticated investors. The principle of buyer beware places some responsibility on the part of investors who could have been expected to question more thoroughly the risks they assumed: "… the breeches stretched from the living room to the boardroom" (sic).[16]

Another point of view is that complex products were so lucrative to bankers and investment bankers that they "created" demand for them, taking advantage of the relative lack of sophistication of many investors.

Risk transfer

The anticipated benefit of credit and asset-backed derivatives was that they enabled risk to be transferred away from banks and toward investors with the appetite to hold it – thereby freeing up capital for more lending to the real economy. Alan Greenspan observed that "… the development of credit derivatives has contributed to the stability of the banking system by allowing banks, especially the largest, systemically important banks, to measure and manage their credit risks more effectively".[17] But in the event, they served to spread the contagion. A reason sometimes given for this is that much of the trading of the instruments took place on secondary markets between financial institutions rather than with either the originator or the ultimate users of the products. "Millions of derivatives of all types between systemically important financial firms were unseen and unknown when the financial system nearly collapsed."[18]

Pro-cyclicality

Pro-cyclicality, or positive feedback loops, is where a fall in an asset price stimulates selling in that asset, and consequently further price deterioration and more selling. This can happen because the holding was itself bought with borrowed funds that are subject to margin calls, or because it is a derivative position, also subject to frequent margin calls that trigger selling when prices fall. It is the bête-noire of regulators, supervisors and central bankers because in stressed market conditions the effect is amplified as the prices of many assets fall in tandem.

Pro-cyclicality is embedded in many parts of the financial system and can be aggravated by established practices. For example, margins on derivatives and geared investments tend to be levied according to the expected volatility of the underlying security – which is, in turn, usually estimated from recent past price behaviour. Since price volatility usually declines in periods of rapid price escalation that often precede bouts of market stress, this virtually ensures that, in the event of a shock, margins that have been posted will be inadequate.

Stress tests

Regulators and organisations rely on stress tests as objective risk measures, despite practical flaws. US bank regulators, for example, argue that Basel III rules are, in themselves, not enough to ensure that banks are in a position to endure a severe economic shock. For this reason they complement the already-complex Basel rules with a series of stress tests that are designed to measure banks' resilience in extreme circumstances. Larry Wall of the Federal Reserve Bank of Atlanta notes that the Basel III rules can demand up to 200,000 risk buckets.[19]

He also notes that the usefulness of stress tests is limited by how well they are designed and specified. For example, the new stress tests rely on accounting data, so will show only accounting measures of resilience, which might not reflect the whole risk profile of the bank. It is widely recognised that poorly specified stress tests can give a false sense of security, which can be worse than nothing at all.

Fragmentation

A response to the perceived contagion of bank failures from one juris-diction to another is to "ring fence" bank activities within jurisdic-tions. Ring fencing demands that subsidiaries of foreign banks set aside enough capital and liquidity to provide a buffer for their risk-taking activities in that jurisdiction. The aim is to ensure that should, say, a US bank fail then its UK subsidiary will continue to operate and so not contaminate the UK banking system through its connections with local institutions and lending activities. Dan Tarullo of the US Federal Reserve notes that over the past 20 years, foreign banks in America have become "more concentrated, more interconnected, and increas-ingly reliant" on footloose wholesale funding, so are perceived as more threatening to local systemic stability than local banks.[20]

This is superficially appealing, but a concern is that it negates the benefits of cross-border banking, such as diversification, whereby the foreign operations of international banks provide mutual support for each other in most market conditions. According to this argument, isolating, or ring fencing, activities in this way actually weakens the bank's ability to deal smoothly with a market event, and increases the likelihood that it might suffer liquidity issues that demand assistance from the local central bank – without necessarily solving the problem of contagion.

The alternative is to craft global rules that would allow the resolu-tion of big international banks from the top down, and to this end the Financial Stability Board (FSB) has produced a detailed set of principles showing how regulators could work together to achieve a top-down resolution of an international bank that applies to the parent as well as to all its international subsidiaries. Similarly, the Bank of England and the US Federal Deposit Insurance Corporation issued a joint paper outlining plans to work together if any of their big banks were to fail.[21]

But such cross-border cooperation demands considerable trust, which tends to erode in times of crisis, so even if a comprehensive multilateral agreement could be reached on how to treat the foreign operations of international banks, it may not work in practice when a crisis occurs.

A 2013 article in *The Economist*[22] agrees with the view that forc-ing big banks to operate as networks of stand-alone subsidiaries would hinder their ability to allocate capital most efficiently, and with the argument that ring fencing potentially adds to systemic fragility by reducing banks' ability to diversify risk and by preventing them from shifting capital from strong subsidiaries to those in need. It goes further, pointing out that it could also distort competition by forcing international banks to hold more capital in aggregate than their domestic counterparts, with the net effect of potentially crimping their capacity to lend to the real economy.

Model harmonisation

The limitations of allowing banks to rely on their own models, rather than some standard versions, to estimate the risk of their asset portfolios is now recognised. An obvious solution is to impose a common model which all regulated banks must apply. For example, Economic Capital is a standardised, objective risk measure across diverse banking operations that is used to facilitate aggregation of bank-level risk, as well as to underpin decisions regarding capital allocation and risk-adjusted performance-based remuneration.

While this facilitates comparisons between banks and can eliminate the danger of underestimation by some banks relative to others, any shortcomings in the common model will be amplified throughout the economy – or economies – leading to unrecognised fragility in the system. Jon Danielsson, in July 2014, observed that "… the potential for different models to provide inconsistent outcomes … [increases with and is caused by] … market uncertainty. During calm periods, the underlying risk forecast models produce similar risk readings; hence, model risk is typically negligible. However, the disagreement between … models increases significantly during market distress, further frustrating the reliability of risk readings."[23]

There is also the danger that the model becomes harder to question, because it is generally understood to be in some sense the "official" model. Some therefore favour some diversity of risk models, which they believe contributes to important system-wide resilience by avoiding the danger of many organisations trading the same things at the same time.

A related proposal is to disclose and share risk management principles and processes between individual financial organisations. This departs from the usual practice of regarding risk management as a part of the organisation's intellectual property, and therefore a secret to be shared selectively. The fact of openly sharing risk management information will, according to this argument, encourage the development of industry-wide minimum standards of organisation-level risk review and governance. Ongoing disclosure is intended to bring to bear the forces of competition and encourage pressure from bank customers and shareholders and, insofar as institutions benefit from public guarantees, the general public. The aim is to encourage banks continually to seek to improve and strengthen their risk management capabilities in order to enhance their competitive advantages and to avoid being seen to "fall behind".

Moral hazard

Moral hazard is the disengagement of reward and accountability: the "heads I win, tails you lose" phenomenon that can result from government guarantees for financial institutions. Organisations that benefit from an implicit or explicit government guarantee are inherently encouraged to take on more risk than they would do without the guarantee. If the risks pay off, the organisation reaps the benefits, while if losses occur as a result of the extra risk, then the government steps in to help, thus disengaging the incentive to take risk from any negative consequences of doing so.

A possible solution is to remove government guarantees so that banks bear full responsibility for their risk-taking activities. Many believe that this would introduce unbearable systemic risk, as failed banks cause further failures through their interconnectedness with other financial institutions and with the real economy.

The other approach is to maintain government guarantees, but on condition that the organisation complies with regulation and is subject to close supervision of its activities and risk levels.

Regulators and supervisors so far seem to have responded by addressing the symptoms of moral hazard through, for example, minimum capital ratios and tightened risk management controls for banks that are judged to be systematically important. The danger is that these restrict the organisation's ability to fulfil its primary function of supporting activity in the real economy while not necessarily dealing with risk.

Once in place, tighter controls can be hard to relax, even if they are ineffective or counter-productive. In an April 2012 report, *The Economist* quips that "[o]ften what starts out as a post-crisis sticking plaster becomes a permanent feature of the system". It recalls that Walter Bagehot argued that "… financial panics occur when the 'blind capital' of the public floods into unwise speculative investments". The authors believe that "…well-intentioned reforms have made this problem worse".[24]

Too big to fail – break up banks

It is argued that some institutions are so large or systemically important that they cannot be allowed to fail because of the impact their failure would have on the financial system and in the real economy.

Some would add that some institutions are inevitably too big to fail because they support international trade and globalisation. For example, Deutsche Bank needs to be big because Siemens is big and it wants to be Siemens' main bank.

Another aspect of the too big to fail phenomenon is that organisations that dominate have a certain amount of pricing power vis-à-vis their competitors, which can stifle competition and increase costs for investors and consumers. Indeed, traders who work in such environments have been observed to behave differently from those working in similar roles in smaller organisations, often engendering an organisation-wide culture of arrogance.

The corollary of the too big to fail institution is that a bank is effectively a utility, in that it provides basic and essential public services by virtue of its importance to the payments system. According to this view, bankers' pay should therefore be commensurate with other utilities; in other words, they should be paid like post office or electricity workers. Under this scenario, the utility would conduct specified activities but not engage in unrelated risk-taking activities, which would be carried out in a separate entity. In effect, the banks would be broken up.

Adrian Blundell-Wignall of the OECD argues that breaking up the banks would be more effective and more efficient than more regulation. He notes that "[b]efore the GFC, many thought hedge funds and private equity firms – the unregulated parts of the financial sector – would be the cause of any crisis, when in fact it was the regulated sector that caused the trouble". He believes that breaking up banks is a better approach than ever-stricter capital requirements: "Assets, liabilities and capital should not be able to shift among the trading and retail arms of banks."[25]

Assets and liabilities

Some recent academic discussion favours regulating the liabilities of financial organisations and leaving the assets to look after themselves. The argument is that liabilities determine both the liquidity and solvency of a financial institution – and therefore the assets in which it invests and how they are managed, not the other way around.

According to this view, an institution is defined by its liabilities. For example, the liabilities of a bank are necessarily short term, including demand deposits, term deposits, inter-bank borrowing and calls for margins on collateral for derivative positions. By contrast, pension funds have much longer dated liabilities and investment objectives.[26] Liabilities-driven regulation for the two types of organisation would therefore differ much more than regulation aimed at their respective asset portfolios.

Both John Cochrane[27] and Gary Gorton[28] argue that because regulation aimed at liabilities targets directly the immediate cause of failures, it is more robust and avoids much of the complexity of trying to regulate asset portfolios, whether of banks or non-banks. It would become an investor relations task to convince institutional investors that managers have sufficiently quantified and assessed assets for the impairment occasioned by specific asset failure, economic downturns and crises.

Unless competence was displayed it would be difficult for an organisation to secure liabilities to support their business plans and model. In the case of deposits attracting a state guarantee, the guarantor would invoke, *inter alia*, certain asset underwriting restrictions that fashion a more utilitarian service model for the payments system and warehousing of precautionary balances. Transparency and simplicity would be the hallmarks of such institutions.

Regulators and politicians

According to the Goodwill Theory of Government, the popular belief is that, in the event of market failure, the government has to intervene in order to find the solution that maximises social welfare and to act to achieve that solution. Yet the most effective solution may not be the most obvious one. And since politicians have to answer to the electorate, whatever solution they put in place has to be something they can communicate to voters. Some see a danger that this encourages regulators to adopt remedies that have superficial appeal rather than to seek solutions that are constructive and effective (and hard to circumvent) in practice.

A related argument is that government contributes to crises through things like low interest rate environments. Edward Kane adds weight to this view by arguing that political forces can compel even independent central bankers to dampen short-term interest rate rises. He believes that the central banker's political purpose is sometimes to serve as an economic policy scapegoat for incumbent politicians.[29] Investors, including many government and semi-government organisations, foundations and pension schemes, who need to earn income through yield in order to meet their investment objectives, can find themselves obliged to assume more risk than is appropriate to their risk appetite and risk tolerance.

Shadow banking

Shadow banking is a term coined to describe bank-like functions carried out by non-banks. Examples range from prime brokers[30] to credit card and mobile phone transactions, pre-payment cards and on-line payment facilities such as PayPal and some money market funds that can operate like current accounts.

The growth of shadow banking can be seen as a response partly to tighter regulation of banking and investment management, and partly as a natural response to new opportunities opened up by technological innovations, especially in computing and improved communications. Some observers believe that the diversity of services and organisations it produces could be a possible solution to the too big to fail problem, and associated moral hazard.

Risk appetite

Another priority of regulators and supervisors is how to decide how much, and what sorts of, risk to take.

One recommendation to the 2009 Walker Report[31] on corporate governance in the UK is that boards of directors agree with senior management the scale and nature of risk acceptable in pursuit of the organisation's profit objective. The IIF report on Risk Culture[32] cites the necessity of communicating clearly the organisation's risk tolerances at all levels both within the organisation and to outside stakeholders.

Risk appetite has four components:

1. Defining, through objective analysis, how much risk the organisation needs to take in order to meet its profit objectives;
2. Defining how much risk can be tolerated in pursuing the profit objective;
3. Apportioning risk to each profit-generating activity within the organisation, according to agreed decision criteria;
4. Communicating risk appetite to investors, regulators and supervisors, and throughout the organisation, as a means of supporting constructive attitudes to risk and risk culture.

And a question: would they do it with their own money?

Risk culture

Bank supervisors are directing attention to how financial organisations engender and maintain a constructive organisation-wide attitude toward risk.

The IIF Issues Paper, Promoting Sound Risk Culture, 2013, says: "The issue of risk culture remains at the forefront of both the industry and supervisory agendas. Its importance has been highlighted by three recent reports ... and a survey of risk management major financial institutions ..." (sic).

The IIF asserts: "A robust and pervasive risk culture throughout the firm is essential. This risk culture should be embedded in the way the firm operates, and cover all areas and activities, with particular care not to limit risk management to specific business areas or to restrict its mandate only to internal control."[33]

A potentially powerful contribution to more robust risk management lies outside the risk management function. Risk managers must take part in risk-taking decisions, while risk takers should assume responsibility for the risk they take. One faculty member believes that "business unit heads, front office leaders, who are also risk managers ... demonstrate ownership or risk", and another that "[r]isk should be owned in the front line and also discussed at board level and senior management level". Many take the view that holding risk takers responsible for the risks they generate is probably the only sustainable way to encourage them to appreciate the ongoing consequences of their profit-generating activities.

For more discussion about these and other issues, readers are invited to visit www.riskculture.today.

Notes

1 Kaplan, R.S., and Mikes, A., The Big Idea: Managing Risks – a New Framework, *Harvard Business Review* (2012) June: 51.
2 Mikes, A., From Counting Risk to Making Risk Count – Boundary Work in Risk Management, *Accounting, Organizations and Society* (2011) 36: 226–245.
3 This is illustrated in Mackenzie, D. and Spears, T., The Formula that Killed Wall Street? The Gaussian copula and the material cultures of modelling (University of Edinburgh, 2012).
4 Stulz, R.M., Six Ways Companies Mismanage Risk, *Harvard Business Review* (2009) March: 86–94.

5 Power, M., *The Risk Management of Everything – Rethinking the Politics of Uncertainty* (London: Demos, 2004).

6 An example of an often-used simplifying assumption is that cross-correlations, within multi-tranched instruments (such as Collateralised Debt Obligations, or CDOs), are uniform in all market conditions.

7 A multivariate probability distribution for which the marginal probability distribution of each variable is uniform. Copulas are used to describe the dependence between random variables. See also Appendix B.

8 Mackenzie and Spears, op. cit.

9 Danielsson, J. et al., Model Risk of Risk Models, Federal Reserve Board, Washington DC, July 2014.

10 Undertakings for Collective Investment in Transferable Securities, a set of European Union Directives that aim to allow collective investment schemes to operate freely throughout the EU on the basis of a single authorisation from one member state.

11 Brunnermeier, M. et al., The Fundamental Principles of Financial Regulation (ICMB International Centre for Monetary and Banking Studies, 2009).

12 Commissioner Byron Georgiou, US Financial Crisis Inquiry Commission Press Release, 27 January 2010.

13 Ifiglobal.com.

14 IFI Global Risk Management in the AIFMD Era, Research Survey, 2014.

15 Alternative Investment Fund Managers Directive. See Glossary.

16 Commissioner Heather Murren, US Financial Crisis Inquiry Commission Press Release, 27 January 2010.

17 Greenspan, A., Risk Transfer and Financial Stability, Remarks to the Federal Reserve Bank of Chicago Annual Conference on Bank Structure, 5 May 2005.

18 Commissioner Brooksley Born, US Financial Crisis Inquiry Commission Press Release, 27 January 2010.

19 Wall, L., Basel III and Stress Tests, www.frbatlanta.org, December 2013.

20 *The Economist,* Inglorious Isolation, 22 February 2014.

21 Resolving Globally Active, Systemically Important, Financial Institutions, Bank of England, London, 10 December 2012.

22 *The Economist,* Balkanisation of Banking – Putting Humpty Together Again, 23 November 2013.

23 Danielsson, J., et al., Model Risk of Risk Models. US Federal Reserve, July 2014.

24 The Slumps that Shaped Modern Finance, *The Economist*, 12 April 2012.
25 Blundell-Wignall, A., The Problem with Banking on the Future, OECD, August 2013.
26 The objectives and investment horizon of an investment fund are, in an important sense, the corollary of bank and investment bank liabilities.
27 Cochrane, J.H., Toward a Run-Free Financial System, University of Chicago Booth School of Business, NBER, Cater Institute, April 2014.
28 Gorton, G., *Misunderstanding Financial Crises: Why We Don't See Them Coming* (Oxford: Oxford University Press, 2012).
29 Kane, E., Politics and Policymaking, *Journal of Monetary Economics* (1980) 6: 199–211.
30 The generic name for a bundled package of services offered by investment banks and securities firms to hedge funds and other professional investors needing the ability to borrow securities and cash to be able to invest on a netted basis and achieve an absolute return. The prime broker provides a centralised securities clearing facility for the hedge fund so the hedge fund's collateral requirements are netted across all deals handled by the prime broker.
31 Walker Review of Corporate Governance of UK Banking Industry, 2009.
32 Promoting Sound Risk Culture. IIF Issues Paper, 2013.
33 Institute of International Finance – Risk Culture, December 2009.

3 | Sir Michael Hintze

London, 8 December 2014

Behaviour and probity are very important, though you do need a thorough understanding of the trades themselves, and to keep operations running smoothly.

Sir Michael Hintze is the founder CEO and Senior Investment Officer of CQS, one of Europe's leading multi-strategy asset management firms. Before starting CQS in 1999, Michael was at Credit Suisse where he was Managing Director in the Leverage Finance Group and at Goldman Sachs where he was Head of UK Equity Trading and where he established and built up Goldman's Euro Convertible and European Warrants business in London.

Michael Rummel, who joins him in the interview, is Head of Communications at CQS.

He describes what sustains a good risk culture throughout the organisation.

Sir Michael Hintze: Whether we talk about risk or we talk about development, the point is you are always a function of your training, of your background, of your mind-set. It comes down to all sorts of things, the probity, risk-taking and just skills in general. If I look at the experience that I have had, I went to Harvard and I studied physics, mathematics, engineering and electrical engineering. I was in the army, which was great. Out of Harvard Business School I went into a training program at Salomon Brothers, which was very important to me, and which was critical because it gave me a good context for the business.

From there I traded fixed income at Salomon Brothers and saw some of the best traders in the world at the time working there. I was pretty junior, trading Yankee bonds,[1] but I saw Lewis Ranieri[2] building the mortgage business, I saw various others, including David de Luca, who was my first boss and Billy White and Billy Voute trading corporate bonds. From them I learned the importance of trading disciplines. Then I was hired into Goldman Sachs into another mini training program, but in some ways I taught myself. Fischer Black[3] had just arrived there and I had plenty of time to speak with him. I was hired by a chap called Bob Freeman, who was running the risk arbitrage there and he showed me some skills and I was able to watch guys like Bob Rubin[4] work. I never worked for him, but I was coming in at 5 o'clock in the morning because I was trading into London and the only other guy who came in at 5 was Bob Rubin. Great discipline.

I soon moved to London and was managing the Euro convertible bond business in London. As part of this we did a lot of syndicate work. I would price transactions off the desk[5] and the capital markets people would do the rest of it. After that I ran UK domestic equities and that was a big deal for me. Again I was largely self-taught because there was nobody to teach me how to trade that market, but again I saw the disciplines. Then I left Goldman and went to Credit Suisse First Boston where Brady Dougan[6] was. Brady was a mentor in different ways but he was even more than that. It was off the back of that, when CSFB and CSFP[7] came together, and I was thinking it was time for me to do something on my own, that Brady said to me words to the effect of: You know, you have made me a lot of money. Courtesy of him, CSFB seeded me $200 million and I returned them around

$500 million and got my own firm. I did it for him but I also did it for myself, and here we are, the firm's there.

Matthew: Did he do it with other guys? Were there a couple of other guys there?

Sir Michael: He backed Alan Howard.[8] He's very successful, he is more successful than I am, I would argue.

So across all those firms what did I learn? Hard work matters, attention to detail matters, operations matter and also understanding risk and sizing matters. So that is the bottom line.

Other people were very helpful and informative in terms of my getting the business. I saw John Mack[9] give a presentation at Harvard Business School on Rule 415, shelf registration, in 1981 or 1982. It was about the power of investment banking organisations shifting from the corporate finance department to the capital market teams in the front office. For me that was quite an insight. Also Professor Robert Glauber, my finance professor at Harvard Business School and who ended up becoming Under Secretary of the Treasury for Finance, gave me guidance; though I am sure that if I mentioned it to him he would have no memory of me at all.

Matthew: What innovations have you found effective in managing your risk? Are there any really important innovations since the tools that you first used?

Sir Michael: Innovation is probably too strong a term, but things always evolve. I think operational issues are always a big deal, I was always very concerned with plumbing. Many have heard me say "You are paid to take investment risk not operational risk." I've always maintained that as a rule and I realise how effective that was, not just in terms of money management, but also protecting clients' investments.

Frances: One of the observations that struck me when I came back to investment management after a break of about five years was that the only real recent innovation in capital markets I could see, since the swap and option markets matured, was the introduction of credit derivatives. I didn't see any other instrument that really had as big an impact.

Sir Michael: There is no question that being able to take risk and apportion risk exactly where you want it is a big deal. That has been happening since we started. To my mind there were two areas where the same technology and similar (erroneous) assumptions were used, the credit derivatives market and the mortgage market.

In the credit derivatives market I think the CDO[10] is a sensible product. However, it was corrupted by the double tranching activities that went on. There is no question that it is possible to take a lot of BB paper and apply Gaussian Copula[11] technology or whatever, and if you assume (incorrectly) they are not correlated, the top end will look like a AAA or at least an AA rated security. However, it is very sensitive to correlation. In fact, it fails if it is heavily correlated. The real problem was that the rating agencies gave the structures their blessing.

Further problems occurred when it was applied to the mortgage market, particularly sub-prime. The problems arose when they took the various pieces of sub-prime and pretended that by taking a lot of CCC pieces and packaging those up, they could say that the top of those CCCs became AAAs. There were a number of things that went wrong. There were sloppy underwriting standards and poor tranching; the mortgage backed securities were held by inappropriate investors and they were also held on bank balance sheets which meant there was a pro-cyclicality issue. I think that at the heart the sub-prime problems were a misapplication of models. That was a massive problem and ended in disaster. It was impossible because they were all correlated.

But I have seen other innovations. For example, when I started we didn't have a swap market and now we have a massive swap market. And we didn't have credit derivative markets. Many different markets didn't exist in the early 1980s and it has changed the world. The SWAPS derivative market is now many times the size of the cash market.

Matthew: *Even with the CDOs there is still that base correlation[12] issue, where everybody thinks correlations are going to be the same no matter what tranche you are in or everybody is going to hold together like a rugby scrum.*

Sir Michael: I agree regarding the base correlation point, but it needs careful managing. I go to a derivative conference most years. When I first started attending everybody was worried about jump diffusions.[13] Then everybody started worrying about the Gaussian Copula distributions because they knew it wasn't right. The risk managers knew there was something wrong, but what they didn't do was to take a step back and ask some basic questions: John Hull[14] usually did that very well, he would delve into the core of the issue. Nobody understood how systematically problematic that could be. Now what they are looking at is capital adjustments, DVA, CVA, FVA or, collectively, XVA.[15] That is the big deal now; it's basically optimising capital utilisation for the banking system.

Matthew: *Are they doing much on liquidity? That seems to be the mother at the door, doesn't it?*

Sir Michael: Yes, they probably should be paying more attention to liquidity but I think that is the least of the problem. Put it this way, sub-prime didn't fail because of liquidity. It failed because of the way in which they'd been structured. It was a credit problem but it wasn't a liquidity problem. When they lost their jobs, people stopped paying their mortgages.

I noticed that in about 2006 or 2007 people stopped talking about derivatives and credit derivatives and they stopped talking about the ability to pay. They started talking about recovery rates. They were tripped up by an inability to pay, which meant that the recovery of outstanding loans went to zero.

Matthew: *What preceded that? There seemed to be a disenchantment with asset-backed paper. Investors pulled pack and entities, such as Northern Rock[16] that relied on these markets for funding, experienced liquidity issues that resulted in a run.*

Sir Michael: I don't think people lost their money once the government intervened. Solvency was impacted by significant mark-to-market challenges despite there being liquidity in the system.

Frances: *They were financing on the short-term markets.*

Matthew: *People stopped buying the paper[17] and they were still buying the CDOs[18] which was a bit bizarre. It was as if the people in the banks that held the "senior" tranches realised it was worthless but they were trying to recover capital by limiting the extension of credit to stronger banks.*

Sir Michael: The problem was that they didn't hold the CCC themselves, they held things that they thought were AAA-rated, but they were effectively CCC. In fact they were D: they were default.

Matthew: They may have pulled back from the asset-backed markets because they knew the other parts of their balance sheets were flawed.

Sir Michael: I thought there would be a ratings migration problem rather than a total bust problem. I knew they would have a problem, which is why we made a good amount of money that year but I didn't realise how big a systemic issue it would be and that they would collapse to zero.

Frances: What would you like to see happen from here ... in the future?

Sir Michael: I don't think there is much that we can change in terms of regulatory framework – and that is the point. Do I believe that the Basel III system[19] is optimal? No I don't. Do I believe mistakes have been made in terms of the Dodd-Frank Act?[20] Yes I do. Do I think the banks are over-capitalised? I think potentially they are. Do I believe that they are enforcing capital adequacy in such a way that is not necessary and has unintended consequences? Yes I do. We have gone from having significant bank liquidity and somewhat inadequate solvency to over-capitalisation (solvency) and dwindled liquidity.

The point that I think has been missed is that it is probity; it is to do with behaviour rather than models. And I think there is a transparency point that has been missed.

Frances: What do you mean by behaviour?

Sir Michael: It's a matter of experience. It is a matter of people thinking that they can get away with it. For example, why did the Australian banks not go bust during the GFC?[21] Why did the banks in Canada not go bust during the GFC? Why did the banks in South East Asia not go bust during the GFC? They all operated under the Basel II regime, so there is no issue about that. The reason they didn't go bust is because they'd seen it before, which is what I mean by behaviour and experience. They didn't need massive rule books to stop them from getting run over by the nearest bus because they had seen it already, they had experience of it.

Going back to the behaviour point, it is all very well to say that people were mis-selling products. That is certainly true, but there was a heck of a lot of mis-buying as well as mis-selling. And why was mis-buying going on? It was because people thought there was money for nothing. And I would say that one of the other reasons for mis-buying was because they thought the central banks would bail them out and guess what? They did. Moral hazard in the system writ large.

Frances: *With respect to behaviour and incentives, I tend to think of hedge funds sort of straddling investment banking and investment management, which puts them into an interesting space. You have the behavioural issues that cover both investment banking and investment management, whereas the two are normally quite different because the incentives for risk-taking activities are quite different. For example, a conventionally-managed pension fund manager's remuneration is linked only very weakly to his or her performance, whereas an investment banker's remuneration is linked very clearly to, mostly, revenue generation. Hedge funds have elements of both. So for this reason you have an interesting perspective on behavioural issues, also from having been in a few different organisations.*

Sir Michael: And not just organisations but through different markets. I also like to read a bit of history. Go back to the South Sea Bubble, or even more interestingly, go back to what went on with the bubble that happened in Louisiana in the early 1700s.

Frances: *John Law.*

Sir Michael: So you look at what happened there and there are two observations. People can go bust quite easily speculating with their own money. People can also go bust when dealing with other people's money. Obviously in both instances there is a greed, fear and stupidity factor going on.

I have noticed this with organisations. Does the organisation make a difference? Does the compensation structure make a difference? I'm not sure I have the definitive answer to these questions, but I do think it is worthwhile to ask who is doing more damage to investment outcomes: an investment banker who is trying to sell rubbish or a lazy investment manager who has been sitting on his haunches and doing nothing.

Frances: A lot of people say it has a lot to do with incentives and it is hard to argue that incentives have nothing at all to do with it. But incentives go beyond compensation. For example, I have a conversation with a friend, who says: Nobody saw this 2007 crisis coming. And I say: Really? I did. I was getting out of equities in late 2006 and early 2007. Why was I doing that? Because I had looked at how much credit spreads[22] had narrowed, it was obvious that risk wasn't being priced,[23] and it was obvious to me that this could not keep going on. My friend asks the perfectly reasonable question: So why didn't the manager of my pension fund do the same thing? I tell her that it is easy to do that with your own money. If I miss the last 15% of the bull market I can rap myself over the knuckles, I have only myself to blame. But if I am managing your money, you might say: Why did you miss the last 15%? You lost me thousands of dollars by selling, and you sack me. And that is a different proposition.

Sir Michael: That recalls what Chuck Prince[24] said: As long as the music's playing we are on the dance floor. Jamie Diamond[25] didn't do that I believe. And note that Chuck Prince is a lawyer and Jamie Diamond more of a trader or risk manager. He definitely was a risk guy, I knew him at business school. He was very risk-aware. And he was very self-confident. But he is not arrogant.

Matthew: There is all this regulation coming forward. Do you think there is a danger that there is going to be over-compliance with regulation and people will miss those signals that you just talked about that Jamie Diamond picked up on?

Sir Michael: There are two problems there. The first is that over-compliance is pushing the cost base of banks up materially. Firms are spending billions of dollars on compliance. The documentation has become so much more complicated. For example, Dodd-Frank is 2,000–2,500 pages of primary legislation *and* with secondary legislation you have another 9,000 pages plus of regulation. It's a massive thing. And that's just in the US. We have similar things going on here in Europe. So costs have gone up.

The second, and in my view bigger, problem you have is that a central bank – or central banks, plural – are taking risk signals out of the market because they are encouraging markets into the same thing.[26] That's when you see distortions because you cannot see how securities are being priced. If you are taking a position against a risky trade you will either under-perform or, if you go short, you will look a total idiot, because there is no volatility to pay for the optionality that you created.[27]

Frances: Is much short selling still going on?

Sir Michael: Short selling or being short the market is very expensive because through QE central bank have killed volatility. Short selling equities, bonds or going long options is probably okay. Going long credit derivatives is expensive because you pay every day as you roll down.[28]

Matthew: And they have extended the liquidity trap.[29] It was probably fair enough when they were trying to rebuild capital in the banks. But now it has gone on for six years and you have left a lot of money on the table.

Sir Michael: More than that. You have not just left money on the table, the other problem is that you have under-called the market. And investors will pull money from you. If you are a hedge fund manager that went short in all likelihood you have lost money. The issue is liquidity versus solvency. And it is one thing for the central banks to provide liquidity (I think that's appropriate), but I am not sure they should be providing solvency. If something really is too big to fail I can see why they are providing solvency – maybe. You can contrast it with (and you are obviously well aware of it) the South Sea and Louisiana Bubbles. That was a heck of a boom and bust!

Frances: There was a transparency issue in those instances.

Sir Michael: There was a transparency issue. There was an insider trading issue. There were all sorts of nightmares there. But the South Sea Bubble flushed out quickly. What happened in France in the early 18th century with Law and the Louisiana Bubble, they didn't flush it out. They bailed it out and what ended up happening in 1789? By 1789 almost every French institution was so weakened that you ended up with the French Revolution. So you can compare and contrast, a tale of the two cities, literally. One where there was a massive rout and the other where they kept the thing going for ever and a day. And, yes, it may have felt better because there wasn't a horrible crash. But this unintended consequence was a revolution. That's a rather simplistic explanation, let's be clear. But the UK became a much more healthy society for it.

Frances: John Law was a Scottish economist, by the way.

Sir Michael: He set the company up but he wasn't the man that kept it going.

Matthew: Do you believe positions should be marked to market[30] or not? Should you mark your book to closing day prices irrespective of the size of the position?

Sir Michael: We spend a lot of time thinking about that question. Firstly, if we are arbitraging, say, between the UK and US, for example Royal Dutch or BP, you want to make sure that both sides of the trade are being marked at the same time. You want to be as contemporaneous as you can.

But in our risk management we are also very aware of liquidity and sizing. Liquidity can move away from you. For example, you might think you have got a two- or three-day volume but you find a year on that [it] can look like you might have a three-month volume. So sizing makes a difference, but I don't know if there is any right answer to that. Much depends on the asset/liability mis-match and the liquidity terms a fund is offering versus the assets it holds.

One has to provide a mark-to-market. But unless there is super liquidity or the position in total sold, that mark is less definite an estimate. Albeit a good estimate, but an estimate nonetheless.

But it's a quite a difficult question and there may not be a right answer. For example, if an investor owns 30% of a company, that investor may never be able to sell this stake at the "market price", so where should you mark that?

Matthew: With inventory in an investment bank, the daily number itself might not be reliable because if it doesn't really take into account the fact that liquidity might affect the price, it can give you a false sense of diversification.

Sir Michael: I think you are right about that.

Matthew: Do you think risk evaluation captures the human response to a crisis, or is it generally regarded as something that is dealt with when it arises?

Sir Michael: It goes back to what you said about liquidity. People get scared. They run away. They do all sorts of things. And things gap.[31] I think it is hard. Tail risk analysis goes a long way to capturing the price action. However, leadership of the trading teams in those times is also a challenge.

Michael Rummel: My recollection of that period was that we had incredible leadership because, first of all you instituted a thrice-daily meeting of a key group of risk managers, operations and communication people. Communication was critical to understand where we were, our positions, the situation with our prime brokers and counterparties, and so on. Second was communication, not only with providers of finance, but also with our clients. We had to be very careful from a legal perspective, but I remember Michael saying: We have got to go and talk to our clients. We have got to provide them the liquidity if they want their money back. It was a matter of doing the right thing; a matter of honour.

Sir Michael: It was. Nevertheless, everyone would have been better off if they had not demanded their money back and stayed invested through the cycle.

Frances: It was precisely because many funds had long lock-in periods, investors were redeeming the ones that didn't.

Sir Michael: It is what it is.

Frances: The other point is that before the crisis everyone was worried that hedge funds would blow up the prime brokers, who were owned by the banks. And it turned out the other way around.

Sir Michael: Exactly.

Frances: So what do the Europeans do in response? They regulate hedge funds.

Sir Michael: Yes, in fact Michel Barnier[32] in effect said in a public forum that it was a political matter, a political issue. What have they done? They have put thousands of pages of regulation in there. It is peculiar. But now what? It is far from clear to me that the system is safer for all the regulation. It has created a barrier to entry for smaller start-ups. That may be good for some incumbents but not for business formation.

And there you have one of the reasons why you now cannot have a fund starting with much less than a couple of hundred million dollars. You used to be able to start with $10 or 20 million. Now you need hundreds of millions.

Frances: *Investors suffer in the end because there is reduced choice.*

Matthew: *Stress testing and scenario analysis, how much do you use that?*

Sir Michael: We do a lot. I have a team that just does that. We do standard VaR[33] one-day 95% and 99%. I have been a user of VaR since we started using it at Goldman. It is a useful tool even though it is not the "truth". I like to say that risk modelling is a great place to start but a terrible place to finish. Whether it is in your risk modeling or in your modelling of securities or whatever, you have got to apply, not just common sense, but an idiosyncratic understanding of the underlying investments. But we do use historic stress testing and we do use historic VaR. We do stress VaR. All these things are very interesting and they will prompt different questions and observations. We have a very rich tableau of where things are.

Now what has ended up happening of course is that there are so many measures that I now have a risk manager who looks at the trends for me. He in turn has a team. I meet with him every day and he highlights them for me, because if I printed everything out I would have a box of stuff which I cannot read. Even without that I have a small telephone book which I can flip through. But I need him to study it.

These tools are very helpful because they do throw up the tail[34] issues and they do allow us to ask where the tail is. And it is getting more interesting as the tools are getting more effective. And the good news is that, whereas when I was at Goldman we used to be nearly a day behind when we ran our risk reports, now, with the increased computing power, it's pretty instantaneous, it's there as we arrive in the morning.

But behaviour and probity are still very important. What you can never get away from is the possibility that there is somebody who is hiding something. When I was at Salomon Brothers in the training programme, the head of compliance said: Look, being a compliance guy or a risk compliance guy means you are sitting there and you are watching all the kids in the pool and you know somebody is doing something they shouldn't be doing in the pool but you don't know who the hell it is. You need to be aware if somebody is breaking the rules.

Somehow you have to make sure they self-police. That goes back to the whole probity thing. There was presumably skullduggery, perhaps you had a chance of knowing where it was. Now you have a situation where you are bouncing into a screen so you don't even know who you are dealing with. It is a counterparty, that's all you know. No: worse. At best it is a counterparty, at worst it's The Market, so you don't even know who you are transacting with or against.

Matthew: *It doesn't look like anybody can or wants to fix caveat emptor, but there seems to be the need for more protection for the buyer.*

Sir Michael: I think that is right. But how often do they say: If it looks too good to be true, it probably is. Come on, guys: it is very hard to cheat an honest man. It still doesn't mean that sometimes bad or dishonest deals don't slip through.

Frances: *It goes back to the mis-selling and mis-buying.*

Sir Michael: When they started regulating SIVs[35] they basically had it right. They wanted to protect the Aunt Agathas, the people who were unsophisticated and retail end-investors; genuine, trusting people. I think that worked pretty well. I don't know that you need thousands of pages of regulation to do that though. Look at what Martin Wheatley[36] is doing now at the FCA, as it is now. I believe he is right. He is effectively saying: Don't think you can rip somebody off by giving yourself a lot of air-cover through the fine print. If you provide a telephone book with the "answer" buried in it, don't think you can behave badly and get away with it.

Frances: *That's the essence of the principles-based approach and that is why many people believe it is so much more robust than rules-based regulations.*

Sir Michael: That's right. Because it's done with 20:20 hindsight it is in effect self-correcting.

Matthew: *So how do you handle complexity now? What's your general approach?*

Sir Michael: With great difficulty, I guess.

Matthew: *There is not a drive for simplicity?*

Sir Michael: In short, no. However, that deserves a longer answer. Let's take two steps back. I think your point is that the simpler the model the more robust the model is going to be. The problem is that when the model becomes way too complicated you will end up picking up model biases, which you will not necessarily know about or understand. But no matter which model you use, you will have some bias inside it. The cool thing that we do here is that we look at models and see how they are biased. For example, there are a whole lot of convertible models that will give you a certain answer. So you can see what is going on there and then you have to think about what's happening. I use derivative models, such as the Gaussian Copula, but then I still need to go back and do the fundamental credit work.

So how do I deal with that complexity? I do simplify it a little bit. I don't throw the complexity away because there is rich data in the complexity, especially when you look at trends. That's important. But what I do is I look at the fundamental credit or fundamental investment story beneath it. And that goes back to sub-prime. If everybody had just stopped and looked at what was behind the model of sub-prime. If they looked into whether people could pay their mortgages that was the key. The other thing is I am not scared of having a horrible, long tail in my portfolio, but I do my very best to ensure that the long tail is identified and properly sized. Think about it this way: I am not going to go down, hop into my car and drive at five miles per hour in a 30 miles per hour zone. The fact is we all drive at 30 miles per hour and there is the chance that we will have an accident somewhere out there. But you make sure you have the right car, the seat belt on, you're cautious.

Frances: *You don't douse your house every morning in water in case it burns down.*

Sir Michael: Correct. Although nowadays we do have fire alarms, smoke detectors, leak detectors and so on. Why? Because we can do it very cheaply. So you do it.

Matthew: *What about pro-cyclicality?*

Sir Michael: Yes I think that is always an issue, it was a big problem with Basel II, there is pro-cyclicality in Solvency II.[37] There is a lot of pro-cyclicality everywhere. But it is more than just the pro-cyclicality. You need to think about the unintended correlations and I think that the Financial Stability Boards are trying to address that. What used to happen with the central banks and market practitioners, the guys who had been around forever, would just say no. Interestingly, Asia and Australia and Canada didn't have a problem to the same extent. Because they were scarred. They were in the same pro-cyclical regime that everybody else was in, but they'd been through the pain and they had thought about it. So they didn't let it build up.

Matthew: The CBA dispensed with its balance sheet holdings of CDOs in 2004 and that was partly my work, although I had a bloody brilliant quant[38] helping me with it. My recommendation was that these things were mis-priced, most of the stocks had been downgraded and they were running on the old ratings. But it took the courage of a guy called Mick Katz. He said: Well we'll get rid of the book. He didn't look at his budget, even though they had quite a big position. Some other Australian banks seemed to hold on to their positions.

Sir Michael: Yes. It goes back to people feeling comfortable enough about it.

Frances: It seems also that it is not just having been through it, but they drew the right lessons.

Sir Michael: I think that is right. But it needs someone like Matt putting his hand up even though there were probably plenty of people who would stab you in the back if it turned out the wrong way. And you also have other people who were very happy to keep dancing as long as the music was playing. They may have known about it but didn't give a monkey's.

Matthew: It is a culture that is hard to wean out, isn't it?

Sir Michael: The experiences of different global banks varied. Interestingly, there were people who saw it and took account of the pro-cyclicality of the regime they were working in. Now did it matter because the world was a Basel II world, which therefore was pro-cyclical? Maybe. But you can't blame the modelling.

Matthew: The models are only as good as the data you feed into them. Some pension funds are still using data samples as short as 90 days to estimate VaR.

Sir Michael: One of the things we do is ask: How bad will we be if we have another Lehman? If we have another auto crisis of 2005? We find that those scenarios can give us a useful view. I had people looking at the Lehman blow-up, but they were all working with percentages, which can give an odd picture. For example, it is all very well to say you have a 50% increase in your credit spread, but that's not what really counts: you have to look at the starting point. For example, if you're at 10 basis points,[39] 50% means it goes from 10 to 15. If you're at 100, it goes from 100 to 150 or 1,000 to 1,500. The yield value, cash rate you have to think about. So we run the scenarios and we think about where that is. We apply judgement. People love to pooh-pooh VaR, but it's not a bad place to be because it gives you one single number. Of course it is not that powerful because the world is just not that simple. But if you keep looking, you look at your VaR trends and you look at the different confidence levels.[40] We will sample back 90 days or 720 days or whatever. But one must also look at historic stress analysis.

Frances: 90 days is probably too short for a pension fund. It depends on what you are going to use it for.

Sir Michael: But maybe it doesn't matter, maybe VaR for them is totally irrelevant.

Frances: Ideally, your look-back data sample should be determined by what you are going to do with the number when you get it.

Sir Michael: Exactly. If you are a pension fund and you are trying to match liabilities out to 20 years or 30 years, which is what these guys are doing, then maybe the VaR is just a box-ticking exercise. Maybe it is more a regulatory shield than a risk management tool.

Frances: I suspect that is exactly what it is.

Sir Michael: I bet you that if it were important to them they would not be using that because it just doesn't get you there. Which I think is your point.

Frances: One of the issues many people say they are facing is that they have so much regulatory box-ticking to do, it is squeezing the resources they have to do genuine risk management. You alluded to this earlier when you suggested that AIFMD is motivated by politics. Do you think there is some playing to the peanut gallery[41] on the part of the politicians?

Sir Michael: The real problem is that you've got to try and have an input to the political decision. For example, when we look at new, proposed regulation in the UK, they usually open it for discussion. You know who you are talking to. The nightmare we had with the European legislation was the fact that there was no single person to talk to. We had at least three groups of people to talk to: you had the Rapporteur, who was meant to represent the

Council, the Council itself and then the European Parliament. So you had three entities and if they were politically motivated you were defeated. They represented nobody, they drove through their own agenda. It's one of the things that is challenging about the whole European project, there was no accountability. Whereas here,[42] if you don't like something, you go to the Bank of England and you talk to them about it. Whether they listen to you or not is a different matter, but if you are credible you have a voice, even if it might not be an effective voice.

We don't lobby in the US, but in the US at least the industry was able to talk to the various decision makers. But the problem there was that Dodd-Frank was passed in lightning speed. There was a political imperative. There were 2,500 or 2,400 pages of primary legislation. I don't believe anybody had read or digested it at the time. I spoke to one of the key legislators and I said: What were you guys thinking when you did it in two weeks? And he said: No it wasn't, it was three weeks! I said: Did you read every one of those pages? He said: My staff did. Well that makes me feel even better. They didn't read it in whole; they couldn't. Look at the original SEC Act. It was written thoughtfully and succinctly. You can see where the cuts and pastes occurred. I blame the word processor, when documents were typed, they required greater care. What you have today is word processing gone mad. This is a peripheral point, but it's what goes on.

Matthew: *What do you hold as the most important thing about culture?*

Sir Michael: Probity. Putting your hand up, keep putting your hand up. We are in a probability world, so you are always going to "make a mistake" or not have the optimal result because you can't be 100% right all the time. By definition you can't always make the right investment decisions. What we want to make sure of is that if there is an issue people put their hand up.

Matthew: *So it is this risk-awareness thing.*

Sir Michael: Risk-awareness, but also honesty about the fact that we all make mistakes. You know Michael hears me in the morning meeting saying: Well I screwed that one up nicely but, look, here is what I have done about it.

Frances: *My experience is that people's willingness to put their hand up depends on what the consequences are of doing so. For example, if they* *think they are going to be attacked they are not going to do it, but if they think everyone is going to say: OK, we can deal with that, let's get on with it and deal with it. Then they will put their hand up.*

Sir Michael: I think that is right. It is not just a willingness to do it but accepting-ness of it.

Matthew: Do you have training, or do you source it from your experience?

Sir Michael: We obviously have compliance training and other training. But I think you have to lead from the front. In compliance, obviously, we encourage self-reporting, which is good. The message is the same thing here, right: you need to make sure that if you put your hand up you are rewarded for it, not punished. Obviously if you have committed a crime you have to be held to account for that.

Michael Rummel: Everyone is encouraged to be a "risk manager" irrespective of their role, whether they are technically managing risk or not, everyone is encouraged to think as a risk manager. I think that is really important. As Michael says, it comes very much from the top down.

Matthew: What three pieces of advice that you would give to, say, a director?

Sir Michael: If you are a director such as I am, a chief investment officer or senior investment officer, one of the things is to be open and fair, to encourage reporting of errors. I think you need to think about your long-term risks and the sizing of those risks. The other thing is to make sure you take the operational risk down to a dull roar: be aware of operational risk: no surprises. For a fund director, make sure due process is being followed; make sure the marking is fine; and make sure that your fund is being treated fairly if you are working with fund-of-funds organisations.

At the end of the day it does come back to that golden rule: How does this feel – either to your investors or to your shareholders? Does this sound right? If it doesn't look right, if it is the sort of thing that would be a worry if it hit the front page of the newspapers, you shouldn't do it. How would you be judged by your peers?

Michael Rummel: I think, Michael, you said this before: Learn from your mistakes. If you make a mistake, share it and learn from it.

Sir Michael: Exactly. You get the bank director, the manager, to encourage people to do that. You see there are mistakes that are made for the right reason not for the wrong reason. There is one thing if someone had done their work, thought about it and made a calculated judgement. It's another thing if it goes wrong because a person just took a punt. As I often say, investors pay us to take investment risk not operational risk. I hate hiring gamblers. Hiring card counters is fine, hiring punters is a recipe for disaster.

Notes

1 A foreign bond denominated in US dollars and traded in the United States (Thefreedicitonary.com).
2 A former bond trader and former Vice Chairman of Salomon Brothers, now of Ranieri Partners. He is considered the "godfather" of mortgage finance for his role in pioneering securitisation and mortgage-backed securities.
3 An American economist, best known as one of the authors of the famous Black-Scholes equation.
4 An American economist and banking executive who served as Secretary of the Treasury during the Clinton administration.
5 Gather real-time market prices, interest rates and currency exchange rates for related securities from the trading desk and apply them to formulae to estimate convertible bond prices.
6 An American business executive. Since 2007 Chief Executive Officer of Credit Suisse and previously CEO of Investment Banking and acting CEO Credit Suisse Americas.
7 Credit Suisse Financial Products.
8 Co-founder of Brevan Howard Asset Management LLP, and a former director of the Conservative Friends of Israel.
9 A Senior Adviser and the former CEO and Chairman of the Board at Morgan Stanley.
10 Collateralised Debt Obligation. Please see the Glossary.
11 A family of models used to estimate the probability distribution of losses on a pool of loans or bonds (Mackenzie).
12 Default correlation parameters implied from market spreads of collateralised debt obligation tranches. The issue referred to here is that

correlations were assumed to be equal across tranches and constant over time (onlinelibrary.wiley.com).

13 A computational method that helps model instances where asset prices gap up or down, that are otherwise not easily dealt with by most asset pricing methodologies. Jump diffusion processes were introduced by Robert C. Merton as an extension of jump models that are computationally tractable.

14 A Professor of Derivatives and Risk Management at the Rotman School of Management at the University of Toronto, a respected researcher in the academic field of quantitative finance (Hull–White model) and the author of two widely used texts on financial derivatives.

15 Please see the Glossary.

16 A British bank best known for becoming the first bank in 150 years to suffer a bank run after having had to approach the Bank of England for a loan facility to replace money market funding, during the credit crisis in 2007. Having failed to find a commercial buyer for the business, it was taken into public ownership in 2008, and was then bought by Virgin Money in 2012.

17 The underlying bonds.

18 Collateralised Debt Obligation. Please see the Glossary.

19 The Basel Accords are global, voluntary regulatory standards on bank capital adequacy, stress testing and market liquidity risk.

20 The Dodd-Frank Wall Street Reform and Consumer Protection Act. Passed as a response to the Great Recession, it brought the most significant changes to financial regulation in the United States since the regulatory reform that followed the Great Depression. It made changes in the American financial regulatory environment that affect all federal financial regulatory agencies and almost every part of the nation's financial services industry.

21 Global Financial Crisis of 2007–2009.

22 The difference in yield between interest rate securities with different risks of default.

23 Incremental risk was not being rewarded with commensurate incremental return. In other words, the prices of risky assets were too high relative to very low-risk assets.

24 An American former chairman and chief executive of Citigroup.

25 Current chairman, president and chief executive officer of JPMorgan Chase.

26 The range of feasible strategies is in effect being constrained.

27 Selling a credit derivative implies buying an option. As expected volatility of the bond price is a factor in the option price, a subsequent fall in volatility causes a fall in the option price.

28 Adjust the associated hedge position.

29 A situation, described in Keynesian economics, in which injections of cash into the private banking system by a central bank fail to decrease interest rates and hence make monetary policy ineffective.

30 A method of valuation derived from the most recent security prices quoted and traded in the relevant market. Also known as Fair Value Accounting.

31 In other words, asset prices can gap up or down in illiquid markets.

32 Vice President of the European People's Party (EPP) and European Commissioner for Internal Market and Services under Barroso.

33 Value-at-Risk. Please see the Glossary.

34 The "tail" of the return distribution that quantifies the likelihood that an asset or a portfolio will deliver extreme losses over a given period of time.

35 Structured Investment Vehicles. Please see the Glossary.

36 A British financier, formerly managing director of the Consumer and Markets Business Unit of the Financial Services Authority (FSA) in the UK, and is currently CEO of the Financial Conduct Authority (FCA).

37 An EU Directive that codifies and harmonises the EU insurance regulation. Primarily this concerns the amount of capital that EU insurance companies must hold to reduce the risk of insolvency.

38 Quantitative analyst, someone who applies mathematical techniques to financial investment.

39 0.10%, thus 0.10% increases to 0.15%, 1.00% increases to 1.50% and 10% increases to 15%.

40 An estimated range of values which is likely to include an unknown return parameter, the estimated range being calculated from a given set of sample data. The width of the confidence interval indicates how uncertain is the value estimated for the unknown parameter.

41 Seeking solutions that are popular but not necessarily effective.

42 In the UK.

4 | John Breit

New York, 19 November 2014

Be curious, gain the confidence of traders and make them explain why their risks will pay off.

Before he retired, John Breit managed risk at Merrill Lynch in New York and at Donaldson, Lufkin & Jenrette.

He tells us why heavy handed regulation may be undermining good risk management practices.

John Breit: I'm a physicist by training. After my doctorate and post-doctorates at The Institute for Advanced Study in Princeton and Penn, I wanted to work in New York. Most of the faculty positions open to me were in the Mid-West, the South, California, but not NY. So I looked at finance and wound up at Security Pacific (Sec Pac), which had a California bank but was setting up what they called a merchant bank in New York. In the Summer of 1986 I joined what they called the Quant Group,

59

where I came in handy solving lots of partial differential equations, but then moved fairly quickly to the swaps desk, which was one of the few really good trading desks. Despite being very much a commercial bank, they had hired the First Chicago swaps team, who were really good. So I hung out with them.

Frances: *Interest rate swaps?*

John: Yes. There I learned what LIBOR was and about what banks did: it was a great learning experience. After that I helped out with the credit department, mainly to help them understand some of the new products. When they decided we should have a market risk department, not just a credit risk department, I got to do that for a couple of years because I'd been helping them and everyone knew me. Merrill Lynch then recruited me to work in market risk. Since Merrill was much bigger than Sec Pac, I was doing much more interesting stuff. There were only six of us in the entire risk management team, so we covered a lot of ground and it was oodles of fun.

By 1998 I was feeling my oats and felt maybe I should run risk someplace, so in the spring of 1998 I became risk manager at DLJ.[1] DLJ was more a loose confederation of warring city-states than a corporation. I loved the place to pieces: it was a great firm. But then Credit Suisse bought us – at an exorbitant price, which made us all rich, no grudges. But DLJ was gone and I returned to Merrill Lynch.

At Merrill Lynch, Dan Napoli, the head of Risk Management retired in 1998, and Richard Dunn[2] became head of risk. He built up the risk team from 7 to over 100. When I arrived in 2001 to run Product Control, Arshad Zakariah was running the group. Merrill had assembled a large collection of former heads of risk management from other firms, Lisa Polsky from Morgan Stanley, Clinton Lively from BT, Steve Schulman from UBS, and me. We were all risk managers by training, so there tended to be a lot of overlap.

Stan O'Neal[3] took over the firm after September 11 and shook some things up. We decided to consolidate the various areas of market risk with product control to save bodies, and I ran the combined unit until 2005.

Frances: How was that?

John: It was fine. By then it was much bigger: there were about 150 people instead of six and the regulatory burden had become much worse. There was also a lot of tightening up to do. After 2005 I hung around and managed the quant group, with a trading desk reporting to me. That went along until the Summer of 2007 when I discovered the existence of the sub-prime positions, began modelling our losses, and in the Fall had to tell Stan O'Neal that we were dead. After Stan left, they put together a group of some of the old hands to see if anything could be done to fix it, but it was too big.

Frances: That was a strange time, we had all seen so many crises.

John: But this was bad. I think it was more complicated because people had lived through many crises. The lesson they had learned was that it's the liquidity that kills you, and it will work out OK so long as you tough it out. But this was a solvency crisis, not a liquidity crisis: this stuff was indeed worthless and was never going to be worth anything. The best thing would have been to take the pain quickly, but of course that went against the grain of what everyone had learned. It's understandable, because all the senior managers had got where they were by being tough and riding out crises. But it was not the right thing to do this time.

Frances: What was curious from an investment manager's point of view was that, while normally equity markets anticipate other markets, this time it was the credit markets leading the equity markets.

John: The equity markets were in cloud cuckoo land. I had long discussions with the equity traders who said the markets are holding up. They couldn't understand why everybody was getting upset. It was 2008 before the equity markets caught up with what had been going on in credit markets a year before. I have a natural selection theory for that, which is that when you have a long run in a one-way market (as equities had done since the early 1980s), everyone who goes the other way dies out and you're left with people who are all genetically predisposed to be long.

I retired in 2008, and then I sort of un-retired in 2011: a colleague from DLJ, Larry Schloss, who was working in the NYC Comptroller's Office as CIO of the city's pension funds, told me they needed a risk manager. So I helped him out. I didn't want to work for the city of NY, so I volunteered. Larry left with the change in administration. I stuck around for a while but when I gave an unabridged version of my views of the risk to the trustees, I wore out my welcome.

If I were doing risk management today, I would never run the official corporate risk function because your whole life is regulatory reporting. If I were running risk management now, I would take a consiglieri approach, but retain veto power, with nothing whatever to do with the official function. These days, in the official function you spend your life running a post office.

Matthew: *Or indeed a police department or something.*

John: But it is a toothless police department. The real meat of risk management is what it once was, a consiglieri function. It's now all about demands from regulators. For example, the Fed wants me to compute, to a 99.99% probability, how much we could lose in a year: that's once every ten thousand years! What are you people talking about? Are you serious? But they are serious.

Matthew: *Now, they are trying to do that with operational risk too.*

John: It is just silly! It is profoundly silly. Sure, we all do silly things in our lives, but when it consumes so much time, when they give you difficult silly things to do, it doesn't leave any time to do what's really needed.

Matthew: *It could be that the regulatory culture is sort of wrong. We know they have their masters and their legislation, but they seem more interested in their internal models than in real risk issues.*

John: They love this stuff! It is manifestly useless, but they love it anyway. But why do they love it? The cynic in me thinks that ever since Barings, the regulators have realised they can't really stop financial institutions from losing tons of money, but they can stop themselves for being blamed for it.

So they have armies of boffins collecting reports and they have umpteen statistical tests, blessed by various academicians. It is all essentially irrelevant to the problem, but it's protective of them. No one loses money because of statistics, you lose money because you do stupid things. When I started out, the risk management mandate was to prevent unacceptable losses. The term "unacceptable" was left very vague: it could mean "monstrously large", but really what it meant was stupid losses that are going to get you on the front page of the *Wall Street Journal*.

It comes down to incentives. Traders are basically honest but they are paid according to the profits they bring. They do fall in love with their own ideas, so you need people who are somewhat removed from it who don't have P&L[4] incentive[5] to take a second look and be sceptical and ask questions. Not because the traders are deliberately trying to commit fraud; they genuinely believe they can spin flax into gold. But you need to check on that. And you need people who have been around, because the same mistakes happen over and over and over again.

Matthew: *I think it may be the degree of freedom that the traders have for their limit structures. Because risk management doesn't want to be in people's faces with overly restrictive limits, they tend to set limits that are a bit broader. But in that broadness there is a degree of freedom. An example is the Saba[6] trading group at Deutsche Bank. They ran a massive position long General Motors credit derivatives and short the common stock, and doubled the position when the trade went against them.[7] It seemed like the group drove the process. It was described in the CDS market as the volatility anomaly of 2007; but it is hard to understand why it seems to be treated as a statistical event rather than regarded as a governance issue.*

John: The regulators can make governance more difficult. I always used to set very tight limits, which I expected routinely to be broken. They were to wake me up and no other purpose: Oops, someone went through a limit. I'd better see how the P&L[4] looks: is there anything queer going on here? Is there some anomaly? No? OK, then I can initial it done. Regulators hate that, they take the view that limits should be much more sacred. So everyone sets them wide enough so they're not driven nuts by constant breaches. But then you lose that little trip wire that serves as a very good way of telling you that something might need more attention. That signal is lost with hard, wide limits.

Frances: *As risk manager I always insisted on two lots of limits. One set were very narrow, soft limits that I expected to be broken frequently, the other set very wide, and were sacrosanct.*

John: It is very hard in today's regulatory environment to get away with that.

Frances: *The clients, the fund trustees, liked it because it reassured them that the positions were getting the attention they needed. The traders loved it because they understood where they stood. It gave them a trip wire too. But regulators would struggle.*

John: The other thing is that the accountants are always overworked. The warning sign that something isn't quite kosher is always there in the P&L: either it's just too smooth for the volatile market you're in, or there is some little drip, drip, drip in an options book, which might seem immaterial, but why is it there anyway? But they are so busy they don't have the time to ask the questions, even though usually the warnings are sitting there in plain sight.

That's my problem again with the regulators. Everyone is busy doing mindless tasks instead of following their noses: What's going on here? Why is this trader making so much money? He's not even trading with customers, he is trading with Goldman Sachs and Credit Suisse. Wow! He is smarter than they are? What's going on? I have never understood the obsession with statistical analysis. We did Value-at-Risk and stuff because we had to, but I had zero interest in it. For me it was more about who's making money, and why is he making money, and can he explain to me in an intuitive way how he is making it?

Model checking is a complete waste of time. The models are not right, they're wrong. Of course their wrong! I think it was Feynman[8] who said: If you think the answer should be something, and the first time you do the calculation and it comes out to what you thought it was, that's the time to recheck your work. In fact I loved it when we had a bunch of models; log-normal, square root-normal, normal with a reflecting barrier whatever. Then I could run things through five different models. But you still relied on the signals from realised P&L, from purchases and sales with other firms, because none of the models are right.

It was much more intuitive than it is now. This grew out of the old partnership days, when everyone understood the businesses they were in. Since then we all grew so big that senior management really can't understand everything. You need people to kick the tyres for you, people whose P&L doesn't depend on the outcome, so they don't have the incentives to convince themselves of things that are not true, which can happen to traders.

Matthew: *What sort of people did you have around you when you were running the practice? What do you think makes a risk manager good? Is it a style, a philosophy? What sort of people did you look for?*

John: My natural inclination, like everyone else, is to seek out people just like me: ex-theoretical physicists. But that's a mistake. You need people with some special skill (mine was to do stupid maths tricks in my head), something that the traders will respect you for. You are never going to know their particular market as well as they do, never. But you need some skill that makes you worth talking to, because the main thing is to get them talking. Beyond that I wanted people who were curious, who had good noses for things that didn't make sense. They didn't have to be maths majors, they just had to be curious, to know how to ask enough questions, to see, get an answer – and know how to follow up on it and keep following up. To see whether they get abdaba, or whether the guy can actually answer the questions. That's all: just be curious.

Matthew: *And now it is so compartmentalised, isn't it?*

John: They've destroyed curiosity.

Matthew: *I'm not sure that the traders really understand their own models. Some of them do of course, but when traders use a model day in day out, they no longer question it.*

John: They're just tools: they are essentially ways of booking things in a convenient way that distills hundreds of trades to a handful of parameters. It should be treated with only so much respect and no more. For example, with credit derivatives, some people thought that the Gaussian Copula model came from God. But it is almost certainly wrong, so you must try to balance things so that you are not exposed to the fact that the model is wrong.

Frances: *What worries me a lot, and this was the issue with the Gaussian Copula model, is that most people using the results that came out of it didn't understand what could go wrong in it.*

John: The way you control that is to control the gross limit: I would say: I don't particularly care for your models, so here you have a notional gross limit as well. Unless you can net[9] things virtually dollar for dollar, date for date, then they're under the gross limit.

Matthew: *Is that a certain style of banking though? When I was a trader I always had an inventory approach to my business: when I was getting too much inventory, it was a sign that something, such as the price, must have been wrong. Now I wonder if traders rely on time. For example, they might say: I can take a trade that looks mispriced to me; I know I am already up to my limit, but I will do it anyway and warehouse it for six months or so.*

John: There will always be opportunities: the market can be out of line. So you keep it for a while but get rid of something else. It's not that big a deal. We always had aged inventory limits but they were very easy to arbitrage so it was difficult to enforce. The regulators hated my gross limits because they are not scientific, they're not new.

Matthew: *Is it because you were sensible, that you took the view that banking is a turnover business rather than a warehouse business, which should be left to the pension funds?*

John: Yes. Dealers are supposed to make money trading with occasional arbitraging, but not warehousing, so that was part of it.

I have a deep distrust of the statistical models, and I'll give you an example of why. I was hired at my first job at the Security Pacific merchant bank because people were worried about some of the new-fangled trading that was going on. They wanted some number that would describe what bad could happen within the merchant bank trading operations. We didn't call it Value-at-Risk then, but that is essentially what we were doing. We were building a variance-covariance matrix of the merchant bank positions and coming up with a one standard deviation,[10] daily move. The vice-chairman in LA loved this thing to pieces.

The programmer did it in APL, I checked the work and it seemed sound. So we launched it, then the programmer went on holiday to Argentina. It breaks. Now we're panicking: Oh my God, we have to give the vice-chairman his number. I said: OK, I'll do it by hand every night (because it wasn't that complicated a bank). So I would stay late and calculate the number by hand and this was the best thing I ever did, because that way I learned what was really driving it, and why it was completely irrelevant. What was driving it was what the chief FX trader was doing in dollar-yen and the head of fixed income in the bond future; and the rest of it was completely noise. They were trading their brains out during the day, so the closing position actually had nothing to do with the P&L.[11]

So this told me that my time would have been much more usefully spent spending three hours a day with those two traders understanding what was driving their trades. This was an epiphany for me. All of this other stuff we were coming up with was meaningless. The other big risk was the swaps desk. It was ancient days, so no one had a zero coupon curve[12] to estimate present value,[13] so what you did was you split out an annuity and then you sort of guessed an annuity rate. The variability in the P&L in the swaps desk between mismatches and annuity coupons dwarfed everything else. So what I quickly learned was about accounting properly for the swaps and to hang out with the traders with big positions. That's what a really good risk manager had to do. A lot of places may be more complicated of course than Security Pacific was, but the philosophy is the same.

Frances: *To know what you needed to know to do the job.*

John: And to understand the dynamics of how senior management budgeted and the pressures they put on traders. Traders had big bonus incentives to exceed their revenue budgets. I remember one year, it was before people aggressively refinanced mortgages, so banks still had mortgages earning 10% on their books that people were happily paying and not refinancing. So we monetised them, securitised them, and sold them. The mortgage desk got the P&L for securitising and selling this treasure trove. The next year they were budgeted to be up 10%, but there was no more treasure trove. So what were they going to do? They were going to trade their brains out and take all kinds of crazy risks.

So it was a great learning ground. We didn't lose money because of correlations or volatilities: they had nothing whatsoever to do with how we lost money. We lost money because we'd done something really stupid. We'd done the same thing 10 years before and we knew it was really stupid. But we forgot, or we convinced ourselves that this time it would be different.

Matthew: *So what do you think about all the stress tests that they are doing now?*

John: I ran stress tests, but I would never tell the traders what the stresses were because if I did, all they had to do was to buy an out-of-the-money put and the stress point would meaningless. I ran stress tests to bring sleeping options to life because otherwise I would never see them. Something struck 20% below the market is invisible, so they needed to be woken up. I can tell you what the regulators will accomplish with all their obsession with capital, particularly risk-based capital. They're human: they will give some things too high a risk weight, and some things too low a risk weight. If they make capital precious enough, everyone will pile into whatever they give too low a risk weight. So they will create a bubble, a disaster, that's all it's going to do.

I told this to the Fed: they didn't like my comment. But it's true.

Matthew: *What do you think of the idea of breaking up the banks? Are they too complex?*

John: Everyone loves the free and fast flow of capital, and they like what you get out of it. Then they said: My God! The banks are big! Why don't you have a whole bunch of little banks? If you make them all little, it makes it easier, I suppose, but we are going to lose something. It will interfere with some of the things that we have come to enjoy from big banks. People like the liquidity of being able to get a bid on a huge block of stock. You are not going to be able do that any more if you break everybody up into little chunks.

Matthew: *Is that a big deal? There is the argument that, for example, Deutsche needs to be big because Siemens is big and it wants to bank Siemens. But if you ask a commercial banker how much he makes out of Siemens, he may complain that it's not much. So it seems to me a funny argument: I have got to be there for Siemens, but I don't get anything out of it and I wonder whether Siemens cares.*

Frances: *It may be to get profile, a kind of public relations, to say they are Siemens' main banker.*

Matthew: *My point is more: So what if you can't bank Siemens, you can get 50% of their business.*

John: It's a worthwhile experiment: break them all up and see what happens. My guess it will not go quite as everyone would like.

Matthew: *And the LIBOR scandal: the regulators are saying: You guys can't control risk and you're breaking the law: we have got to break you up.*[14]

John: This is a profoundly silly thing in my opinion. When I was risk manager for Merrill I probably was in the best position of anyone to take all the various bits of the firm; the marked to market parts, the not marked to market accrual books, the funding desk, the insurance subsidiary, the notes we'd written to retail; put it all together and I would have found it all but impossible to say whether the firm did better if LIBOR went up or if LIBOR went down. What I could tell you was whether the smart guys on the swaps desk could rip off the stupid guys on the FRA[15] desk by diddling a rate setting. But that was just one part of Merrill robbing another part! Who, outside of Merrill, cares about that? The odds that people were actually going to rig LIBOR to help their entire organisation at the expense of the outside world are zero, no one would know that much. What they could do was to rig it to get one up on the trader across the hall. So I think it's a tempest in a teapot.

Frances: *Was there an element of competition-like bravado in that, or was it really just to score against their colleague-rivals?*

John: It was more the Oxbridge vs the barrow boys.

Matthew: *The barrow boys always win.*

Frances: *They are often quicker, but the Oxbridge boys are better connected.*

John: But that's what it was.

Matthew: *Technology makes a difference too. I suspect that many of these things that they are now finding fault with existed before. The difference is that in 1986 there wasn't an on-line chat room, there was a pub. Now it's in chat rooms rather than pubs, so they are finding things out that they wouldn't otherwise.*

John: Yes, there is a paper trail, whereas before it was over a pint. And banks are predisposed to settle things to make them go away. Regulators can make their name by suing and getting a settlement, but I don't think it is going to change the world in any way to make it materially better. I particularly love the recommendation that, because banks are rigging LIBOR, we should use the Federal Funds Rate[16] instead: what more rigged rate could you possibly think of than Fed funds?

Frances: I never quite understood the logic of panels[17] to get "market" prices. LIBOR is just a giant panel. How easy is it? That these guys know they don't have to trade at that price? They can quote anything if they know they don't have to deal at that price.

John: It is wildly out of whack.

Frances: Next they are going to discover that the gold price, or something else, is rigged too.

John: I'm sure all of them are. We saw it all the time. Huge trading around IMM[18] dates, huge trading around the four o'clock[19] fixing of currency. There was usually someone who had an option position such that it was worthwhile to move the price of the underlying a few bips[20] so it came through the strike.[21] They would work like mad to manipulate the fix. But this was just battles between the professionals.

Matthew: What do you think about caveat emptor and packaging of CDOs and so on? We are having a financial sector enquiry in Australia and one of the submissions was to make institutions liable for the products they sell. This has come about because CDOs were sold to many people, some of whom wanted them but maybe didn't fully understand them. As a consequence, some US local governments had to cut school and fire department budgets. So it turns on the question of caveat emptor. Is there a qualified investor?

John: I was not a big fan of our Asset-Backed CDO desk even after I left risk management. I was still chairing an internal Merrill committee that looked at institutional suitability, and I spent a lot of time looking at sales practices surrounding the equity tranches of the CDOs. But to a considerable degree the proximate cause of pension funds and others being in trouble was rates were down to two or three per cent, while they had seven per cent bogies.[22] They desperately needed an investment grade product that gave them yield. This turned everybody into yield hogs, they will go for it as long as it's rated BBB or above (which they are allowed to hold in their portfolio) and it's got yield.

And perversely, the way the rating agencies looked at it was that they looked at the default histories and how quickly money came into, and built up, the reserve fund. This meant that, the worse the mortgage pool, the better it fit a CDO, because it threw off more yield and replenished the reserve fund more quickly. So that's why they mixed in those crappy ones. Not because they were desperately trying to cheat. It was what made the deals work according to the rating agency models.

Now, should people have stepped back and said the rating agency models were obvious crap? Perhaps, but that wasn't their job. Their job was turning out something rated BBB or better and had a nice coupon so people would buy it. No one wanted the stuff yielding LIBOR plus a nickel. This means that the banks will end up owning all the low-yielding paper in order to create the thing that everybody wants. If you create enormous incentives for people to chase yield, they will.

Matthew: *Like now.*

John: The temptation is to view the people creating these things as evil geniuses. They aren't, I know the guys. They were trying desperately to move stuff out that the sales force was screaming for. They had all these people who desperately needed yield, so they needed to generate product. And so they were doing it. And they believed it: the rating agencies say it's AAA, so it's AAA. How did the rating agencies believe it well into 2008? The meetings were monologues then: No, it's OK, it's not OK. It might look like you're insolvent, you're dead. No, no, no: these models say it's all going to converge. It will be fine. Yes, it was deceptive. But people first deceive themselves.

Matthew: *They never looked at the expected loss. They looked at the probability of default.*

John: All the models were based on historical experience, which is precisely what the Fed and everybody else wanted you to base models on. And so you would look at geographical diversity, and say: Even when Michigan had a bad time, people still paid their mortgages. We had never been in an environment where so many people had refinanced and had taken out so many second mortgages. A lot of the losses were on second mortgages. People were being encouraged to grow the economy by taking money that was locked up in home equity and spend it on stuff. And no one could believe that these mortgages would not, could not be repaid. People always pay their mortgages. It was inconceivable to an awful lot of people that you could have loss rates that were as high as they tuned out to be.

And we are still doing it. The new rules are going to encourage second mortgages yet again. When you have an economy that lives on asset bubbles, this is a consequence of it. The risk manager can look at it till the cows come home, but it won't change anything.

Now a big problem with the build-up of sub-prime at Merrill was regulators finally got their way, we got rid of all the gross limits and replaced them with ratings-based risk limits, which did not give the signal the old gross limits did.

Frances: The other thing is that they typically used two years of historical data in their models and it's not enough. You have to go back too far to see any real volatility in markets.

John: In mortgage losses you have to go back to the Great Depression to see people defaulting on mortgages. They could go back 10 or 20 years but it won't tell them anything. They could do standard deviations across regions: Michigan vs California and stress it to three standard deviations. It's irrelevant to the problem. But that was best practice according to regulators and everyone else.

And I knew the guys at the rating agencies, they were not the world's greatest quants but they weren't venal. They weren't doing it because they got fees, they were very diligently doing what they thought was the appropriate thing to do.

Matthew: In 2004 we thought the model looked wrong. How we got there was by sort of starting with the price, the margin, that we thought it should have been at properly to reflect the expected loss.

John: You've got to wade through that, I prefer looking at markets. For example, with the ABX,[23] you had various tranches. There was no set of loss assumptions that would have them all fairly priced, so which do you pick BBB, BBB+? And they all came out with different answers. So they'd then pick their favourite tranche and assume that that was the one that was predicting default rates for all tranches. And people who said they were wrong, were thought to be completely insane in 2007.

Matthew: *When did they call the end of the world? Was it when Lehman fell over?*

John: No, no. Oh well, people did. But gosh, when did I find out about it? I had a buddy who was a regulator at the FSA. He and I were chatting about this supposedly AAA stuff and every bank is stuffed to the gills with it. This is July 2007, and he said: It is the end of capitalism as we know it. Now it took a year to unfold, but it was obvious then that this stuff was going to bring down a lot of institutions.

The irony is that I don't think we ever made that much money from this product. It wasn't a lucrative thing, it was something the sales force really, really wanted, because they had all the yield hogs to service. But it wasn't a particularly profitable business. It was viewed as a very safe business, a fee business: you sell stuff to people and collect the spread. And it was easy to convince yourself that it's just impossible for it to go wrong. The other thing was that as you moved up in the firm, and I am sure it was the same in every firm: people didn't really realise. They thought: We own the super senior stuff so we own the top 40%. No: you own the top 40% of the bottom 5%, because this has already been tranched three times before. It begins super senior. But that would get lost as you moved your way up in the firm.

Matthew: *Because of the aggregation, the time, the date?*

John: People didn't really understand the asset-backed market and the initial tranching or, yes, sometime mortgages. All right, so you have Fanny Mae taking the most senior pieces. Then you have Japanese banks come in, and then you've got this tranche down here. And you slice and dice that like mad to try to get some yield. And then take some of the yield and you'd stick it in something else, and you tranche yet again and you have a super senior part of this piece, which is really the rotten core. But that would get lost because it had AAA, it was magic.

Matthew: *So what chance do you think directors have got of running these things? Most people would think you'd be a great director because you are asking different styles of questions. If you're a director, you are grateful for* *the work people do in giving you all these numbers, but you know that's not the story.*

John: You know it's hard, it's very hard to know what questions to ask some people. When Tom Patrick[24] senior was at Merrill, he had a reasonably strong background: he'd taught, he'd been a banker, but he wasn't quant by any means. But boy, he knew how to ask questions of a quant to see if he was being bullshitted. That's a rare talent. You could not expect that of most directors. They need a risk group that's not burdened with idiocy and can go round and ask questions and let you know if something troubles them.

At Merrill and DLJ, I had silver bullets. I could veto anything and make it stick, but I also realised that I probably didn't have a full chamber of bullets. I could do this a few times before there would be a revolt on the trading desk. But it never came to that because I never had to use a silver bullet: the traders knew I had them, so we would negotiate. That's crucial: if they think all you can do is enforce limits, and you can't just veto something when you don't like the smell of it, it's very, very hard: how do you get them to open up? You horse trade. But of course the regulators wouldn't like the way I horse traded either. If a trader had got himself in trouble to a modest degree: a million dollars or two, I'd give him a "Get out of jail free" card because I wanted them to tell me when it was still only a million dollars and not 20 or 50 million. Would the regulators stand for that today? No, it's a pity.

Frances: *It's a question of police vs colleagues.*

John: It is partly collegial it's partly just the guy: he's trapped, you know, he's in something which is only going to get worse. You've got to get him out of it.

Frances: *He has got to be able to trust you, but also respect you, it's the Teddy Roosevelt saying about carrying a big stick.*

Matthew: *Does this come back to the special team you mentioned earlier? You need people walking around asking questions with the authority. You don't want to talk only to the trader, you want to be able to talk to the accountant, to the quant guy.*

John: My day would be walking the trading floor and sitting down with some of the quants and then going for a drink with the accountants. What are you seeing, what's going on?

Matthew: *And that is a very informal process.*

John: But that's what has to be: it's an internal spy network. It's what's really happening that you are trying to find out. Now, internal audit.

Matthew: *Probably too authoritative?*

John: They don't have the judgement and they became very politicised, very quickly. They know who is supposed to be at fault in any disaster and any post-mortem, so I never had much use for internal audit. Generally the skills and the judgement are not there.

Frances: *Interesting, because I got on very well with them, probably because where I worked they were not like that. They knew that I understood what a portfolio manager was doing because I had done that job before, and they knew that portfolio managers opened up to me. I'd say: Give me a bit of slack and I'll tell you what's going on. And I want you to come and audit me because I also want to know if I'm missing something. We had a very good relationship, partly because they understood they didn't have the skills.*

John: And that can be very helpful and every firm is different too. At Merrill, compliance was a complete backwater and the legal department was where the people actually understood stuff and you would talk to them. When I went to DLJ compliance was all-powerful and legal was the backwater. And it took me months to realise that I was insulting this very important person who runs compliance by ignoring him.

Frances: *Tell me if we have got it all wrong, but when planning for crisis management (it's like a disaster recovery applied to markets), everybody worries about which puts are going to be invoked if rates go haywire. But does it take into account what people are going to do about that? A lot of models that I have seen just assume that portfolio managers are going to sit there and do nothing.*

John: Deer in the headlights.

Frances: *And they don't do that.*

John: I think people misunderstand fundamentally why big market moves sometimes lead to terrifying losses. It is not that you're positioned so that a "Black Swan"[25] kills you. I don't believe in "Black Swans". But you have been doing a lot of things wrong over time, you have stuff mis-marked over here, stuff mis-booked over there, and it's got lost in the shuffle until the market moves enough that suddenly it becomes obvious what has been going on. So then you get those losses starting to flow in, and every trader that has a position he doesn't like might say, for example: We've already lost $100 million, so I won't be noticed if I lose another $5 million. And so they take the opportunity to clean up their book.

That can be a wonderful event for a risk manager even though it is not favourable to the firm because you can see everything that you have been missing that was just below the surface or under the water. But that is why they lead to big losses. It is not that we all think the position in a 10 standard deviation event will kill us. But the 10 standard deviation event, or whatever you want to call it, does reveal all the things that we got wrong over time and hadn't seen.

Frances: *Warren Buffett said: Only when the tide goes out do you discover who's been swimming naked.*[26]

John: So I view "Black Swans" as an excuse. Senior management loves to think, "Oh my God, something that no one could have anticipated happened and cost us money." No we were doing something really stupid and that event revealed it. Don't kid yourself.

Frances: *I remain bemused by the expression: being Australian, I was 23 by the time I saw my first white swan. In Australia, all swans are black. It seems to me a cop out to say that nobody could have foreseen it.*

John: An act of God took down our bank. Yes.

Matthew: *The regulators are starting to push across to the liability side, total loss absorption capacity, do you think that's a better way?*

John: Well in the old way of doing it, with tier one tier two capital, you can have kinds of really complicated things that would count as capital but sure felt like senior debt. We are all endlessly creative. If you really want to constrain the banks, make the senior bond holders suffer, sure, why not? I doubt the regulators have the balls to change that much. But if they did, it would have some impact.

Matthew: *But how do they get to the number in the first place? The capital number: do they model their way there?*

John: I'd say: Don't obsess yourself with it. Let the market do it. Make it clear that senior debt is not going to be protected, only depositors and then the market will quickly correct. Again, it may lead to consequences you don't want in the flow of capital, but then that's life. The history of the banking system is of very powerful banks going under. I'm reading something now about the Spanish Empire and the great Fugger Bank of Nüremberg.[27] They were bankrupted by sovereign debt. There is a long history of this. What was the best-capitalised stock market in the late 1800s? Vienna! Do we ever think of a Vienna stock market?

Matthew: *Where to from here?*

John: It makes me want to cry what has happened to risk management, which was such a wonderful thing to do and has been turned into regulatory reporting of a particularly inane and complicated form. It's just a shame. The Feds don't understand that risk management people are on their side. Take the London Whale. This was not a risk management problem. If I had been the risk manager and I had seen the VaR model for that, I would have overridden it. It was crap. It was an accounting issue that they were shaving their mark, shaving their mark so you weren't getting the signal you were a roach motel.

Frances: *One of the things that exercises my mind is that to do risk management properly you need a lot of common sense. You have got to really know the models so you can say what is wrong with them. Ideally you should have some experience in risk-taking as well, so you understand what these guys are dealing with, even if you can't possibly know exactly what signals they are responding to day to day. So you need a very clever person to do risk management properly. I am not saying all risk managers are really clever, but it involves many skills, and to do it properly, quite a lot of experience. Yet we have also seen that being a risk manager is a bit like having a sold put: unlimited downside potential. If you want to have a bought call,[28] you become a trader. So why would somebody who is really clever sign up for a sold put when they could easily have a bought call?*

John: Every time I saved the firm $100 million, did the traders jump up on the trading floor and say: Oh my God, I was going to do something really stupid and John stopped me? No. If I stopped them from doing something and it turned out that Goldman did it and made $20 million, it's: Oh my God what an arsehole! Look what he did to me, taking money out of the mouths of my children! Yes, so you need a thick skin. I think people go into it because in the end traders only get to know one thing. They know it really well, but it is boring. The sort of person who wants to be a risk manager likes to know a little bit about everything, and would be bored as a trader. That's why I was saying I always look for curious people, because that's what you need.

I always thought that Maureen Miskovic[29] was one of the best risk managers I know. She ran risk at Lehman when I was running it at DLJ. We had this informal network. What would happen is you tell traders: No, no you cannot do that in that size. Is Lehman doing it? I'll find out, I'll call Maureen. We would share stuff. She was solid, and eventually she was succeeded by Madelyn Antoncic.[30] UBS, how could you possibly fault her for what went on there? Sacrificial lamb. But as a risk manager you get to learn an entire firm. So if you are a curious person it is a lot of fun. We get to go to the insurance subsidiary and look at their risk, the trading desk, the bankers and salesmen. The bankers and the salesmen were always the enemy to me: I am going to get a fee and all the risk is left with the trading desk.

Frances: *Yes, but they were just responding to their incentives too.*

Matthew: *How can a risk manager ever win an argument, about an illiquid position, for example, because he's not there. He doesn't have the same information as the trader.*

Frances: *You are not responding to the same signals.*

Matthew: *For example, this position is stale, it's been on your books too long. The salesman will pipe up and say: Oh we will clear that in the next couple of days. You can hold them to it, but that's about all you can do. Then, if you can't clear it then you are stuck with the exposure.*

John: That should be marked down until it does clear at some point: enough is enough.

Matthew: *One suggestion would be to ratchet the marking price down so if it is not gone in a week it goes down by so much, and so on.*

John: But then there is always an exemption for arbitrageurs. And then: what's really an arbitrage, and how much does it exist only in the trader's mind? This is why you need the mutual respect, so you can have these discussions. Then you are not just parachuting in with the sheets of computer printout. There [are] always one or two or three important things going on, on a trading desk. I wanted them to tell me the joke, I want to get the joke and then I will be OK. But if I don't get the joke then I don't know what you're doing here, and I am not going to be happy. So walk me through, tell me why this is so brilliant. If it's such a great trade, you can tell me in very simple language why it's so great, how are you actually going to realise all this money? And telling me that the model says it is, is not a good answer.

At one point, I think it was the FSA who had demanded that the traders on one of the London currency desks use only an official, approved model. I had considered that silly, but OK. I watched a trader mark his book, and he was inputting volatilities to six significant digits. So I asked him: What is going on here and the laptop comes out where he has the model he likes and he had to torture the official model to return those prices.

If the books are so dependent on a model, then forget it. The models are not that good, and are never going to be. That's why they are called models, not reality.

Matthew: *The risk consultants of the world would be distraught though: they have whole teams.*

John: Well it's a good living for people but it's silliness. I loved the regulators in the old days. When I was still at Sec Pac I ran both risk and the model development group. So the regulator comes in and says: Wait! Wait! You are developing the models as well as checking them! I said: Yes, what could be more efficient? And they went away happy.

Frances: *Is it generational, that we're so like-minded?*

John: It may be a generational thing, only because the young ones don't know how wonderful it used to be.

Frances: *They don't know what they missed. We have seen it work properly and now we see it not working, and we can see that it can't possibly work unless we drop the meaningless risk statistics or at least put them in a commonsense context.*

John: And eventually it will all come around. But how many disasters have we had where Value-at-Risk was completely irrelevant? And we still don't get it: Oh well, we have to go more standard deviation or multiply it by something else. We have something that has proven it's irrelevant and then you multiply by something, I don't get it!

Matthew: *And you spend 95% of your time producing it.*

John: I told the SEC years ago that we found Value-at-Risk incredibly useful as a contra indicator. If our desk is making a lot of money and the Value-at-Risk is tiny, very small, that's a desk I am going to spend an awful lot of time with. If someone has a big Value-at-Risk and they are making money and their P&L is very volatile, fine: they are never going to hurt us. They are in something liquid; they are marking to market, great!

Matthew: *I remember at a GARP Conference in 2009, I think, one of the guys said: I am pleased we've had this crisis because finally they will listen to me. I have been warning them about this all along and now it has happened. Finally they will take me seriously. Guess what: You have no chance.*

John: Near death experiences for management of banks has exactly the opposite effect of what you would think. It makes them feel immortal.

There's a famous short story about a New England town, where the bells chime and they kill all the old people, like a horror story. One reason I was attracted to risk management, aside from being curious, was because I'd come out of physics and I was wandering around the trading floor. I feel like I am in this short story: I don't see anyone with grey hair, what became of them all? The credit department and risk management have grey haired people. And that's where I am.

Notes

1   Donaldson, Lufkin & Jenrette was a US investment bank founded by William H. Donaldson, Richard Jenrette and Dan Lufkin in 1959. Its businesses included securities underwriting; sales and trading; investment and merchant banking; financial advisory services; investment research; venture capital; correspondent brokerage services; online, interactive brokerage services; and asset management.

2 A member of Merrill Lynch's Executive Committee and Head of Market and Credit Risk. He was instrumental in the Wall Street "bail out" of hedge fund LTCM. Prior to this, Mr Dunn was Co-Head of Merrill's Equity Division, Head of European Debt and Head of Asian Debt and Equity.

3 An American business executive who was formerly Chief Executive Officer and Chairman of the Board of Merrill Lynch & Co. Inc., having served in numerous senior management positions at the company prior to this appointment.

4 Profit and Loss.

5 Whose remuneration is linked directly to revenue or profit generated by risk-taking activities.

6 Saba is Hebrew for grandfatherly wisdom. This refers to the trading group led by Boaz Weinstein, an American derivatives trader and hedge fund manager and founder of Saba Capital Management. He worked at Deutsche Bank from 1998 to 2009 and rose to prominence in 2006 and 2007, when one of his trading groups cleared over $1.5 billion in profits. Weinstein was promoted at age 27 to become Deutsche Bank's youngest ever Managing Director. His proprietary trading group was widely reported to have lost about 18% on $10 billion of capital in 2008, his only losing year out of his 11 years at Deutsche Bank.

7 See Deutsche Bank Fallen Trader Left Behind $1.8 Billion Hole, *Wall Street Journal*, 6 February 2005, http://www.wsj.com/articles/SB123387976335254731.

8 Richard Phillips Feynman (11 May 1918–15 February 1988) was an American theoretical physicist known for his work in the path integral formulation of quantum mechanics, the theory of quantum electrodynamics, and the physics of the superfluidity of supercooled liquid helium, as well as in particle physics. For his contributions to the development of quantum electrodynamics, Feynman, jointly with Julian Schwinger and Sin-Itiro Tomonaga, received the Nobel Prize in Physics in 1965.

9 Offset bought and sold exposures.

10 Standard Deviation indicates the range of outcomes that can be expected to happen 68% of the time.

11 Profits or losses generated by their trading activities.

12 A theoretical yield curve describing pure interest rates for a range of maturities, excluding the effects of coupon payments.

13 The current value of a stream of future cash flows, given the interest rate. A related concept is Net Present Value.

14 See Dudley, W.C., Opening Remarks at the Workshop on Reforming Culture and Behavior in the Financial Services Industry. Federal Reserve Bank of New York, 20 October 2014.

15 Forward Rate Agreement. An over-the-counter contract between parties that determines the rate of interest, or the currency exchange rate, to be paid or received on an obligation beginning at a future start date. The contract will determine the rates to be used along with the termination date and notional value. In this type of agreement, it is only the differential that is paid on the notional amount of the contract.

16 The interest rate at which depository institutions actively trade balances held at the Federal Reserve, called federal funds, with each other, usually overnight, on an uncollateralised basis. Institutions with surplus balances in their accounts lend those balances to institutions in need of larger balances. The federal funds rate is an important benchmark in financial markets.

17 The practice of obtaining an indicative benchmark price or rate by conducting a "survey" whereby selected market practitioners are asked to quote a price or rate for a given, hypothetical transaction.

18 Quarterly dates of each year that serve as scheduled maturity or termination dates for most futures and option contracts. They are typically the third Wednesday of March, June, September and December.

19 GMT.

20 Basis points, or hundredths of a percent.

21 The exercise price of an option.

22 Target investment returns.

23 Asset-Backed Security Index, a credit default swap contract that pools lists of exposures to mortgage-backed securities.

24 Served as an Executive Vice Chairman of Finance and Executive Vice Chairman of Administration at BofA Merrill Lynch (Merrill Lynch & Co., Inc.) from November 2002 to July 2003. He now serves as Head of Equity for North America at Deutsche Bank AG, is a Co-Founder and Co-Owner of New Vernon Capital, LLC and serves as its Chairman and Principal (Bloomberg Businessweek. Investing.businessweek.com).

25 A term coined by Nassim Taleb to describe rare, unpredictable events that have a big effect, and are often inappropriately rationalised after the fact with the benefit of hindsight.

26 Brainyquote.com.

27 Founded by the Fugger family in the fifteenth century.
28 With unlimited upside potential.
29 Maureen J. Miskovic served as Group Chief Risk Officer and Member of the Group Executive Board at UBS AG from January 2011 to December 2011.
30 Madelyn Antoncic is Vice President and Treasurer of the World Bank.

5 | Bill Muysken

London, 2 December 2014

You only get so far analysing the risk, you need to communicate it to other people and understand the biases that can affect human judgement.

Bill Muysken is Global Chief Investment Officer for Alternatives at Mercer in London.

He tells why commonsense and reasonableness checks are as important as ever.

Bill Muysken: I trained as an actuary, so mathematics is my forte. Like a lot of actuaries, I started out working in insurance, for Prudential in Sydney in 1981. In 1985, seeking more variety, I went to work for the Australian Government in Canberra, first in the Government Actuaries Office, then after two years in the Department of Finance because I found that those folk had more influence over policy and the way things were done.

While I was there we became a client of Mercer and in 1992 I joined Mercer in Melbourne as an investment consultant. During my period in Canberra my work had gravitated from actuarial to investment and I liked the investment side, so when I came to Mercer it was pure investment and has been ever since. In 1997 I moved to Mercer in London and became Global Head of Research. In 2007 I left to take up a fund management role, but came back to Mercer in 2010 as Global Chief Investment Officer for Alternatives, which is what I do now. The attraction there was it combined the knowledge of Mercer's research network that I built up with the practical implementation skills that I picked up during my time in funds management. I'm still doing that because I enjoy it immensely.

Frances: *Who were the people you were influenced by in that period?*

Bill: I think the person who has most influenced me is Tony Cole,[1] one of my early supervisors. Tony was the head of Investment Consulting business at Mercer in Australia, before which he had been Secretary to the Treasury in Canberra. He gave me a very good piece of advice very early in my career, which was that the value you add in your job is not just picking good investments, it is convincing other people that they are good investments, and I have thought about that ever since. It is no good just convincing yourself it's a good idea; to translate that into value, you have got to convince other people that it is a good idea. That might not tell you anything about risk, but it does tell you something about communication, which is I think important in risk management.

Frances: *What innovations have you seen in the last 10 years that you believe have been effective in managing risk?*

Bill: I will be a bit bold here and say none at all. I think there is a lot to be said, no matter how much quantitative analysis you do and how fast you do it and how good your data is, you still need to give everything a very careful reasonableness check and a commonsense overlay. If people think more data and more computing power and so forth helps them manage risk more effectively, they are probably not seeing the wood for the trees. In that sense I think some of the basics haven't changed. The way you do it has changed a little bit but the most important thing is common sense and reasonableness in thinking about what can go wrong.

One of the things that was drilled into me early in my training as an actuary was the importance of doing reasonableness checks. I trained at a time when computing power wasn't great and you didn't have many chances to run your program through a system. The key thing that was drilled into me was standing back, running reasonableness checks, trying to triangulate the results you see with what logic tells you. You ought to see the connection and if you can't figure it out, you need to start asking questions. So that's something I have tried to apply ever since. It is one of those old practices that has stood the test of time. Sometimes, when things go wrong, I think people have forgotten those basics.

Frances: *Who do you think are the most important thinkers today?*

Bill: Out of all the stuff I have read over recent years, the person who really stands out is Howard Marks,[2] one of the founders of Oaktree Capital Management in California. He has written some great stuff, treatises and essays on risk, and of course he's written books in his own right. I'd like to think he has influenced my thinking, although I have only come to his writing relatively recently, so it's more a sort of confirmation: he confirmed what I thought I already knew. A lot of very sensible stuff has been written about risk, but his work really stands out. It entices you to think about the subject, I think.

Frances: *What would you say has changed since 2007?*

Bill: Probably the biggest change is when we do our quantitative analysis on risk we have a much richer data set than we had in 2007. To start with, we have another crisis in our data set that we didn't have before. So, whereas you used to have to imagine extreme events, you don't have to imagine them anymore. But that's not to say that it's the only thing that can happen.

It is probably worth mentioning one other thing that probably influenced my thinking on risk very early in my career, which was the October 1987 stock market crash. I wasn't managing money at the time but I was watching plenty of people who were and reading a lot about it. A lot of people active in the market today don't believe something like that can happen. So one of the risks that worries me most these days is that there are a hell of a lot of investment strategies that seem to rely on an assumption that you will be able to head for the exit door when the time comes and get out. And the more people there are who rely on that assumption the less possible it is going to be. And I think the risk of that sort of thing happening again: it either will or it won't, but I think it's underestimated.

Frances: *A lot of people think that the way liquidity risks are measured misses that point. When you came into work the market was down 25%–40% if you were in Australia. And that was if the market was open at all: most markets around the world closed for at least part of the day because of the crash.*

Bill: I was working in Canberra at the time, so I was sort of sitting on the sidelines rather than an active participant; but I remember it very well. For example, CTA[3] strategies are a popular strategy for hedge funds, and I'm very comfortable investing in them, but I'm aware that they comprise many of the characteristics of the CPPI[4] strategies that are known to have contributed to the severity of the 1987 crash. With these limitations in mind, as with anything else, we do it in moderation.

Matthew: *Man Financial used to have a product that guaranteed capital and they'd put the rest in a portfolio of CTAs.*

Bill: And that sort of layers trend-following upon trend-following. We think there is a place for them in portfolios, for example they were very effective in 2008 to provide a hedge against a long drawn out market crash. But I don't think any of the CTA managers would claim that they'd provide a hedge against a 1987 type crash.

Frances: *A bit of gap risk.[5]*

Bill: So I think people underestimate that sort of risk simply because it hasn't appeared in the data for a long while. We had some mini flash crashes over recent years but nothing of the same extent.

Matthew: *I think also they underestimate the intra-day risk that they take on. They rely on the margin system to protect their capital. And this works to some extent, but if they are taking eight times that risk during the day, which some are, that's quite scary.*

Bill: And as with CPPI back in 1987, the more people that do it, the greater the risk becomes. So that is one of the types of risk that worries me most these days.

Frances: *What are your observations about the role of risk management in the organisation?*

Bill: I think the best risk takers are very aware of risk and very good at monitoring and managing their own risk. I do think there is a role in investment organisations for someone independent from them to oversee what they are doing and maybe give advice on how to do it better, as well as to check that the way they are doing it is sound. Not so much taking over risk management from the risk takers, which would allow the risk takers to think they don't have to worry about risk management. More coaching and coordinating.

Frances: *Like a mentor.*

Bill: Yes. I think good risk takers have to be risk-aware to do their job properly. They have to have a good understanding of the risks they're taking, otherwise they will be good risk takers for a while and then they will be extinct. They have to believe in risk management themselves rather than having it imposed upon them by an external risk manager. So I think a large investment organisation should have a dedicated risk team, but they should operate in that way rather than taking over from the risk takers and telling the risk takers they don't have to worry about risk anymore.

Matthew: *Do you see that happening much?*

Bill: I see elements of that happening. It calls to mind those personality tests that you sometimes find you have to do as part of soft skills training. You get to become a little bit more self-aware during these things. One thing I found out about myself is that my results on these personality tests have evolved. For example, one particular aspect is introversion versus extroversion. I started out my career at the extreme end of the introversion scale, and more recently I'm sort of right in the middle of that dial. I have an untested hypothesis that I think extroverts tend to be more risk takers, less risk-aware and introverts tend to be too risk-aware for their own good. I remember early in my career, every time the equity market went up I thought it was getting over-heated and throughout my career my bias has been far too much on the bearish side. But over time I feel my views have become a bit more balanced, in line with the change in my personality type from introverted to in the middle of the scale.

Frances: Your risk appetite and tolerance have changed.

Matthew: I think I'm a bit like you in the way the 1987 crash got seared into my brain. I was trading at the time, but after some years I began to think of it more as a point on a broader distribution. I had been modelling my own tail loss on that extreme event, whereas the markets had moderated and the data had settled down. I think that is sometimes what can happen, you fail to look dispassionately at the data. For example, if you were just walking into a new job and you ask to be shown the distribution or returns you would probably come out with a different perspective than if you were wholly reliant on that single tail loss. Perhaps the same thing has happened to you, you've seen many moves now and you know which ones are important and which ones aren't.

Bill: Maybe that is just one of the things people learn with experience. I'm sure there are people who started at the other end of the scale and gravitated towards the middle as they get burnt by experience. That's an observation: I haven't done any detailed analysis to test that hypothesis; it is really based on a sample size of one, with that one being me.

Frances: Going back to the importance of the buy-in of the portfolio manager, where you said you think the risk takers have to be risk-aware, do you think it's not just the portfolio manager, but also the CIO and senior management? How many senior managers in hedge funds do you see who actually buy in into that?

Bill: A lot of the best risk takers that I come across are very risk-aware and that's why they haven't gone out of business yet. I met some who aren't very risk-aware and then over time they don't last, which might be fine by them because they may well be retired on a lot of money. But on a net basis the clients might not have made much money. So I do find a lot of good risk takers are very risk-aware: that if you are not careful it might be the last risk you get to take.

In my job I spend a lot time meeting risk takers and that's a trait I see in some of the better ones. They're not just all guts and no brain. I think it also helps them when things go the wrong way in a position. It's probably important to be positioned so that, when things go the wrong way, you are not forced to liquidate positions to protect yourself. If you have calibrated things right to start with, you are in a position where firstly you can hold your positions and secondly you might even have some buying power to exploit the situation. I know that this is easy to say and hard to do, but it is something I see in good risk takers. They also tend fully to appreciate the value of good risk management and certainly when they are hiring, they look for those traits.

Frances: *How do organisations manage the balance between the technical skills necessary effectively to interpret the output of sophisticated risk models and the political skills to ensure that they are taken as seriously as they need to be?*

Bill: Occasionally you come across an organisation where there is a risk manager who's very good technically but they don't get taken as seriously as they should be. But I wouldn't describe what is required there as political skills, I would say it's presentation skills. This goes back to what I was taught by Tony Cole, who said: You know you only get so far coming up with good investment ideas. You have got to convince others. I think it is the exact same thing on risk: you only get so far analysing the risk, but the key thing is how best to communicate it to others so that they understand the key points of your findings.

Communications skills are what I think a good risk manager has to have to be able to convey their understanding of risk to the people that matter. And some people do that very well. Both on the risk-taking side and the risk management side, a lot of the people in the industry come from technical backgrounds like myself. You tend to be of the personality type that focuses on the details and not so much on the big picture and part of the skill is to sort of step back from the detail and summarise the big picture in ways that people can understand. That's a challenging part of the job, both for the risk takers and for the risk managers.

Matthew: *Does risk evaluation capture the human response to a crisis, or is it generally regarded as something to be dealt with when it arises?*

Bill: I had a very interesting conversation with an investment team that used to be part of a hedge fund that blew up in late 2007 even before the 2008 crisis. This hedge fund had a lot of quantitative models, both for taking risk and for risk management, but they had an approach of applying a judgemental overlay to the output from those models. What they found when the crisis really hit was that the pressure was just too great and the judgemental overlay tended to amount to staring at the ceiling and wondering what to do. As part of their systematic model they'd coded a systematic response to a crisis situation. So rather than leave it to judgement when the time happens, they'd come up with a set of rules to respond to a crisis, which I think made sense. Whether you do it systematically or judgementally, I think you need to think in advance how you will respond when a crisis happens rather than wait for it to happen and then stare at the ceiling.

Going from what I said earlier, if you have calibrated your risk well in the first place, hopefully you won't be forced to liquidate everything in response to a crisis. You will be able to look at things rationally, decide what if any positions have to be cut and what can be retained and come out of the other side.

The worst thing in a crisis is to take the big drawdown and have no capacity to come out the other side. That happened in October 2014. Anybody who liquidated at the bottom got burnt, whereas whoever made it through to the end tended to come out okay.

Matthew: *What kind of structure would prepare an organisation to respond smoothly to a crisis?*

Bill: I think you have got to have clear accountability so that the people who are responsible for dealing with crises know that they're responsible. Ideally you would prepare in advance some responses, for example to a scenario you imagined as one that your organisation just couldn't tolerate. You have really got to think about how you size your positions so that you don't get yourself into that situation in the first place. Clearly you can't foresee every possible crisis but there are plenty of permutations of past events you can look at for an idea of what might happen. And it's probably not good to assume that the worst crisis that's ever happened in the past is the worst that can ever happen in the future, because as we've seen over the years, it can get a lot worse than it ever has before.

Matthew: *Why do you think that is, given the increased focus on good risk management over the last 20 to 30 years?*

Bill: I think part of what drives fluctuations in markets is human behaviour and that's something that doesn't change that much over time. It evolves over generations but not over shorter periods of time and if you read the behavioural finance folk, the nature of human behaviour is that if it was something that was easy to fix it wouldn't be a behavioural issue. And I think there are plenty of players in markets who have incentives that are given them to take risk and it's sort of heads I win, tails you lose. That doesn't help things either.

Frances: *Do you think there is a check, anything you can do about that? What would you do about that if you could?*

Bill: I think organisations really have to have the right culture. The incentives structure is part of that, but I think that the people at the top of an organisation have to lead by example and set the culture in such a way that people behave for, if you like, for the greater good rather than for individual incentives.

Frances: *Do you see a tendency toward regarding very complex risk models – such as those with embedded copula analysis – as a black box?*

Bill: Quantitative risk analysis does advance over time and I think that's great. But going back to what I said earlier, it's really important that whoever interprets the risk output applies commonsense and reasonableness checks and tries to triangulate the results they see in front of them with the things they see in the real world. One thing that I've noticed in the risk models we use is that the time horizon tends to be quite short with short look-back periods used for data sampling. That's a bit of a problem right now because we are coming out of a period where risk, as measured by volatility, has seemed almost non-existent. Risk has been there, of course, but it just hasn't manifested itself in a disaster.

Frances: *What is your look-back period?*

Bill: Some of the tools we use they have a six-month look-back and they will tell you that the volatility of equity markets is in single digits. If it tells you that, then nothing else is going to make sense either. If you are in a period of extended low volatility you need something in your framework to allow for the fact that it is not always going to be like that. There are different ways of doing it, but you can never rule out the fact that you might get another 2008 or another 1987 and if your risk model relies on the last five years being as risky as it gets, then you are probably going to get into trouble at some point.

Frances: I thought it was one of the big problems with the 2007/2008 crisis because the longest-look back period was, as you know, 60 months. Even that was far too short because that took you back only to 2002. Taking a longer look-back period is no panacea either, but there is a widespread tendency to use short look-back periods with more frequent observations, and that implies correspondingly shorter investment horizons. Horizons of a day or so make good sense for investment banks and trading portfolios, but not for longer-term portfolios such as pension funds.

Bill: And when you talk to the people who built the risk models, they'll tell you that there are so many new securities that you can't get data going back so long. It's driven by technical issues rather than common sense. There are various ways to address that and I've seen people do it different ways. For example, some people look at short-term risk but they also have a long-term risk model, and they take whichever gives them the greater, which is fair enough. Other people just do commonsense things like setting limits on absolute position sizes so that if their risk model happens to underestimate risk, there is a backstop there. Some people set limits on how low their correlation assumptions are going to be, so that if correlations end up being higher than expected (or lower as the case may be, depending on how the mathematics works), there is a backstop there. But you need some commonsense check in the framework that says that if your risk model is failing you for whatever reason there is a backstop.

Frances: A good example of that is in 2007, when an investor was concerned that there wasn't enough risk in the portfolio to achieve its target returns. The models used 60 months of look-back and they were telling us that the market volatility was in single digits. I pointed out that that was atypical, in view of market volatility observed over longer periods and that it implied that portfolio risk was understated by at least 50% and so was unsustainable. The investor accepted the argument and we kept risk at that level rather than increase the risk of the portfolio. That turned out to be the right thing to do, and I think it illustrates your point.

Bill: Whoever uses the tools has to apply some common sense and interpret them properly and look for things that the risk tools and risk horizons aren't covering.

Matthew: *Because in some organisations, there is an agenda to produce the reports on a timely basis for various purposes, such as daily review by management, strategic review once a week, board review once a month. It becomes a job of just churning out numbers with very little opportunity to sit down and think about what it might be telling you, particularly if risk management is seen as a cost that needs to be watched.*

Bill: I think it's good to have hard position limits so that if your risk model fails there is something to fall back on.

Frances: *But can nominal position limits over-simplify things? Sometimes you need to take into account how much the positions are contributing to risk, which is not the same thing. For example, in a portfolio I worked on recently, nearly 30% of its risk was coming from a position that represented 2.4% of the value of portfolio. So if you limit that position to, say, 5%, you are still going to allow up to about 60% of the risk to be concentrated in one stock – and not a very liquid one at that. Have you come across that?*

Bill: I think if you only use hard position limits you will find yourself limiting risks that don't need to be limited and being too loose on others. I would just advocate position limits as a loose backstop. Proper risk models are a better guide in most circumstances, but just in case they are pushing you to the limits, I would apply some hard limits to stop things going totally off the rails.

Shortly after I joined Mercer, I remember meeting with a new client. This was quite a large fund and at the initial meeting with this client we asked them if they would like us to run an ALM.[6] The client said: Please do anything you like, but not an ALM. The last consultant did an ALM and we ended up with 40% in real estate.

Frances: *How effective do most practitioners think ongoing stress tests can be?*

Bill: I think stress tests are useful, and one reason for that is that they don't necessarily require any particular look-back period. You can stress against actual periods in history and things that actually happened. Even if you've made up scenarios, it doesn't matter what the look-back period is or how volatile the markets have been recently. Because they're fixed scenarios, I do think they are

useful not only for making sure risk doesn't get off the rails, but
also for communicating the risk analysis. For example, I have a risk
report here, and most of what's in it I couldn't explain to a client
without their eyes glazing over. But you can explain it in terms of
scenarios in the past and how the portfolio would have done. And
that makes sense to them. After all the whole definition of risk is
not clear to a lot of people. It's not just volatility, it's really a
probability of a serious loss of capital, however you might want to
quantify that. Presenting people with stress test scenarios saying: In
this circumstance, this is how much capital you would have lost,
are you OK with that? And the key question is: If that happens to
you, are you going to be happy to hold your positions? Because if
not, then the positions may be too big. So I think stress tests and
scenario analyses are very useful. Both are free of any recent data
bias and also they are something that you can explain to
people.

Frances: *Most of your clients, the funds that you are working with now, are*
they mostly hedge funds or some kind of alternative? Are they captured by
the AIFMD?[7] *What are they saying to you about that?*

Bill: Actually very little because most of them are in America. Hedge
funds based in the US are now very cautious about approaching
entities in Europe and inadvertently breaking the law. Fortunately
with us, they just approach our US people and they don't run a
risk of breaking the law so it's easy. If our organisation were
wholly in Europe, that would be a problem. But I have been
getting a lot of emails from people who are worried about
breaking the rules through unsolicited tele calls or whatever it's
called, saying: Unless you tell us you want more of these emails,
this will be the last one you get from us. They need some reverse
inquiry on file to be able to keep the communication going.

Frances: *So does that mean that your clients are feeling relatively unaffected*
by encroaching regulation?

Bill: There is no doubt that the cost of regulation is going up, and I
don't mean the cost incurred at the regulators, I mean incurred at
all the organisations they regulate. It's increasing the hurdle for
running a small boutique firm. There is so much that you have to
deal with, no matter what the size of your firm, which increases
the fixed cost element. It makes it more attractive for the

multi-boutique platforms and that sort of thing to evolve. So some people would say that that is the cost you have got to pay to have properly functioning markets. But as with everything else, I think there is always scope to do things more efficiently. Hopefully the regulators will learn that over time, and hopefully their political masters will incentivise them to do that.

Frances: *Do you think that, by ruling out a lot of the small players, which means in many cases emerging hedge funds, it's going to make it really hard for small, emerging hedge funds. Some people worry that it could limit investor choice, especially if you take the view that the new ideas and new strategies emerge with new hedge funds.*

Bill: Maybe there is a role in the market place for someone to run the infrastructure that risk takers need to sit within, such as these multi-boutique structures.

Frances: *The hedge fund hotels.*

Bill: One thing that has struck me recently is family offices and how much risk appetite they have. I started asking myself why they have such a big risk appetite. But when you think about how they came to be in a position where they have a family office, it must be that they're really wealthy and somewhere along the line they must have taken some really big bets. And the bets must have paid off. That's how they got to be really wealthy, and that's how they come to have a family office. If you took big bets and they didn't pay off, then you wouldn't have a family office to worry about. So people who find themselves with a family office – at least in the first generation – are people who have taken some big bets in their life that paid off, and so their natural inclination is to take big risk.

Matthew: *They may have a different time horizon too. For example, listed funds are subject to quarterly benchmarks and so on, whereas the family office doesn't care as long as it works out after three years or so.*

Bill: And I guess it's different taking risk with your own money as opposed to other people's: you can take a longer-term view. But I think part of it also is some people have got themselves in a position where they have created family offices who have never known a risk not to pay off because otherwise they wouldn't have got in that position.

Frances: At least on balance they might have paid off.

Bill: And part of the education they need is that not everybody is as lucky as they are. Sometimes risks don't pay off and that has to be managed, no matter how long term you are.

Frances: Do you discuss risk appetite with your other clients?

Bill: Not me personally. It is generally discussed by another member of the team.

Frances: Have you observed any common approach to assessing risk appetites?

Bill: Yes. It tends to be driven primarily by scenario analysis. There are various types of modelling that can be done to look at the probability of losses below certain levels. This isn't original: you can find it in the Howard Marks stuff. I can talk about the probability of rain tomorrow, but it's either going to rain tomorrow or it's not. And yesterday it either rained or it didn't. Talking about the probability of something happening is a concept that people find difficult to come to grips with. It's probably a little easier if you give them a scenario that says this might plausibly happen, although we don't know what the probability is. But if it came to pass, how would you feel? That's probably a better way to get people to think about it.

There are various sorts of biases too. I find it interesting reading the behavioural finance stuff about various biases people have in their judgements. One of them tends to be a confirmation bias. Sometimes when the risk managers prepare the standard quantitative analyses and send their reports down the line, people who receive them just want confirmation that everything is OK. This can be dangerous as it clouds judgement. Related to that is anchoring bias. Anchoring bias is where the report tells you something that you didn't believe beforehand, and you tend to ignore it because you are anchored in your previous opinion.

You have to be aware of the potential for biases when you are talking with clients. Sometimes it's just a matter of trying to frame questions the right way. A famous psychological experiment concerns a scenario where there is a ship about to sink. You might ask someone: How do you choose between a 90% chance of saving 10% of the people and a 10% chance of saving 90% of the people? Which one is more attractive to you? Another way of framing the same question is: How do you choose between a 10% chance that 90% of the people will die and 90% chance that 10% of the people will die? Even though it is the same question, framed in different ways, you get very different responses.

So in talking to people about risk appetite it is important to frame the questions the right way, think about the different ways a question can be framed and the different responses you will get. Sometimes you need to ask the same question in two different ways to get a balanced response. If you say to a client: Do you want to take a lot of risk or a little bit of risk? They'll say: A little bit please. You have got to really frame it in a way that gives them a proper understanding of the trade-off that they face.

Matthew: *What about the trustees?*

Bill: I think certainly in the pensions funds world, governance in general is a topic that people are thinking a lot more about. What is the best sort of governance structure to have in place? Firstly, you must ensure that the key issues get focused on, and secondly, you must ensure that decisions get taken properly. There are often situations where the discussions get dominated by one or two key individuals and the rest are bystanders. That's fine if everything goes right but, if something goes wrong, all the trustees are accountable – even if it was really just one or two people driving the decisions.

It's a major topic for discussion: how to get the governance arrangements right so that everybody who is held responsible for a decision is actually involved in making that decision, and also that decisions that should be delegated are delegated so that trustees can focus on the important decisions.

Frances: *That's an important point. Do you have much to do with hedge fund boards?*

Bill: We generally check to make sure they exist and who's on them. But it's not often you see them taking material decisions.

Frances: *That's interesting because we read in, for example, the Walker Review[8] of corporate governance, about how they should be more pro-active in overseeing risk management. Yet you also hear about individuals serving on sometimes hundreds of hedge fund boards. It begs the question of how pro-active can they be on so many boards?*

Bill: Yes, I'd agree with that.

Frances: Do you think directors are being held accountable?

Bill: My sense is that in today's world they do feel the accountability very much and they are being pro-active in making sure that risk is being looked after. In any well-governed organisation there is someone whose primary responsibility is to look after those sorts of things. The people doing those jobs are seasoned professionals, who know what they are doing and know how to do it properly in practice. That might be too rosy a view of the world but I do think that it's generally being well looked after; you can have organisations that are dominated by over-bearing individuals who override their peers and there are plenty of examples where that has happened in the past and it will probably happen again. But that's a sort of culture thing to be aware of.

Frances: Are there any other events or instances that have really stood out?

Bill: The other thing I've learned that can be important is what the behavioural psychologists would call recency bias, which you come across quite often. In 1981, when I started my career, we had just had a decade of double digit interest rates and double digit inflation. At that time, people couldn't understand why actuaries were assuming that, over the long term, interest rates and inflation would be in single digits. Everybody was extrapolating from the last decade, which at the time was the 1970s, and assuming that we'd have double digit inflation and interest rates forever. More recently the opposite has been the case: where people are finding it difficult to imagine that one day we might have material positive interest rates and inflation rates again. Whereas in reality it is somewhere in between. I'm not sure what the best way to address recency bias is, apart from growing old like me, or studying longer-term history.

Frances: It could be an argument for mixing age groups in teams: you don't want everybody to be at a similar stage in their careers. It can be good to mix young, middle-aged and older to broaden that perspective.

Bill: Hopefully younger people don't have to wait 30 years to learn those lessons. Hopefully they can read a bit about the history and gain some of it through education so that they can be more effective earlier on in their careers.

Frances: Another example of recency bias is in October 1987. After the crash, we found that nobody, including among the bond dealers, nobody short of the partners in the firm, had ever seen a positively-shaped yield curve. We had read about it in text books, but that was all.

Bill: There are parallels these days. Until 2008 people hadn't seen a credit spread spike and more recently there are again people now who haven't seen one.

Frances: What value do you think is added to an organisation by risk management? From the perspective of organisations, from the clients' and from broader stakeholders' perspectives?

Bill: Well certainly at the top level of a large organisation the directors and senior management need to have some comfort that risk is being looked after properly. So they need to get some sort of independent advice about the risk being taken. It's important to make sure the people at the top of the organisation are properly informed about the risk being run. And I think these days, directors are very conscious of their liability and what might happen if risks get out of hand. It's probably one of the things that is upper-most in their minds. Asking: Everything seems to be going well, but is it really going well and are we taking undue risk in doing this? And if things do go wrong they need to demonstrate to regulators and others that they did actually take appropriate precautions and set an appropriate culture to minimise the risk of things going wrong. Otherwise they may be found liable.

And certainly the customers' long-term interests must be looked after by risks being properly managed. Many customers have a limited understanding of risk and probably underestimate risk, because risk by its nature is something that doesn't manifest itself all the time. It is a bit like when you take out insurance on your house. For example, I have insured our house against fire every year for the last ten years. It hasn't paid off of course, but I think it was good risk management, and when it comes up for renewal I will be renewing it again next year. You can say that it costs something but it is a cost I am happy to bear because I know what the outcome might be if I don't. And I think people need to think of risk in those terms when they're attaching a cost to risk management. It's a kind of insurance premium that you pay to protect against disaster. For the customers, risk management is like giving them some insurance against things going badly wrong, protecting the taxpayers against having to bail out organisations when things go wrong.

Notes

1   An Australian who served as a senior World Bank official from 1979 to 1981 and principal private secretary to Treasurer Paul Keating from 1983 to 1985. From 1991 to 1993, Cole was Secretary of the Department of the Treasury and then Secretary of the Department of Health, Housing, Local Government and Community Services.
2   An American investor and writer. After working in senior positions at Citibank, Marks joined TCW, an investment management company, in 1985 and created and led the High Yield, Convertible Securities and Distressed Debt groups. In 1995, he left TCW and co-founded Oaktree Capital Management.
3   Commodities Trading Adviser. CTA strategies sometimes refer to option replication strategies that rely on a dynamic hedge to protect a conventional market exposure.
4   Constant Proportion Portfolio Insurance is a method of protecting a portfolio against adverse market fluctuations while permitting participation in market growth. It relies on a dynamic hedging strategy. See also Appendix B.
5   Dynamic hedging strategies rely on progressive fluctuations in the prices of underlying assets. They can suffer when market prices "jump" or "gap".
6   Asset-Liability Management, an analysis that takes into account not just the assets, but the liabilities and expected liabilities. This sort of analysis is often applied to defined benefit pension schemes, where the fund is obliged to meet prescribed pension obligations.
7   Alternative Investment Fund Management Directive. An EU initiative to regulate hedge funds and other alternative investment funds.
8   The Walker Review of Corporate Governance in UK Banks and Other Financial Institutions. 2010.

6 | Hugo Bänziger

Geneva, 3 December 2014

Risk management is about understanding the whole organisation and cutting through complexity.

Hugo Bänziger managed risk at Deutsche Bank and before that Credit Suisse. He is currently a partner at Lombard Odier.

He explains why regulations that are becoming more complex will make risk management less effective.

Hugo Bänziger: I have to admit but I became a banker by accident. All started at my Alma Mater in Berne, the Swiss capital, where I was reading modern history, constitutional law and economics. At a seminar on the relations of Switzerland and Nazi Germany in the 1930s, my professor asked me to present the economic policy of the Swiss government and how it differed from the German response to the Great Depression. Of course, the subject made me look into the failure of several major Swiss banks and how they were restructured. The seminar eventually resulted in my master

103

thesis, which included a chapter on the establishment of banking regulation and supervision in 1934. I had no idea that the then head of the Federal Archives passed my thesis on to the President of the Federal Banking Commission, who offered me a job as his assistant and asked me to edit his book *50 Years of Swiss Banking Supervision* in 1984. Writing about banks triggered my interest for working in finance. I decided to join Credit Suisse, where I worked in retail banking and corporate finance before joining the derivative house Credit Suisse Financial Products, which was set up in London in 1989.

When we opened for business in London's West End, we generated about twenty tickets a day. Thus, we could calculate all the sensitivities and Greeks in a spreadsheet at the end of a working day. This entailed manually entering each trade with the relevant information and subsequently re-valuing the book. But in the1990s, derivatives trading volumes grew sharply. Within a year, there were more than 5,000 trades in my little Lotus spreadsheet. Clearly a proper system was needed, so I set about building one. This was less complicated than I thought. It entailed building a scalable database that performed essentially the same functions that the old spreadsheet had done before. One by-product of the exercise was that I learned a lot about system architecture! The main point about data management is to preserve its integrity and always work with the complete set of available data. Retaining the base data gave me the flexibility in later years to access and arrange it to answer questions that had not necessarily been anticipated, but would subsequently demand answers.

This lesson stayed with me when I moved to Deutsche Bank (DB) in 1996. I quickly realised that the existing risk systems used only extracted data, which meant that some valuable information was discarded. For example, it was not possible to view the complete set of data of an individual trade ticket, which limited our ability to answer questions about sensitivity of transactions, where it had been booked, the sales credit that went with it etc. We had to rebuild the data structure of the risk system to get access to this type of information.

Conceptually, risk management is not difficult. It comprises recording of all positions, a complete data set of both cash and derivatives, and calculating their sensitivity to market price movements. Since interest rate swaps make up 85% of all derivatives, sensitivities are mostly linear. Options of course aren't, but even at a large bank, they comprised less than 10% of the volume.

The accepted method for calculating the risk of a position was to use Value-at-Risk (VaR), usually based on Monte Carlo (MC) simulated market price movements. At Deutsche, we ran MC simulations overnight to get the VaR by next morning. But as we observed over time, these numbers were not much different from simulations based on historic market prices. For both, the MC and historic simulations, the starting point was the benign market of the pre-crisis years with very low volatility, tight spreads and seemingly abundant liquidity. The look-back period with 220 trading days was short – too short – and excluded market upheavals from previous crises. VaR numbers did not reflect the true riskiness of a position. Much worse, it said nothing about how liquid a position or a book really was. Luckily, we moved DB to stress-test-based risk management before the Great Financial Crisis. When you look at the VaR charts in DB's annual report during the Great Financial Crisis, it looks as if there was no crisis!

Frances: *How did you do stress-testing?*

Hugo: Revalue your books at minus 10, minus 30 or 50[1] of current book value and look at the impact. The important thing is to use simple assumptions that everybody understands. And then play with the numbers. Like on a keyboard. You will quickly discover the sensitivity of your books. Most people don't understand the assumptions used in VaR models, and thus do not understand what the number tries to tell them. Understanding your stress assumptions is the first step to risk managing your positions. When stress tests are used in a coherent manner, the results are really useful. I also love reverse stress-testing, when you start with the question, what events could make your bank breach minimum capital and liquidity requirements? I found these results always very refreshing and thought provoking.

A lot of thought has to be given on how to report risk to the Executive Committee or the Board of Directors. I always found it useful to start with the P&L of the bank. Asking how big your loss could be before you face a significant widening of credit spreads or a rating downgrade or lose your re-financing capability in money and capital markets provides you with a good starting point to establish your risk appetite. Looking then at the strength of your balance sheet tells you how much time you have to take decisive action to restructure and recover. Talking about risk in this context is conceptually straightforward, intuitive and easy to communicate, which in turn simplifies the subsequent decision process.

Banking history is also a useful tool in making an institution risk aware. Most people know a bit about the Great Depression of the 1930s. But few remember what caused the international banking system to collapse. It was by and large the same balance sheet mis-match that triggered the Great Financial Crisis. When American banks cut their money market lending to European banks in 1931, most lost their refinancing capacity. Having engaged in massive maturity transformation with almost no duration on the liability side, they lost their refinancing capacity. Sounds familiar? The difference to 2008 was that now both the US and European banks engaged in massive maturity transformation and that their short-term funding depended on money market funds instead of banks. The actors were different but the root cause was almost identical. Who forgets his history is condemned to repeat its mistakes. Knowing a bit about banking history is thus quite useful. 2008 was neither the first banking crisis nor will it be the last one. It is important that regulators and supervisors understand this too. Improving the capitalisation of banks was absolutely essential after the Great Financial Crisis, as was the introduction of a leverage rule and minimum liquidity requirements. But history also tells us that over-complex institutions fail first together with banks with volatile revenue streams or aggressive business models.

Matthew: *What do you think has changed since 2007/08?*

Hugo: There are many positive developments since 2008. To mention just a few apart from the regulatory reforms under Basel III: Money Market Funds are much more prudent when lending to the banking system. Banks have massively upgraded their liquidity management. The MIS[2] inside banks is much better than before the crisis. Balance Sheet and Risk Weighted Assets are now actively managed. Also, financial transparency has improved considerably. Whilst annual reports from banks continue to have 400 pages and more, they are now easier to read and the narrative has improved. Also, the analytical depth of bank equity analysts has improved. They understand bank business models with their respective risks and opportunities much better.

Matthew: *How effective can a risk manager be at the same time as being independent of risk-taking activities?*

Hugo: Banks run a risk–reward business, thus under the prudent check and balance rules of corporate governance, someone on the C-level must own risk. The independence of risk management, however, comes with the risk of an organisational silo. During the Great Financial Crisis, whether risk management was organised independently or within business divisions, did not make a difference. Both failed. And most CROs were replaced. If too independent, risk management lives in an ivory tower, which is detached from reality. If too closely aligned with business, it may become "native". In my view, risk managers should be independent in their decision-making but remain closely aligned to the business. Really good risk managers are people with both front and back office experience. People who know the organisation, have run a business and also are experienced IT project managers. Moving people in and out of risk is a good policy. More important is actually the integration of risk MIS into everybody's activity. Every trader and banker should know how much risk their business contributes, how much capital and liquidity they consume and be accountable for it. Accountability for risk has to be part of a bank's culture.

Matthew: *Do you think there's a danger that, even if the risk person has front office experience, as soon as that person moves away from the risk-taking activity, they tend to lose perspective and end up having only an historic view of liquidity. So if you are running a swap book, say, and the risk manager comes and says: I think that position is too big, the front office person could say: Well I think I can clear that in an hour and a half. Is it sufficient just for the risk person to say: I think it's too big, or is their argument muted by the fact that the risk person is not trading the markets.*

Hugo: There is always a risk that this may happen. But if every trader has his risk and liquidity budget and is accountable for it, the risk is much mitigated. Important is a bank-wide policy on how to handle liquidity risk. With the exception of Treasuries, Bunds, JGBs, Gilts, a few major currency pairs, some large stocks and the principal commodities, nothing is really liquid. Specifically not in a financial crisis. A bank's risk policy has to take this into account.

Frances: *That gets on to an almost philosophical question about what liquidity is. For example, people say that they could clear a position in an hour and a half. That might be the case in a calm, well-behaved market, but when you have got to clear it in an hour and a half, then it's probably not a calm, well-behaved market. Then suddenly it isn't liquid.*

Hugo: Even bonds such as Swiss government bonds can be difficult to trade in calm market conditions. When trading larger lots, you quickly move the bid–offer spread. You thus have to trade in several tranches. During the Great Financial Crisis, we experienced illiquidity in ways we did not expect. Take corporate bonds. We hedged our portfolio with CDS for protection from first order risk. But because bonds are cash instruments, they became much more illiquid than CDS. We assumed that the basis risk of a corporate bond and its corresponding CDS would never exceed 50bp. It was 500bp in October 2008!

Matthew: *It's like pushing against the balloon, but it seems that's all the regulators could do. What about the role of the board?*

Hugo: Risk management starts with good corporate governance, accountability and culture. Managing risk by issuing very detailed guidelines does in my view not work. Banking is a risk–reward business. As long as it is transparent, up to the board, how much risk a bank assumes and how the bank gets compensated for it, there will be no nasty surprises. Nobody deliberately breaks a bank. But this requires sophisticated IT. It is rather extraordinary that the manufacturing industry has developed very sophisticated software to calculate and track its labour unit cost. Try to find such a system in a financial institution! A well-balanced and independent board is perfectly positioned to act as check and balance to the executive committee's risk taking.

Frances: What you said about the relationship and the independence and the relative authority of a risk manager raises the question: Why would somebody be a risk manager? You have already observed that a good risk manager needs to be able to do the job of the risk taker, so the person needs to be pretty skilled. But if you are a trader or a portfolio manager, you have a pay-off function that looks like a bought call option: you have unlimited upside and limited downside. The risk manager has something like a sold put: they have limited upside, in that all they are going to get is a salary – and arguably their bonus can't even be related to the profitability of the risk-taking activity they oversee. At the same time they have giant downside risk. So why would somebody with all the necessary skills buy into that?

Hugo: Under the system you describe, indeed. Why would anyone want to become a CRO under such circumstances? But the framework you describe is incompatible with good corporate governance. If the trader you describe would have to fully compensate the bank for the capital and liquidity his book consumes, his P&L would be much smaller. The reason his bets were so profitable is because they were backed with the bank's liquidity and capital for which there was no charge. I assume with Basel III this will change. Banks will have to charge traders for the use of their balance sheet. Once this is done, the asymmetry between trader and risk manager, indeed between traders and banks, disappears. As I said, internal capital and liquidity pricing require good systems. That is where banks have to catch up most. It is fair to say that even Deutsche Bank's systems were not perfect in 2007. But we had some idea of our customer profitability and return on equity per customer. I became CRO at Deutsche Bank because we had good checks and balances and because of the esteem in which I hold Joe Ackerman.[3] He was a leader, who enforced good corporate governance. Of course, we did not agree on every transaction. But when I said no, he sought to understand my reasoning, and I could trust him not to override me. My experience in the industry, unfortunately, is that he was the exception.

Frances: Yet we are now seeing the emergence of a generation of professional risk managers, most of whom do not have, and never will have, any direct experience in risk-taking activities. What are your thoughts about this?

Hugo: I do not really believe that risk management as such is a profession. I think you need to have professional bankers, who can be developed into risk managers.

To train aspiring managing directors in risk at Deutsche Bank, I put them through three weeks of intensive training. The initial test was whether they understood the bank's financials. To find out, I asked things like: how much capital do we have? How liquid are we? The expectation was that anyone aspiring to become an MD should know the essentials of the institution. Surprisingly, close to 50% had to re-sit the test, often amid complaints about the stressful environment. But, as with any other profession, bankers need to understand their business. You cannot be a doctor without understanding medicine. You cannot become a heart surgeon without passing through years of demanding training. Before you perform heart surgery on humans, you do several heart transplants on mice, and then on chickens, and then on a pig and finally on a calf before you get to patients. We must insist on professional expertise for bankers and this comprises far more than some specialist trading or banking skills.

Matthew: *A lot of bankers come up on the asset side: they just go and get the loans. I suppose they think their technical expertise is in understanding the customer balance sheet requirement. But if you talk about treasury to them, they wouldn't know much detail.*

Hugo: True. That is the reason why bankers have to understand how much capital a loan absorbs and how it is refinanced. Keeping this information in a silo is risky. If a banker has all this information at their fingertips, the banker will make the right decision since their performance report will also measure their capital and liquidity consumption. Those who grow their loan book with fewer resources will get more performance pay.

Matthew: *Well they are all put in silos as well, aren't they? There's financial institution risk, counterparty risk, operational risk; they all tend to get compartmentalised. At Deutsche Bank, for instance, how did you get a full view?*

Hugo: By working hard to integrate the risk functions. By creating common language, platforms and systems. Risk silos encourage specialisation at the cost of risk managers losing the overview.

Risk can move from liquidity to market to credit to capital. A risk manager has to understand that. So we had common systems, joint risk meetings, joint off-site conferences, joint training programmes. It was a lot of effort but worth it. Enterprise-wide risk management is more than just a theory. It actually works if you bother to implement it. But oh boy do I remember my credit staff complaining when they had to understand option pricing or be able to price a swap manually. Or my market risk managers when I asked them to learn how Basel II worked. Why would they have to learn about default risk when they could use credit spreads instead? The Great Financial Crisis answered these objections.

Matthew: *So do you think that is why the risk management organisations, such as PRMIA[4] and GARP,[5] are struggling?*

Hugo: I don't think so. You have a pretty holistic approach. But I noticed that many CROs are now very busy implementing new regulations. But regulation is not risk management. It is time consuming, however. A lot of senior risk people in the industry are so stressed with their day job that they hardly have energy left to talk about risk in their spare time. Plus, let's not forget, risk management was a spectacular failure in the Great Financial Crisis. Our image as risk managers has been severely damaged. We promised a lot but did not deliver. Graduates and younger bankers noticed. I guess an open and honest debate about the reason as to why risk management failed in so many banks would be a first step to address this. Why could we not cope with the complexity of trading? Why did our systems not provide the information we needed? Why were so many of our assumptions wrong? This is an interesting and necessary debate.

Matthew: *So with CSFP,[6] before it became part of Credit Suisse, how different was running that risk management? Did you have your own balance sheet?*

Hugo: We were a subsidiary, thus we had our own balance sheet. Plus, we were also regulated by the Bank of England. They were demanding – much more demanding than the Swiss regulator at the time. We were also lucky. We were a green field operation. Nothing was there. No legacy system or process to bother with. We could build our own.

Frances: Do you see a tendency toward regarding very complex risk models, such as those with embedded copula analysis, as a black box?

Hugo: We cannot run banks by black boxes. We need to understand what is going on in our models. Many of our models failed in the Great Financial Crisis. And there were too few people who understood how they worked. The models supporting correlation trading were so complex that most people on the trading floor did not understand them. And they were full of assumptions, which no independent party had approved and verified. Yes, correlation trading was innovative. But it was also rolled out too quickly before people understood its risk. A new medical drug has to undergo years of clinical trials before it is sold. We did not do enough testing on correlation trading, which became my biggest nightmare in the crisis. We need less complexity. And where complexity is unavoidable, we need to seriously test it until we learn how to deal with it.

Matthew: When you say that innovation was too fast, do you think it's because the push to be innovative and to come up with new ideas, new ways of packaging risk, tends to get led by the traders?

Hugo: It's worth remembering that structured trades were devised to tailor investments to the risk appetite of investors, to offer better returns in a low interest environment or to save investors the expense of having to assemble it all by themselves. Customers asked for structured products. But then they took on their own life and I wonder how many of them got sold without any of the three benefits mentioned above. You will have to interview traders who sold them to get an answer.

Matthew: Do you think they suffered brand damage?

Hugo: They really did. But they remain interesting investment instruments if properly managed and with the appropriate level of disclosure. Structured trades were a significant source of revenue for the banks. But that is unlikely to return. With the range of offerings now available in exchange-traded derivatives, investors have what they need to assemble their own structured products using basic, liquid components. Contrast this with the bespoke approach, whereby the bank puts the product together. This means that the product can only be closed out or modified by dealing with the issuing bank. If the bank is unwilling or unable to close or modify the position, the investor has no other choice than keeping it until it expires. Investors do not like to be at the mercy of banks.

Matthew: *Do you think that the short horizon of investment bankers is a necessary consequence of their business? Is that simply the business that they are in? In London they are debating about structuring remuneration to have a long tail, to try to make decisions take more account of long-term risks.*

Hugo: I think institutional investors, together with the new regulatory requirements, have already corrected much short-termism. Many activities in banking are actually long term by nature. Investment bankers, who issue shares on behalf of clients, are interested in the long-term success of the issues. Private bankers are interested in the long-term performance of their customers. Commercial bankers want to save their clients money with their transaction banking products. We just have to get the incentive system right.

Matthew: *You talked about regulation before, but do you think the regulators themselves have a cultural problem in the way they prosecute their business?*

Hugo: I think the intentions are good but they are often quite removed from business. That said, I believe they are improving. I know many leading bank supervisors personally and can vouch for their integrity. They do not have a personal vendetta against banks. They want to make the financial system stable. Something their political masters ask them to do. Detailed regulation is actually a response to the failure of the FSA's light touch approach. In that respect, we bankers have only ourselves to blame.

Frances: *When politicians have to answer to voters, whatever solution they put in place has to be something they can communicate to voters, which might not be the most effective one. Do you think the regulators are at the mercy of this?*

Hugo: Politicians are in the business of winning elections. So, they have to explain their policies in understandable terms. Do they sometimes overshoot? Yes, of course. Some of the capital rules for retail and commercial banking business are now rather draconian. But we now pay for the sins committed by the Spanish and UK banks, which had their risk undercapitalised and knew it. That tougher capital rules hurt the banks' ability to grant credit is undisputed. But also undisputed are the economic and social costs of the Great Financial Crisis. The loss in GDP since 2007 was substantial. It is probably worth paying the price of slightly slower growth if it helps to avoid a big financial meltdown. But whether we really need a regulatory rulebook with more than 10,000 pages (Dodd-Frank), I wonder. Many of the detailed rules do not really serve a purpose. With the establishment of CCPs,[7] the OTC derivatives business was made safe. There was no need to segregate that business from the parent bank.

Matthew: *What about the complexity of regulation? The burden of compliance with regulations almost becomes an end in itself, to the point where very little resource is left to do real risk management.*

Hugo: I share your concerns. Compliance with regulation is not risk management. Risk management is dynamic. Regulation is not. We unfortunately missed the chance to eliminate a lot of outdated regulation. Would you believe that German banks still inform the German Bundesbank monthly about every credit exposure larger than EUR 5 million? I always wondered who was reading these reports and what they learned from them.

Frances: *Lots of people observe that the increase in regulations is crowding out real risk management.*

Hugo: I wouldn't say "crowded out". It is a mistake to burden risk management alone with the implementation of regulation. The regulatory framework applies to the entire bank. Thus, it should be implemented by the front line, by the business divisions. We have to do business within the regulatory framework. It is just one of our ordinary constraints.

Frances: *It must be very galling for a historian to see people learning so little from the past.*

Hugo: It does not have to be like this. Who cannot remember his own history is condemned to repeat it. This sentence was true for centuries. Anybody who runs a bank should have some understanding of previous financial meltdowns.

Matthew: *What are your thoughts about too big to fail (TBTF)?*

Hugo: Nothing should be too big to fail. Rescuing large institutions is motivated by the desire to avoid the impact a bank failure would have on the real economy. It is important to understand how a bank crisis spreads through the system. We need to fully understand the interconnectedness and then restructure the translation mechanism. OTC derivative trading was de-risked by establishing CCPs. The risk of spreading failure through short-term borrowing was reduced by introducing large exposure rules for short maturities. The risk spreading through settlement risk in FX was addressed by establishing CLS, the joint DVP[8] settlement venture between commercial and central banks. There is still work to be done. CLS now clears only about 40% of FX trades when it should clear 100%. And the issue of payment systems, which flow through banks' balance sheets, remains unaddressed. In my view, the Financial Stability Board's "Too big to fail" paper did a very good job on recovery and resolution. With all these new rules, banks will eventually become less complex and thus easier to resolve. For corporates, we established workable bankruptcy rules a century ago. If we believe in Schumpeter's principle of "creative destruction", we have to be able to resolve banks without damaging our economy.

Matthew: *Some would say you need TBTF because large institutions support international trade and globalisation. Linked to that is the argument that the systemic cause of crisis is government policy, such as low interest rate environments and things like that. According to this argument, there needs to be TBTF because the governments themselves are not well risk-managed.*

Hugo: Switzerland lost its mechanical watch industry in the 1970s, because Japan could produce cheaper and more precise electronic watches. It was devastating for the Swiss watchmakers. But the collapse of the Swiss watch industry was resolved under commercial law. Today, Switzerland has with Swatch a thriving mass producer and also a booming luxury watch industry. It would not have been possible without the traumatic experience of the 1970s. There is no justification for too big to fail except protectionism, which ruins competitiveness.

Matthew: *Do you think regulation made the financial sector more pro-cyclical?*

Hugo: Yes, I do. It already started with the Basel II framework. Fair value accounting, VaR-based capital requirements and Basel III all reinforce pro-cyclicality, which has many unintended consequences and exaggerates a crisis. But that doesn't mean that it is unmanageable: I think you can provide for it by forcing banks to hold more buffer liquidity and capital. And through stress tests you can calculate how much that needs to be. When Basel II was introduced, we created at Deutsche Bank the first contingent capital and successfully issued about USD 5 billion in 2006. They came in very handy in the Great Financial Crisis.

Matthew: *What about collateralising, for example the SPAN margining mechanism?[9] They are trying to keep the margin as low as possible, but what about saying: Even though the data from the last 90 days or three years may be benign, certain collateralisation ratios are mandatory.*

Hugo: I do not know this well enough. But calibrating collateral requirements with only 90 days of data seems to be a flawed approach. You definitely need to look back to the last big market event.

Matthew: *What about shadow banking? Do you think institutional investors have changed the market to the point where activities are not so much leaving the regulated banking environment as that they are just not being done anymore?*

Hugo: I think its likely effects are largely over-stated. The last report on shadow banking by the FSB[10] is long in analysis but draws very few conclusions. Shadow banking is very diversified. Private equity funds, which make or buy loans, are not big players. A few hedge funds, such as Citadel, act as market-makers in traded options, but they are rather the exception. And note that the leverage of a hedge fund, typically two and a half times, is closer to the levels seen in industry rather than in banking.

Frances: *Do you believe that investors' interests would be served by more transparency in the products offered by financial institutions such as banks and investment managers?*

Hugo: The Financial Stability Board's Enhanced Disclosure Task Force (EDTF)[11] made substantial progress on disclosure of sensitivity of business models and the performance of business divisions. If we really want capital market discipline to work, we need to be transparent and provide the essential information an investor needs. If you know how to read an annual report of a bank and are prepared to look, you will now find most of the information you need. But non-specialists can still get lost in the

400–500 page documents. We thus asked the banks to provide a simple narrative to make the reports easier to read and understand. In my view, bank annual reports could be half their size and be better. There is too much clutter.

There is another type of transparency, which the private sector cannot create by themselves. Bond issuance is highly fragmented today and reminds me of the stock market in the 1930s, before the SEC established standards. General Electric has now more than 7,000 different bonds outstanding. I wonder whether this is really necessary and whether we could not live with standard bond maturities of one, three, five, seven and ten years only. Such an approach would definitely deepen the market, make issues more comparable and create liquidity.

Frances: *There is another argument about standardisation of risk reporting. Some people believe that if everyone uses the same underlying model then it encourages a concentration of reactions: everybody heading for the same exit at the same time, so to speak.*

Hugo: They do this anyway as we have seen in 2008 when everyone wanted to sell exactly the same at the same time. So let's deal with the root cause instead. Let's make sure that investors buy instruments that they fully understand and which they can keep in a time of crisis when markets turn illiquid.

Matthew: *If we were in this room in ten years' time, looking back, what do you think we will be surprised by?*

Hugo: By the way digitalisation will have changed our industry. We may well have our Nokia moment within the next ten years. The technology giants could already today move into the financial business if they chose to do so. Banks will have to produce at much lower cost to survive. Our large compensation packages will revert to the mean of the service industry. Risk will be much more transparent than today. Financial services will be mobile. Banks will be less complex. Most will look like utilities. Banking in 2025 will still be banking, but it will be different.

Matthew: *There's an argument, mainly in America, that banks need to be big so they can make big loans to the big global companies.*

Hugo: I tend to disagree. With proper preparation, a bank syndicate can be put together very quickly. Very large deals are months in preparation. I do not really buy the argument that when it comes to putting the financing together, it needs to be done in 24 hours. Ask yourself: do we really want to have a bank which carries a concentration risk of USD 25 billion? At Deutsche Bank, we imposed rules limiting the size of individual underwritings. And guess what? I made one exception and that was the very deal that went sour!

Notes

1 −0.10%, −0.30%, −0.50%.
2 Management Information Systems.
3 A Swiss banker and former chief executive officer of Deutsche Bank. He has also been the Chairman of the International Institute of Finance, an influential Washington-based financial advisory body.
4 Professional Risk Managers International Association.
5 Global Association of Risk Professionals.
6 Credit Suisse Financial Products.
7 Central Counter-Parties
8 Delivery Versus Payment.
9 Standard Portfolio Analysis of Risk is a system for calculating margin requirements for futures and options on futures, developed by the Chicago Mercantile Exchange in 1988.
10 Financial Stability Board.
11 Of the FSB.

7 | Carol Alexander

Brighton, 27 November 2014

Risk managers need to be better trained and better rewarded. Risk takers need to be held more accountable. Some of this is happening.

Carol Alexander is Professor of Finance at the University of Sussex and Managing Editor, with Geert Bekaert, of the *Journal of Banking and Finance*.

She talks about what still needs to be achieved in Risk Management.

Carol Alexander: My academic background, briefly, is undergraduate in maths with experimental psychology and a PhD at Sussex in algebraic number theory supervised by Walter Ledermann,[1] followed by post-doctoral work in Amsterdam with Hendrik Lenstra[2] and then a move back to London. There were very few jobs in algebra so I worked for Phillips and Drew (later UBS). In the early 1980s I programmed BBC micro-computers[3] and wrote a paper on the valuation of index-linked gilts using

119

inflation forecasts. Then I returned to academia at the London
School of Economics studying for a masters in mathematical
economics and econometrics, which included time-series analysis
with James Durbin[4] and Andrew Harvey,[5] and game theory with
Ken Binmore,[6] Avner Shaked[7] and John Sutton.[8] There I met
some famous economists, including Willem Buiter,[9] Charlie
Bean[10] and Mervyn King[11] and worked as research assistant for
some members of the Monetary Policy Committee:[12] Stephen
Nickell[13] and Richard Layard.[14] I also learned about GARCH[15]
and co-integration from Rob Engle.[16]

   Then I moved back to Sussex as a lecturer and taught
econometrics, a bit of micro-economics, algebra and game theory.
I started consulting with Hill Samuel Bank (where I built the first
GARCH models in London) and then with Equitable House
Investments (alpha strategies), Robert Fleming and Shell pension
funds (risk systems). Consulting took off via publications in *RISK*
magazine and talks at many practitioner conferences. In the 1990s
I worked part-time as Academic Advisor for Algorithmics, Inc.
and then full-time as a director and Head of Market Risk
Modelling at Nikko Global Securities. Whence to Reading's
ICMA[17] Centre as Professor of Risk Management, when I helped
David Koenig[18] to develop PRMIA. I was the Chair of the
Academic Advisory Council, I edited their *Handbook of Professional
Risk Management* (covering the syllabus for the PRM[19]
qualification) and for a while I became Chair of the Board. I also
started their magazine *Intelligent Risk* – not quite as nice a title as
NetExposure – the journal I started while working for
Algorithmics. Three years ago I returned to Sussex.

Matthew: *From your consulting, how do you think boards are dealing with
complexity and the way risk builds up through everyday transactions?*

Carol: I recently watched an Horizon programme about individuals
who became great physicists of the 20th century, such as Einstein
and Hawkins. The programme contrasted the way these people
did research, almost by themselves, with modern-day research in
physics at CERN[20] and similar large-scale laboratories. Here a
large team is required to work like different cogs in a complex
mechanism. That's the only way to conduct the type of
experiments that are needed today to bring us closer to

understanding the Universe. In other words, as a discipline evolves, it requires more and more specialised parts to perform specific functions. Rather like the human body, really.

This message applies to today's risk management team. It's required to delegate different types of responsibility to the junior analysts, who specialise very much in their own areas (e.g. in exchange-traded products such as equity-like things, another team of analysts that specialises in derivatives: options and so forth; with another team on swaps and so on). Senior managers should have all that technical knowledge plus experience of working in the front office, where the risks are actually generated. A CRO should have a huge amount of experience to be able to view the big picture, especially the crucial co-dependencies between risks. Most importantly, this person should focus on the major risks rather than getting bogged down in details, which is what regulation is pushing towards. Identifying the major risks and managing their co-dependencies is key to cutting through complexity.

There should be more government funding for developing proper industry qualifications, and legislation put in place to ensure risk managers have these qualifications. Risk management is not like accounting or law, which are much older subjects, where there already exist good qualifications. Until proper qualifications exist, of a much higher standard than those existing today, salaries will not be commensurate with the experience actually required to do a proper job, and many of the best individuals won't choose risk management as a profession.

Frances: *How can organisations manage the balance between the technical skills necessary effectively to interpret the output of sophisticated risk models and the political skills to ensure that they are taken as seriously as they need to be?*

Carol: First of all, if it is difficult to interpret the output of a risk model then it is not a proper model. The analyst's job is to design a model, which may be quite complex, but if it is built on proper mathematical principles the output should be simple enough to interpret.

There is a lot of hocus pocus about metrics and this adds unnecessary complexity. What is the point of having 101 different

metrics? Underneath all is one distribution and this distribution
is all we need to estimate. Metrics are typically point estimates,
which are not only misleading, they ignore valuable
information.

   Also, risk is not objective, it's subjective. It has to be because it
is forward-looking and nobody has perfect foresight. Therefore
risk is represented by a distribution – and this distribution is
always based on the risk analyst's beliefs (or, better, those he
receives from his senior manager, who in turn is led by the
board). This is universally true, whether or not so-called
"reliable" historical data exist and are used to form one's beliefs.
There is too much reliance on historical data anyway; risk
managers should think out of the box to explore the effects of all
sorts of beliefs. That's scenario analysis.

Frances: *When you say distribution, you mean of outcomes, returns, that
kind of thing: probability distributions?*

Carol: Yes, that's what risk is, it is a probability distribution, isn't it?
A very big joint probability distribution. There is far too much
focus on data. What we need are experienced senior managers
that make informed decisions based on scenario analyses. Still, the
difficulty will always be assigning probabilities to outcomes. We
are still at the very start of a new discipline – a very important one
though, for the global economy.

   Financial risk is so much more complex than nuclear power or
aviation or other types of risk. There are so many human factors
involved with financial risks and each factor needs to be modelled
by a distribution. And whereas in other subjects one tends to look
at expected loss, in finance we need to model an entire, very large
joint distribution of interacting factors within credit, market and
operational risks. No wonder people lose sight of the wood for
the trees. They get bogged down in details.

   In my view there should be no distinction between risk and
uncertainty. All this discussion about knowable and unknowable
unknowns, Knightian uncertainty[21] and so forth is adding
unnecessary complexity again. In my view you may have a
distribution that is very narrow and the outcome fairly certain, or
an extremely wide distribution where you have no idea of the
outcomes. It is still a distribution! In finance outcomes always

correspond to profits or losses. So you know the outcomes, however uncertain you may be about the probabilities. There is no distinction between risk and uncertainty because, once you have fixed your view, there is only one distribution for a risk factor. An "unknowable" risk just has a uniform distribution on a very, very wide range of profits and losses.

Matthew: *It seems to me we need an individual or it could be a number, whose job is to talk about co-dependencies, almost walk the floor, trying to spot the real risks. There is so much pressure on people, particularly now, to conform to regulatory demands, which is to some extent reinforced by the models that they use, in that they're hard-wired into risk systems. You can lose sight of the assumptions in them and you can't easily tweak the assumptions. And with the necessary compartmentalisation, risk gets confined to various métiers, and it can lack vital collaboration.*

Frances: *I think that also comes back to the point you are making about co-dependencies. A lot of where regulations are pushing encourages the view that risks are additive and we know they're not.*

Carol: That is a very conservative view. If they're additive it means that you have perfect co-dependence. But in practice, it is the core business of a risk manager to net risks.

Matthew: *But this is the way the regulation seems to be heading.*

Carol: Regulations have an over-reliance on risk metrics. But, because regulators recognise that the metrics are very inaccurate, they are added up as if there is no netting of risk. The final number representing regulatory capital could mean anything or nothing. I honestly think this bottom-up approach is completely misguided.

Regulators should take more stock of the top-down approaches advocated by Ken Rogoff,[22] Nouriel Roubini,[23] Rob Engle and so forth. This means using scenario analysis with competence. But we don't have enough people who have the requisite knowledge, mainly because risk management is such a young subject. It only really started in the 1980s. That is why governments should step in by financing the development of professional industry qualifications, in collaboration with academics. For example, decision theory is a fundamental and integral part of risk management, which is completely ignored at present.

Frances: What do you think is the industry view of compartmentalisation of risk functions into investment, counterparty, operations, legal and compliance, reputational risks and so on?

Carol: This is poor practice. Focusing on the co–dependencies of major factors and accurate netting is far more important than working out the detail within those silos because, mathematically, that is what is going to determine the probabilities in this joint distribution far more than just looking at the marginals.

Frances: Within an organisation such as a bank or an investment manager, the trader or the portfolio manager has a position that resembles a bought call option, in that they are rewarded when things do well, while the worst that can happen to them is they can lose their job. By contrast, the risk manager has a sold put: they get blamed when things go wrong. And we have just noted that the technical skills required to be a competent risk manager are not trivial and in many ways much more advanced than what is required to be a portfolio manager or a trader. So the question I ask is: Why would somebody who is so talented go into risk management?

Carol: Indeed. I really like that question.

Frances: You know only when it is not working. You can measure the cost of risk management, but measuring the benefits of risk management is virtually impossible.

Matthew: If you save $80 million, $100 million, $500 million, nobody really knows about it.

Frances: You know only when risk management hasn't worked and even then you don't really know, because without risk management it might have been even worse.

Carol: Indeed! And the other thing is that risk managers still don't have a real voice at board level – that needs changing. I think that you have got to the crux of the matter here: unless portfolio managers and traders are held accountable for their own actions they may continue to make reckless decisions. There is nothing like a Sword of Damocles above their head to help them do a good job.

Frances: Can the emergence of career risk managers, often with little or no experience of risk-taking activities, aggravate the natural tension between risk-taking and risk management and control functions or are the advantages of specialisation and independence more important?

Carol: This just goes back to what I said before. The profession needs more specialisation and quant skills, yes – but it also needs more trading, hedging and portfolio management experience. We need teams where middle office analysts progress into the front office and then move back into the risk team as a manager after having gained the relevant experience.

But, you made a very good point earlier: Why would someone with the skills and talent to succeed in (usually better rewarded) risk-taking positions choose to return to risk management?

Matthew: *Unless it was a requirement for a trader to have some years in risk management.*

Carol: Good idea, but that's at the lower level – senior risk managers with trading experience need to be better rewarded.

Matthew: *How effective can a risk manager be at the same time as being independent of risk-taking activities? In other words, can the risk manager be on an equal footing with the trader in judging the future course of a market or when to cut a position?*

One risk manager told me that risk disappears. What he meant by that was: Do I make a big hullabaloo about this position now, when perhaps a client will take this position away in the next five minutes? The risk manager might judge it better to keep quiet, keep his powder dry for a more important risk. He doesn't want to be accused of crying wolf.

Carol: I'm not sure how much I buy into the independent oversight concept, except insofar as the manager's remuneration should be completely disengaged from the success of a deal.

But, he/she is still bound to have an emotional interest in the success (or otherwise) of a deal assuming they have been party to its construction at all stages.

There should be a well-structured hierarchy in risk management. The senior risk manager needs to have held the jobs of risk analysts, senior analyst, trader, senior trader, risk manager … this way he or she should be in a much better position to judge risks than the traders. Rooky risk analysts just need to know the models inside out. But senior managers need to have held positions that give them a better understanding of risk than anyone else in the company. And because of this, they should be included in the construction of deals, giving advice to traders where appropriate. And be a full member of the board.

Frances: *It's a debate and there are arguments in favour of both independent and collaborative risk managers.*[24]

Carol: There is not nearly enough attention to psychology in risk management today. If behavioural finance is to contribute one thing, it will be to improve the knowledge that risk managers have of the psychology of decision taking.

Matthew: *Do you think risk evaluation captures the human response to a crisis?*

Carol: Now this is interesting. This is where I think that there is insufficient understanding of behavioural finance. For example, I don't think that people really understand what risk tolerance is.

Frances: *Yet risk tolerance can be very difficult to communicate.*

Carol: All the performance metrics that we use, whether Sortino[25] or Sharpe[26] or Omega Ratios[27] … performance metrics are just simplifications of the certainty equivalent.[28] You can think of this as a monetary amount that you associate with an optimal expected utility. Everybody has a utility function. Some people are more risk loving, some are less risk loving. Academics tend to be risk averse: they go for their secure pension (or at least they thought they did, until recently).

Risk tolerance is just a simple parameter in a utility function. It's possible to measure risk tolerance (very approximately) easily. Let me measure your risk tolerance. You don't have to tell me what your net worth is, but keep it in mind. Add up all your wealth. Not in the future, now: your house, your car, your savings, whatever. That is your net worth. Now I am going to enter a gamble with you. I am tossing a fair coin, it doesn't cost you to enter, you can just say yes or no. I am going to give you $100 if it's heads and you give me $50 if it's tails. Will you take it? (***Matthew***: Yes, I think I would.) Now I am going to give you $1,000 if it's heads and you give me $500 if it's tails. (***Matthew***: Yes.) I am now going to give you $10,000 if it's heads and you give me $5,000 if it's tails. (***Matthew***: No.) OK, what about less than $10,000? (***Matthew***: Yes.) OK so $10,000 is your risk tolerance, in absolute terms.

Your risk tolerance is a monetary amount relative to your wealth. If you want a percentage risk tolerance then you divide, say, $10,000 by your wealth and you come up with 0.25 or something. The inverse, 4 say, is your risk aversion. And so this is a parameter of a utility function, whether it is logarithmic or exponential or so forth. The board of a bank should employ experts in behavioural finance, people that understand behavioural decision-making to educate the decision-makers. This means the board of the bank and the shareholders: the people who make the decisions about the balance of risks, the major risks. Everything boils down to business risk really, whether it's market risk, credit risk, operational risk. It's all to do with the running of the business.

Frances: *This came out in the Walker Report,[29] which said the board ought to establish with the shareholders what risks are integral to the business, what risk is superfluous, how much of it should be taken on, and then letting the organisation get on with taking those risks within the agreed parameters.*

Carol: The same risk tolerance – the preferences of the board – should be fed down through the entire organisation in a systematic way.

Frances: *And it is linked to a business outcome, a business objective.*

Carol: But the difficulty is always translating to the traders and the portfolio managers, because they don't think in terms of certainty equivalent.

Matthew: *In setting a firm's risk tolerance, do you think that most firms take human responses into account?*

Carol: That's premature – at present firms don't understand risk tolerance, sufficiently. The sort of structure we need is one where there are top-down allocations according to clear decision processes and maximum transparency.

Matthew: *At CERN they were getting so much data that they built some new statistical program to spot the important aberration rather than try to analyse everything.*

Carol: That is exactly right. That is what I think we need to be thinking about when addressing the challenge of big data issues arising from all this data capture of clearing OTC transactions.

Matthew: *So what is the technique they use?*

Carol: Signal processing, wavelets, genetic algorithms, machine-learning techniques.

Matthew: *That is your point about the data. Perhaps that is a new area of research.*

Carol: Well there are two areas of research that have been ignored: the complexity of the data – handling big data in a complex system, and the decision processing side of it – the importance of behavioural finance in decision-making.

Matthew: *How can an enterprise-wide, truly top-down approach to risk measurement fit with regulatory reporting requirements, which seem to encourage compartmentalisation?*

Carol: Regulations get lost in rules; for example, this historical simulation-type approach, where you had to use a year of data, was giving extremely high capital requirements for the year after the crisis. But it is expensive to adapt a legacy system. For instance, adding a simple exponential weighting could cost millions of dollars even in a moderately large asset management outfit.

Matthew: *And there is usually an assumption in those legacy systems that never gets challenged, for example the one year of data and historical simulation rather than exponential weighting.[30]*

Frances: *Do you see a tendency toward regarding very complex risk models – such as those with embedded copula[31] analysis – as a black box?*

Carol: Not given the right communication. I can remember writing the chapter on copulas in Volume II of my books *Market Risk Analysis* (Wiley, 2008) and I didn't know much about copulas at first. I went through the literature, read the papers and bought all the books and, goodness, it was obscure! I thought: It's no wonder people are saying it's a black box. It took me months to produce something that was accessible to people even with fairly highly-trained mathematics, let alone the intended readership. The thing is, it takes time for complex things to become simple. So in my books I wrote an Excel spreadsheet for every concept – there's about 5,000 of them in total – this way, you can actually get to use the ideas in practice and that leads to a much deeper level of understanding than just reading.

Matthew: *How does one prioritise the testing and adoption of complex valuation and risk measurement techniques in an environment, such as an investment bank, where many transactions are bespoke?*

Carol: I think that you just need to prioritise simplicity, make a model as simple as possible as long as it is realistic. If it is not realistic, then you do have to go up one level. Copulas are one example of that because correlation is a symmetric form of dependence and you do need a copula to get asymmetrical dependence.[32] By the way, a copula that was blamed for mispricing collateralised debt obligations (CDOs) during the credit crunch was the Gaussian[33] Copula, which is the same as correlation! Mathematically, it applies only when the marginals are normal (or Student t,[34] at a pinch) – and I assume this point could have been misunderstood – so the only point to use a copula is not to use the Gaussian one. There are some very beautiful ones – see the pictures in my books.

Frances: *How do you guard against creeping complexity in valuation and risk-estimation models?*

Carol: That goes back to focusing on the major risks and the co-dependencies in their joint distribution. I'd forget about the idiosyncratic risks: focus on the major risks. Some people tend to latch on to metrics, which don't mean much, especially when they are aggregated in a mathematically incorrect way.

Matthew: *Is there too much emphasis on expected default rather than expected loss in estimating credit risk?*

Carol: These are just two parameters of the loss distribution. But when you disengage these parameters from the distribution almost any number can be used as a parameter.

I think one of the reasons why Value-at-Risk has become so ubiquitous is because it is simple to understand. It corresponds to a loss that you anticipate to make once every hundred days if you don't rebalance your portfolio – this is something that almost everyone can relate to. Things get more complex when you go beyond that, looking at expected tail loss, particularly in margining. While it is important to look beyond VaR (because it is not just exceeding the margin but it is by how much you exceed it that matters) it is also important to use a metric that is tractable (if you have to use one at all). For instance, median tail loss, which is just VaR at a higher level – is much easier to backtest than expected tail loss.

Frances: *Is the short horizon of investment banks an inevitable consequence of the nature of their business?*

Carol: I think it is a consequence of their reward structure and that's down to their shareholders and investors. Mostly, these people have short-term time horizons because they seek a quick return on their investment, and so they are willing to give rewards that are fairly immediate. If we can shift the investor's focus toward longer-term rewards then the risk horizon will also be longer term.

Frances: *Do you believe that it is possible to ensure that ongoing risks are taken into account at the point where investment banking positions are established?*

Carol: Are you thinking about the valuation of existing positions, like mark-to-market valuations of the trading book versus cash accounting in the loan book? Accounting practices become very difficult without mark-to-market accounting. For instance, look at what is happening with our pensions in the USS[35] at the moment. There is a huge question mark about the value of the fund. It all depends on the discount rate and long-term discount rates are very difficult to determine.

Frances: *Do you think there is a danger that crises can encourage regulators to adopt remedies that have superficial appeal rather than seek solutions that are effective and hard to circumvent in practice?*

Carol: Yes. We don't have the infrastructure yet, we can't implement lasting remedies. And regulations can have lasting consequences. For example, the repeal of the Glass-Steagall Act[36] – at the time could we have foreseen what would happen as a consequence?

Frances: *What would you say has changed since 2007?*

Carol: I don't think we've seen many fundamental changes so much as knee-jerk reactions. There is a permanent increase in capital requirements and more committees being set up, processes to look ahead, the stress testing programme and so forth that is coming out of the Financial Conduct Authority and the Financial Policy Committee. But I'm not sure how much thought has gone into this process.

One of the better developments is top-down Economic Capital[37] allocation. This is basically a good concept, whether it's based on risk-adjusted return on capital or another risk-adjusted performance measure like RAROC.[38] But then at the end you get to the options trader who thinks in terms of delta[39] and gamma,[40] and the interest-rate swaps trader who is thinking about durations[41] and convexities,[42] and it's for the risk manager to be able to translate these things into a meaningful metric: that's one of the many reasons why a senior risk manager needs to have trading experience as well as risk analysis skills.

Frances: *What developments would you like to see?*

Carol: Criminalising reckless gambling and also proper accounting for risk management. What is the cost of risk management? To bring in the lawyers and criminalise certain activities is much less costly and would be more effective.

For instance, during Alan Greenspan's extremely long interest rate regime US banks were deprived of their normal yields, so they invented new high-yielding products, such as CDOs. If CDO creation at source (i.e. selling mortgages that had little hope of being repaid) had been criminalised there wouldn't have been such great proliferation of these financial bombs and the economy in the Eurozone might have been much healthier today.

Matthew: *Is there a pervasive expectation that authorities will step forward to support markets and their participants in the event of a shock.*

Carol: Yes. Limited liability for senior managers is a critical issue. Risk management would be much simpler without this form of moral hazard.

Matthew: *Is complexity a necessary feature of modern financial markets?*

Carol: No, I have been saying that all along. Risk assessment can be less complex and regulations can be less complex and less susceptible to loopholes as a result.

Frances: *How do you see the balance between rules-based risk management and principles-and-judgement-based risk management – with a dose of caveat emptor – that reflects the intention of the regulations?*

Carol: Regulation is very rules-based now. But it is better to allow for the fact that risks are not objective. They are forward looking. Risk is a distribution and it is subjective. Possible outcomes are objective in the sense that you choose your portfolio and trading horizon so that its potential profits and losses are set within some range. You may be very confident or you may be very uncertain about this range: it is a personal view. So the outcomes are relatively objective but the probabilities associated with each outcome in this range are entirely subjective.

Matthew: *What balance would avoid the process becoming antithetical to clear thinking?*

Carol: Sue those who take reckless risks, whether they win or lose. Look at the trades and judge if there is a significant probability of losing a very, very large amount over a long-term horizon. If so, that is reckless. The regulators need to make that judgement, it is subjective.

Matthew: *How effective do most practitioners think ongoing stress tests can be? How do you think they overcome the necessary subjectivity of their design and composition, their tendency to respond to the recent past and the associated danger of "fighting the last war"?*

Carol: I am a great advocate of stress tests. And there is no substitute for good scenario analysis. Regulators use stress tests to get an aggregate view of risk across the whole system. They need to be focused on solvency and systemic risks: that is how their stress tests are designed. But I think there are insufficient resources being put into this area and too much focus on the measurement of minutiae. Stress testing individual portfolios may be important for the head of desk, but it is less important for macro prudential regulation – provided we can trust portfolio managers not to take reckless risks.

Regulators need better models for systemic risks. That is where Rob Engle's Volatility Lab is very good. In the *Journal of Banking and Finance*, which I edit, more and more papers are being submitted on systemic risk and network analysis. Some very interesting academic work is emerging in network analysis and contagious networks.

The translation from finance academia to banking takes much longer than the translation of academic medical research to medicine, for instance. Partly this is because the knowledge base of people in the industry is just not adequate to understand the papers being published on finance research. And there are not enough rewards for industry to link with academia in finance, to encourage the right people to invest time in doing the right type of research. This is very different to pharmaceuticals, for instance, where there is much less of a divide been practice and academics.

Frances: What do you think are the limitations of scenario building?

Carol: It is the probabilities that are very difficult. As I said before, the outcomes can be more or less agreed on because they are more or less determined by the positions. It's the likelihoods of those outcomes that are very difficult – because they are subjective.

Scenario analysis based on worst case outcomes is a complete misnomer. How can there be a worst case outcome? Is it that we get taken over by aliens from Mars? Or that all life on Earth dies? Or maybe there is something worse than that in a black hole at the end of the Universe. So there is no such thing as a worst case loss. Six sigma[43] is better. But the question is – what is sigma?

Frances: Do you believe that regulations aimed at dealing with the risk attached to credit and asset-backed instruments, for example the requirement that they be traded on an exchange, address their potential to spread risk as well as to transfer it?

Carol: The requirement that OTC[44] transactions be cleared is having two rather important effects. One of them is the amount of data being generated: we don't know what exactly to do with it all, but increased transparency should have positive lasting effects. Then there is an advantage in moving OTC transactions towards exchanges. For instance, it used to be impossible to find out how much had been traded on variance swaps,[45] and risk management was almost non-existent. But now we can look at the market capitalisation of VIX[46] futures; and volatility exchange-traded products are marked-to-market on the balance sheet.

But I still worry that volatility[47] might be the new credit. A problem with CDOs was that there was no agreed-on model to price them when the liquidity dried up, and this is what's happening with volatility at the moment. With volatility exchange-traded notes and funds[48] we are going through the characteristics of a bubble: when the product gets transferred into the public's hands outside the pool of large institutional investors, and the growth becomes exponential. Then the situation is ripe for a panic situation, unless you have a proper model for pricing these products. Otherwise, when the liquidity goes and there is no market price, how else can we find a price that everyone agrees with? The trouble is that traditional variance swap models have huge errors during volatile times, which is exactly when we need them to be accurate!

Matthew: *When I traded options, I used to try to work out what I call the supply of volatility in the market place: how much capacity is in the market to absorb changes in volatility prices? So this is a rough-handed way of saying: who's going to be there to write this option when you need it?*

Carol: Trading volatility is rather like selling out-of-the-money puts. The volatility risk premium is generally rather small and negative because volatility is a great diversifier, so people don't mind paying to add to their portfolio. If you have a position in equity and volatility, when equity goes down, volatility goes up: great negative correlation. So you don't mind if the risk premium on volatility is negative most of the time, provided you get that payoff when equities plummet. Banks that issue these variance swaps generally go short swaps, to get a small negative premium most of the time. If volatility spikes and they see it coming, they should put on a hedge; but I wonder how many "hedge" funds involved in volatility actually hedge? Sooner or later, when the volatility risk premium shoots up to 80–100% again we might see some major losses in hedge funds.

The headline losses last decade were about CDOs but I bet the losses on variance swaps following the Lehman Brothers closure were also massive. Not easy to tell, since it was all OTC. Now that volatility is traded on exchanges I am getting concerned for ordinary investors. I became quite alarmed at trading on VIX futures[49] when they were introduced in 2006 – and about options on VIX futures. At first, the market was pricing the options off the spot[50] not the futures, but the spot and futures on the VIX are completely different: there isn't a no-arbitrage relation.[51] It is not like the S&P 500 spot and the futures (and the SPY[52]), where scalpers arbitrage between them so that the basis is tiny.

Also, trading along the curve of VIX futures is very unusual. Whereas most futures go between backwardation[53] and contango[54] quite regularly, this no longer happens in VIX futures. It is almost always in contango now – only 1 day in 20 does it go into backwardation, and then it returns to contango almost immediately. This means there is a very large negative roll yield.

(MATTHEW: That you can lose your shirt on.) Yes, or win, if you're always shorting.

That is exactly what happened when the first volatility ETNs were brought in. They track a constant 30-day position so each day the S&P indices, which give their indicative price, sell a little bit of the shorter and buy a little bit of the longer maturity futures, at the two 30-day straddling maturities. At the beginning purchasers hadn't read the fine print in sufficient detail to understand this roll cost. But now the issuers have big warnings in their terms and conditions on volatility ETNs: "this should be held only as a short-term, speculative investment. It should not be part of a long-term portfolio strategy." Because the negative roll yields makes you lose money every day, unless there is a crash and volatility shoots up.

A big problem at the moment is front-running[55] of the volatility ETN hedges. There are now about 40 exchange-traded notes and funds on volatility with an overall market capitalisation of about 4 billion USD and about 120 million contracts are being traded every single day. Every year more and more products appear, and most of these have a value that deteriorates unless there is a spike in volatility. But as soon as volatility goes up their value shoots up, especially the leveraged ones like TVIX[56] or UVYX.[57] Volatility is pretty low at the moment but as soon as we have a surge in volatility everyone will be in there to redeem early – because they have been losing all the time on the hidden roll yield.

Seeing a spike in volatility, the front-runners know this surge of early redemption demand will come, and so they sell short-term VIX futures during the day then use an algorithmic trade to buy them back just after the provider has sold their very large hedge portfolio of VIX futures. It is this behaviour that is forcing the term structure back into contango all the time, hence exacerbating the negative roll yield especially at the short end.

Matthew: *Should regulators guard against this kind of risk being transferred to non-financial parties that may not be in a position to evaluate and manage it, or is the principle of caveat emptor more important?*

Carol: Whereas previously, demand for volatility was from large institutional investors (variance swaps being OTC), now, with the move to more exchange trading, ordinary investors are being drawn into the honey pot. But there are plenty of health warnings being published now – especially by academics – so yes, caveat emptor, I would agree.

Notes

1 Walter Ledermann FRSE (18 March 1911, Berlin, Germany–22 May 2009, London, England) was a German and British mathematician who worked on matrix theory, group theory, homological algebra, number theory, statistics and stochastic processes. He was elected to the Royal Society of Edinburgh in 1944.
2 A Dutch mathematician who worked principally in computational number theory and is well known as the discoverer of the elliptic curve factorisation method and a co-discoverer of the Lenstra–Lenstra–Lovász lattice basis reduction algorithm.
3 A series of microcomputers and associated peripherals designed and built by the Acorn Computer company for the BBC Computer Literacy Project, operated by the British Broadcasting Corporation. Designed with an emphasis on education, it was notable for its ruggedness, expandability and the quality of its operating system.
4 A British statistician and econometrician, known particularly for his work on time series analysis and serial correlation.
5 A Fellow of the Econometric Society and a Fellow of the British Academy (econ.cam.ac.uk).
6 A British mathematician, economist and game theorist. He is one of the founders of the modern economic theory of bargaining (along with Nash and Rubinstein), and has made important contributions to the foundations of game theory, experimental economics and evolutionary game theory, as well as to analytical philosophy.
7 A Visiting Professor at CERGE-EI since 1998. From May 2000 a member of the Executive and Supervisory Committee of CERGE-EI. State Street Distinguished Visiting Professor at CERGE-EI from Autumn 2001 to Spring 2009 (cerge-ei.cz).
8 The Sir John Hicks Professor of Economics at the London School of Economics.
9 A Dutch-born American-British economist. He is currently the Chief Economist at Citigroup.

10 Deputy Governor for Monetary Policy at the Bank of England.
11 Was the Governor of the Bank of England and Chairman of its Monetary Policy Committee from 2003 to 2013.
12 Of the Bank of England.
13 Stephen Nickell CBE is a British economist and former Warden of Nuffield College, Oxford, noted for his work in labour economics with Richard Layard and Richard Jackman.
14 A British labour economist, currently working as programme director of the Centre for Economic Performance at the London School of Economics.
15 Autoregressive conditional heteroskedasticity (ARCH) models are used to characterise and model observed time series, from which came Generalised ARCH models.
16 An American economist and the winner of the 2003 Sveriges Riksbank Prize in Economic Sciences in Memory of Alfred Nobel, sharing the award with Clive Granger, "for methods of analysing economic time series with time-varying volatility (ARCH)".
17 International Capital Market Association, a centre of higher education in the UK.
18 Previously Chair of the Board of Directors, Executive Director, and President of the PRMIA Institute (PRMIA.org).
19 Professional Risk Manager, a finance certification offered by PRMIA.
20 The European Organisation for Nuclear Research.
21 Risk that is immeasurable. Knightian uncertainty is named after University of Chicago economist Frank Knight, who distinguished risk and uncertainty in his work *Risk, Uncertainty, and Profit*.
22 Ken Rogoff is the Thomas D. Cabot Professor of Public Policy and Professor of Economics at Harvard University.
23 Nouriel Roubini is an American economist. He teaches at New York University's Stern School of Business and is the Chairman of Roubini Global Economics, an economic consultancy firm.
24 Independent risk management that is removed from risk-taking activities and collaborative risk management with frequent interaction between risk manager and risk taker.
25 Measures the risk-adjusted return of an investment asset, portfolio or strategy. It is a modification of the Sharpe ratio but penalises only those returns falling below a user-specified target or required rate of return.
26 A measure of risk-adjusted return, measured as return variation from the risk-free rate of return divided by return volatility.

27   A risk-return performance measure of an investment asset, portfolio or strategy, defined as the probability weighted ratio of gains versus losses for some threshold return target.

28   The guaranteed amount of money that an individual would view as equally desirable as a risky asset.

29   The Walker Review of Corporate Governance in UK Banks and Other Financial Institutions, 2010.

30   A technique used in sample data analysis that gives more importance to recent observations, thus avoiding bias due to atypical events that occurred very early in the sample.

31   A multivariate probability distribution for which the marginal probability distribution of each variable is uniform. Copulas are used to describe the dependence between random variables. See also Appendix B.

32   So that the relationship between two assets, say, varies at different levels of return.

33   A family of copulas.

34   Ibid.

35   Universities Superannuation Scheme.

36   The US Banking Act of 1933.

37   The amount of risk capital, assessed on a realistic basis, which a firm requires to cover the risks that it is running or collecting as a going concern, such as market risk, credit risk, legal risk and operational risk. It is the amount of money that is needed to secure survival in a worst-case scenario.

38   Risk-Adjusted Return on Capital.

39   The change in the price of an option associated with a change in the price of the underlying security.

40   The change in the delta of an option that is associated with a change in the price of the underlying security.

41   A measure of the maturity and timing of cash flows of a fixed interest instrument.

42   The change in duration of a bond or portfolio of bonds for a small change in the interest rate.

43   Sigma is a standard deviation, representing the 68% range of outcomes. Six sigma indicates a probability of less than one in 150 million.

44   Over-the-counter.

45   Investment instruments that become more valuable when market swings increase, making them an attractive choice for traders seeking to protect gains in equities.

46   A popular measure of the implied volatility of S&P 500 index options.

47 For example, variance swaps.
48 ETN and ETF, portfolios of investments that are traded on exchanges as single instruments.
49 Futures contracts that are settled against option volatility.
50 Physical instruments that underlie the derivatives.
51 To ensure they are traded at or near economic parity with each other.
52 The Ticker symbol for the SPDR® S&P 500®, an ETF Trust seeks to provide investment results that, before expenses, correspond generally to the price and yield performance of the S&P 500® Index (spdrs.com).
53 The market condition where the price of a forward or futures contract is below the expected spot price at contract maturity.
54 The market condition where the price of a forward or futures contract is higher than the expected spot price.
55 A practice whereby traders transact on their own account in anticipation of client orders, thereby deriving a personal profit. Front-running is illegal in most developed markets.
56 An ETF that seeks to replicate, net of expenses, the returns of twice the return of the S&P 500 VIX Short-Term Futures index (money.conn.com).
57 Ultra VIX Short-Term Futures ETF that seeks daily investment results that correspond to twice (200%) the performance of the S&P 500 VIX Short-Term Futures Index (Bloomberg.com).

8 | Mark Lawrence

Melbourne, 5 January 2015

Regulators are setting the agenda and much has changed and is changing as a result. But the real risk culture question is about how to "maintain the rage" when the pressure from regulators is off.

Mark Lawrence is an adviser to banks and bank supervisors on risk appetite, risk culture and governance. He previously worked at McKinsey and was CRO of ANZ, a large Australian bank. Prior to that, he managed risk at Merrill Lynch in New York.

He explains the thinking behind recent regulation and where it is heading.

Mark Lawrence: I grew up in Australia and studied pure mathematics and theoretical physics at the Australian National University. My first job was with the Commonwealth Bank of Australia in Sydney from 1982 to 1983.

Then I went to the USA to do a PhD in mathematics at the University of Wisconsin-Madison. For my minor subject I chose finance, which was refused initially on the grounds that there was no connection between mathematics and finance (!). But fortunately, armed with the Black and Scholes paper I was able to persuade the dean otherwise.

My graduate studies were interrupted in September 1986 when I joined Merrill Lynch Capital Markets and unwittingly became a member of the first generation of "rocket scientists", or "quants", working on Wall Street. I was put into a newly formed group called the Hedging and Arbitrage Group, which consisted of seven or eight quants attached to the main trading desks. Although there was no formal job description, our job essentially was to add value to the trading operation. I was to provide analytical support to the Global Arbitrage trading desk.

In March of 1987 a colleague who was attached to the Mortgage-Backed Securities trading desk went skiing for a couple of weeks and I was asked to cover for him during his absence, generating a daily duration-adjusted risk report based on each day's closing trading positions for the mortgage-backed book. At just that moment one of the traders on the desk took a huge naked long position in a single stripped, Principle-Only "Ginnie Mae" mortgage-backed security ("GNMA 11% PO"), in addition to several other big positions in individual securities. Back then, there were neither written limits nor a formal risk management control framework for the mortgages trading operation. At the time, US interest rates had declined steadily for two or three years and this was a big leveraged bet that yields would continue to fall further. The position couldn't even quite fit on the report. I was worried: how big is too big? There wasn't any guidance about this and my position was quite junior. I spent a weekend with an analyst from the mortgage research department and we figured out that if interest rates declined by about 50 basis points[1] we would make something like $40–$50 million; but if interest rates were to rise by 50 basis points, we would lose about four or five times that much, due to a modelled slowdown of expected pre-payments on the underlying GNMA 11% MBS collateral. Prepayment risk brings a lot of negative convexity[2] to these securities, which are in effect cash flows arising from pools of 30-year underlying mortgages. As near as I could tell, few people understood the significance of this. I started trying to talk to various senior people on the mortgage desk about it, but they did not want to talk to me. So at the end of my second week, the mortgage research analyst and I wrote a memo showing the results of our stress-testing analysis and highlighting the risks of the big position in question, which I sent to several senior people. This was not well received, to say the least; incredibly, I was forbidden by my manager to have any further conversations about the position. This was the end of the third week of March 1987. In the middle two weeks of April the US yield curve experienced an upward parallel shift of approximately 80 basis points over about 10 days; I watched this unfold from my position across the trading floor, hoping that the size of the huge mortgage position had been reduced. Unfortunately it hadn't; the trader concerned was suspended on April 20th and on April 29th the *Wall Street Journal* reported: "Merrill has $250 million loss on unauthorised trading."[3] The memo from five weeks earlier was of course awkward, lots of people were fired or left the firm, and a big shareholder lawsuit followed.

Following the announcement of the loss, the head of the government bond trading desk, Dan Napoli,[4] was co-opted to sort out the position and I was tasked with providing analysis to continuously adjust the hedge on the position as it was being progressively sold down. After a month or two of this, the first risk management group at Merrill Lynch was created with Dan Napoli as Head of Risk, reporting directly to the President, Dan Tully.[5] Today we would call it market risk, but back then it was called risk management. The team comprised three guys who were well established in their careers and me, in my mid-twenties at the time, overseeing fixed income derivatives trading globally, mortgage-backed securities trading in the US and global foreign exchange trading. Initially we didn't even know with any certainty what the positions were, whether we were net long or short on each trading desk. This meant that we had to invent what today would be called a daily market risk process. We experimented with several different approaches; over about a year we developed some IT infrastructure and processes to collect all end-of-day positions from the back and middle offices and some initial analytical algorithms for adjusting and aggregating the risks of the positions. This enabled us to produce some rudimentary daily risk reports. After 18 months, we had a pretty good view of all the trading risk, not just in New York but globally, including London, Tokyo and the rest of Asia.

It took a long time to build that technological and analytical infrastructure, but the core of the risk management processes were the conversations. Napoli would call a meeting at 7:30am each Wednesday with all of the heads of businesses and senior traders in New York. He had our two to three page report with the gross positions and net delta-adjusted position for every major product and every major desk, and he would ask the head of each desk to talk about the position: "I see you are much longer than you were a week ago. Is that intentional? What's the strategy? How long do you plan to hold the position? What do you think about the market? Let's talk about the risk, are we comfortable with that? What is the exit strategy? Are customers giving you this position or is this an intentional, proprietary position?" etc. The meeting would sometimes go for 90 minutes and he would discuss everyone's positions in front of everybody else. This created a culture of openness and transparency about risk taking, and heaven help you if you showed up at that meeting without being articulate about your risk. This process worked very well, albeit at 7:30 in the morning with strong coffee! I stayed in that role and enjoyed myself thoroughly while learning a great deal, until 1990, when I returned to the University of Wisconsin to write my PhD thesis.

After graduating with my PhD in 1995, I worked a short time in the Mathematics Department of Penn State University, and then in the Finance Department back at the University of Wisconsin. In the second half of 1996 I joined Bear Stearns as a Managing Director in Market Risk. I had expected it would probably be very similar to Merrill Lynch: characterised by openness, transparency and dialogue about risks; however, I was very surprised to find the culture at Bear Stearns was quite different – indeed, the exact opposite. The Bear Stearns experience really opened my eyes to the importance of culture in underpinning – or indeed sabotaging – effective risk management.

In late 1997, I went to Société Générale (Soc Gen) in New York, where I became Head of Market Risk for the US securities subsidiary.

Soc Gen had recently expanded the trading operation, but it didn't have a robust, independent market risk oversight function. I was hired to create that, essentially from scratch. The idea was to set it up in NY, and then replicate that at the Soc Gen Head Office in Paris and elsewhere. What was great was the genuine commitment from senior management and trading management to building a strong and well-resourced market risk capability. With talented people in the team, we built the relevant risk reporting infrastructure quite quickly. We would generate risk reports overnight and use them as the foundation for conversations about risks with traders and trading management early in the morning and throughout the day.

I really enjoyed that experience, but subsequently moved in 1999 to Melbourne, Australia, to become Group Chief Risk Officer at ANZ, which had just lost a large sum of money in August 1998 when Russia defaulted. Of course, lots of banks lost money when Russia defaulted, including Soc Gen. The difference was that ANZ's leadership appeared not to know that it had a substantial position in Russian bonds at the time, apparently because the majority of the risk-taking in emerging markets in 1998 was taking place in ANZ's Investment Banking operation in London, while the bank's leadership was in Melbourne.

My time as CRO and a member of the Executive Committee at ANZ was challenging, thoroughly enjoyable and rewarding; in retrospect, the risk management piece was mostly about building capability and repositioning the function as a centre of excellence and an important contributor to the group's overall performance, in partnership with the business. Together we built a strong team and capability in risk management, delivered consistent performance and growth, changed the culture, and oriented the group strategy towards Asia; all of which positioned ANZ well for the future. I greatly appreciated having the support of ANZ's leadership to become actively involved in the development of Basel II from 2001 to 2004, especially the operational risk part.

At the end of 2004, I left ANZ and quickly found myself consulting, first independently, with major clients in Australia and China, and subsequently for McKinsey as an expert partner in their risk management practice from 2006 to 2008.

Matthew: *Who would you say influenced you most in your early career?*

Mark: I've worked with and for many great, inspirational people, but I'd have to say that Dan Napoli at Merrill Lynch was one of my biggest influences. He believed that analytical models can be useful and that reports are sometimes interesting, but "risk" is ultimately best understood in dialogue and conversation. His approach was to walk around the trading floor talking to the heads of trading desks and senior traders, and even individual product/junior traders. He talked to them about their positions, trying not only to understand the strategies they were employing and how they were trying to make money, but also assessing how well they understood the risks they were taking.

I believe the "Napoli approach" really reflects what works best in risk management today.

Matthew: *You currently work as a consultant?*

Mark: Yes, and I have done so for more than 10 years now, since leaving ANZ. Since leaving McKinsey in October 2008 (a chaotic time for financial markets!), I have advised clients in both developed and emerging markets around the globe on all aspects of risk management and risk governance, including credit, market, operational, liquidity, strategic and reputational risks, and regulatory issues (including Basel II and III strategy and implementation). My primary focus over the last three or four years has been advising clients on risk appetite and risk culture, as well as risk governance at board level (including director training) and also some supervisory training.

Matthew: *One thing we find interesting from the supervisors' point of view is the complexity of modern banks. In particular, there is a sharp contrast between the lending activities of a traditional bank and its trading activities. For example, the models for traditional lending activities are relatively straightforward: you estimate things like default rates and loan-loss reserves. The maths entailed is pretty well understood. But modelling trading activities is much more complex, combining mark-to-market and estimates of volatilities, and whether you sample your* *data from 90 days or, perhaps, 17 years or some other period. We wonder if risk modelling for trading activities is being led by the traders themselves. And this brings up the question of culture. Do regulators believe that risk modelling and reporting can be made much more powerful when there is someone actively engaging with the traders to understand what they are doing so that risk concentrations can be headed off? The Napoli approach, if you like.*

Mark: There are two important points contained in your question. The first is the complexity of modern banks, which I agree is certainly an issue. The financial crisis very clearly demonstrated that some of the largest, most complex banks were just too big and complex to manage effectively – in particular, as documented by the Senior Supervisors' Group in their very important October 2009 report,[6] the aggregate, integrated risk profiles of some banking groups proved to be much too complex and opaque for their management and boards to understand, especially when they were changing rapidly during the time of great market stress.

Indeed, even individual dimensions of risk were not properly understood and managed. During the financial crisis, many large firms discovered that they could not aggregate all of their exposures to their largest counterparties quickly and accurately at the group level, which limited their ability to make prudent business decisions and effectively manage risks in fast-moving markets.

Secondly, the structural limitations of risk models, including their dependence on history, can sometimes make it more difficult for management to understand risks, particularly at those times when the historical conditions and relationships, which are captured and reflected in the models, no longer hold true ... For example, at some of the worst-affected banks, some of the most important forward-looking risk numbers in management risk reports immediately prior to the crisis (e.g. expected losses on US residential mortgage portfolios) turned out to be dramatically wrong, particularly after US house prices fell substantially. Some actual, realised losses turned out to be orders of magnitude greater than the earlier loss estimates, which were derived from models that were built during an environment of rising house prices and that may have provided false comfort to management.

These examples demonstrate some of the substantial challenges associated with producing good risk reports for management, which need to be complete, accurate, timely and actionable. To answer your question: the best chance to catch potential weaknesses in risk reports – and to identify unacceptable risk concentrations, so that these can be headed off in a timely fashion – is by actively discussing the contents of the risk reports on a very regular basis. This also applies to the risk reports for trading activities – which should be produced by the independent risk function! That was essentially the Napoli approach.

Matthew: *Could we talk a little bit about the culture and capability of supervisors?*

Mark: My main observation is just how much has changed in that regard since 2007. Pre-crisis, in some jurisdictions, there was almost a supervisory deference to industry, with "light touch" regulation in vogue in some important countries … that has obviously changed dramatically, post-crisis.

A particularly important development since the crisis, which has recently been emphasised by the Financial Stability Board (FSB), is the need for banks to implement effective risk appetite frameworks and strengthen their risk culture. These are both complex topics, which are very challenging for both industry and supervisors. In May 2013, I coordinated an APEC[7]-funded training programme for supervisors from APEC economies in Shanghai; the topic was enhancing supervision of risk appetite and risk culture in large financial institutions. In that programme, many of the supervisors who were present discussed the importance of more deeply engaging with bank management and boards on a regular basis, going forward. This by itself represents a major change in supervisory approach for many.

With regard to supervisory capability, a key conclusion of the Shanghai training programme was that supervisors in the future will need to have significantly strengthened skills and knowledge, including an ability to better understand risks associated with specific business models, and highly developed "soft" skills to assess and evaluate risk culture. Everyone present agreed that these (non-traditional) "soft" skills are "hard", and that a substantial amount of supervisory training will be needed to deliver these strengthened capabilities within the supervisory agencies. I expect this substantial uplift of supervisory capabilities, which is really necessary in many countries, will take at least five years, if not longer, to achieve.

Matthew: *What do you think are important innovations and developments of the last 10 years and what developments would you like to see?*

Mark: I can think of at least eight major developments related to or impacting the discipline of financial risk management over the last decade.

The first is all about the risk management challenges and developments arising from the explosion in volume, complexity and sophistication of derivatives, including credit derivatives, structured and exotic products. This includes lessons learned during the crisis about their valuation and liquidity.

Perhaps linked to this is the continued emergence of operational risk management and control as a specialist risk discipline in its own right. Despite substantial difficulties with operational risk measurement – which I think has been driven in a wholly wrong direction by some regulators enforcing "loss distribution" approaches to measurement, in their jurisdictions – this discipline of operational risk management and control will continue to grow in importance and maturity.

Also, post-crisis, we have seen very significant advances in both the conceptual approach and the tools and processes for measuring and managing funding and liquidity risks.

Matthew: *You are talking about XVA: DVA CVA and so on?*

Mark: Here I am mainly referring to the bigger picture regarding the recent advances that have been made in all aspects of liquidity risk management – this I would name as the second significant development of the last decade. The world was awash in liquidity for many years prior to the crisis, and liquidity risk didn't get much attention. Of course, the ALCO[8] committees in major banks would always look at the funding structure, cash flow schedule and cost, but liquidity risk management itself (including measurement, management, and control dynamics) was not well developed as a discipline.

Matthew: *I think it was on the regulators' agenda for 2008. Too late, of course.*

Mark: Yes. Actually the Institute of International Finance (IIF) also had a working group on liquidity in 2006, which published an extensive set of recommendations about good practices for the measurement and management of liquidity risks in March 2007. Unfortunately the ink was barely dry on those recommendations when the crisis hit ...

The third big trend since the crisis is the emergence and elevation of the Chief Risk Officer (CRO) role in major banks, together with a significant strengthening of the broader, end-to-end risk management capabilities in almost all banks. Risk management prior to the crisis often struggled for resources and to get the attention of senior management in many institutions. CROs were, in reality, sometimes more like "chief reporting officers". The CRO was often not at the table when big risk-taking decisions were taken. Happily, that is mostly not the case today.

Fourth, since the crisis, we have seen the birth and development of the notion of "risk appetite", which as mentioned previously is a very difficult concept, but one that is now better understood and widely appreciated as a crucial component of effective risk governance. Obviously, you wouldn't drive your car on a road without first deciding how fast you can drive it, given the conditions and your capabilities as a driver. In an exactly similar way, if you are running a bank, it makes complete sense for you to try to determine in advance how much risk you can take and manage (of each risk type, and in aggregate) in pursuit of your revenue objectives; while making sure that in all reasonably foreseeable conditions (including conditions of extreme stress) you are going to stay within your tolerance for downside and loss.

That is the essence of defining risk appetite, and I think some banks are now becoming very good at this. Early on, not a lot was known about how to do it; in fact, there was some scepticism about whether you could do it at all. An IIF working group asked whether or not risk appetite was doable; and, if so, what are the four or five key challenges that need to be addressed, and what works in overcoming those challenges. Its findings were reported in June 2011, along with four detailed, named case studies,[9] which proved very helpful to industry.

The fifth important, post-crisis development is the emergence of "risk culture" as an important consideration for management, boards and increasingly also for supervisors. There is now widespread recognition that culture is a crucial enabler of effective risk management or, conversely, is a constraint on its effectiveness. The title of the Ernst and Young (EY) Risk Management Survey of 2014 *Shifting Focus – Risk Culture at the Forefront of Banking* makes the point. EY has been doing this survey for six years now, with risk culture becoming an ever bigger priority and focus each year. Indeed, I believe it is now truly front and centre for most large banks.

Matthew: *Is that aimed at more efficiency or cost control?*

Mark: I don't think so. Often, when thinking about risk management we focus on the obvious things – IT systems, data, risk policies, quantitative models, limits, risk reports, etc. However, while these are all important, the largest banks that collapsed as a result of the crisis had most or all of these things in place. In 2009 the IIF Risk Management Working Group defined risk culture as "[t]he norms and traditions of behaviour of individuals and of groups within an organisation that determine the way in which they identify, understand, discuss and act upon the risks the organisation confronts and the risks it takes".[10]

So risk culture is really about organisational behaviours with regard to risk. Personally, I like to think of "risk culture" as being like the crucial, largely hidden, software that makes risk management processes really work effectively – or not.

Matthew: *It could be a good way of dispensing with things that you are really not comfortable with or not very good at. Do you see that happening?*

Mark: That's a very interesting question. A number of major banks, especially those that have had challenges with capital stress testing and so on, have exited certain business lines or specific geographies for various reasons, but on balance, I think those decisions are typically more about risk appetite – including considerations of return on scarce capital, commercial priorities and management capability strengths and weaknesses – than about risk culture. But perhaps culture has also played a role in some cases.

The IIF put together a crisis committee in late 2007, and the first principle of conduct in the final report of that committee was Principal I.i: "A robust and pervasive risk culture throughout the firm is essential."[11]

Yet, how do you do that? If you're the CEO or on the executive committee or board of a major bank, how do you even know what your risk culture is? You know the culture in the executive committee; you probably know it at a level down, maybe two levels down in your particular business line, but below that you probably have little idea.

In my experience of working in this area with clients, large-scale staff surveys are typically of limited use for shining a meaningful light on risk culture, so a different approach is needed. Yet the industry, backed up by the Senior Supervisors Group, and more recently by the FSB and all major regulators, says that the culture of how an institution understands and behaves regarding risk is crucial for making risk management effective. So if you want to ensure that your expensive risk management processes and systems are contributing to effective risk management, you need to know whether your culture is supporting that central objective, or is somehow undermining it. In my conversations with CEOs and directors, many of them don't know the answer, and they don't know how to know. In 2014 the FSB published guidelines to help supervisors begin to assess the risk culture in major financial institutions. However, while helpful, I believe these guidelines represent just the first step on a very long journey to a deeper understanding of risk culture and its impact on risk management effectiveness.

The sixth major, post-crisis development is a significant change in the role of boards in the oversight and governance of risk. Not long ago, some of the biggest banks in the world did not have a board-level risk management committee. Today it is unthinkable that a major bank would not have a risk committee, and most major regulators now require it. That's challenging many directors, who may have been captains of industry and very successful in their fields, but are in some cases perhaps not very well equipped for extended discussions about risk. So I am seeing a big change in the increased demands made of boards and of individual directors in the area of risk governance, which includes – among other things – the challenging topics of risk appetite and risk culture, mentioned previously.

Frances: *Are you seeing much shareholder activity in this direction? Are shareholders demanding that boards improve, or is it mainly from regulators?*

Mark: No, I don't think that shareholders have been the major force acting here, which leads to my seventh major observation of change, which is that essentially, the entire agenda is now being set by national and international regulators, and I expect that this will continue for at least a few more years. The end of the period of substantial regulatory change, post-crisis, is not yet in sight. This dominance of regulators in setting the agenda has been largely driven by political pressure coming from the G20, going right back to 2008/2009. Some of it, in my view, has moved too fast. For example, with some of the new liquidity requirements, I think there are likely to be unintended consequences, especially in Asia.

Returning to my earlier point about increased demands being made of boards and of individual directors in the area of risk governance, I will highlight one specific example: risk models. What should be the responsibility of directors and boards in the oversight of models? Reading the press, you might perhaps be tempted to think that models are all about calculating risk-weighted assets (RWAs) and minimum capital levels. But most risk models principally exist so that management can understand the performance, pricing and risk characteristics of products, customers and portfolios, and therefore successfully manage risks on a day-to-day basis. So what should be the responsibility of boards to enquire into and understand all of the risk models, including key aspects like what they are used for, how they work, and their important limitations? In many jurisdictions, boards are required to sign off on certain aspects of the risk management infrastructure, which includes the risk models, to say that it is all good and it works appropriately. For most part-time, non-executive directors, this is a very big ask and frankly is not very realistic. I believe that little comfort should be taken from such declarations.

Another, broader example of the increased demands now being made of boards and directors is the consultation document from the Basel Committee entitled *Guidelines: Corporate Governance Principles for Banks*, dated October 2014.[12] The draft Corporate Governance Principles that the Basel Committee published for comment are 36 pages long with 169 paragraphs. In my experience, I think it is almost impossible for any director of a large, complex, international bank to properly meet all of these requirements with less than (say) 80–100 days a year of work. In practice, most directors are unlikely to devote that much time to the task. So – if I'm right – what are the consequences of this for governance at individual banks, and for the financial system as a whole?

Perhaps part of the answer is that many large banks will need to find new directors over the medium term, but if so, where will these appropriately skilled and qualified people come from? The medium-term consequences of these increased burdens being placed on bank directors have not yet been widely understood, and I think this is a very big issue.

Matthew: *Is this going to eventually push us to a simpler world? Is one of the corollaries to say: It is just too hard?*

Mark: That's a great question. Will these developments lead, over time, to a simplification of banks' business models? As a first step towards answering this question, I think the increased accountability for directors and for boards, combined with the strengthening of the role and function of risk committees, will lead many banks to develop a stronger risk governance capability after a few years. As that stronger capability gets built, and the regular risk appetite processes become more closely linked to strategy and operational planning, those processes also become more familiar to members of the risk committee and hence can be conducted in progressively more detail.

When this happens, I think that in many cases there will be an increased realisation that many of the more marginal and complex activities, while apparently profitable on a "top line" basis, are perhaps not quite so profitable when you factor in all the costs of stronger risk management, IT, modelling, governance, control and everything else, including increased capital requirements.

Consequently, I expect that for some institutions, it will make more sense to revert to a simpler strategy, where both the governance of risks and the associated regulatory requirements are less complex and less burdensome.

Over time, I do think that more institutions will look to simplify their business models, and regulators will presumably be happy about this. However, there will always be some banks that have confidence in their capabilities and will be comfortable continuing to carry more complex products and business lines.

Eighth on the list of big developments is the substantially increased level of sharing of good risk management processes and approaches by industry. Prior to the crisis, risk management was very closely guarded and very tightly held: banks typically didn't disclose much about their risk management. Perhaps surprisingly, the way different banks manage risks varies significantly and many banks rightly or wrongly (often wrongly, I believe) thought their own risk management was a source of competitive advantage, so they didn't disclose much about their risk management processes.

For example, if the crisis ultimately led to the conclusion that Goldman Sachs' risk management was better than that of Lehman Brothers or Bear Stearns, then good for Goldman's shareholders. But the financial crisis also showed us that if Lehman Brothers' or Bear Stearns' risk management capabilities and processes were not strong enough, that affects us all. Viewed through this lens, the secretive approach to risk management is neither effective nor sustainable.

A key development occurred in July 2008, when the industry published the first ever consensus set of principles and best practice recommendations for risk management. This report set out some important principles. For example, Recommendation I.20 says: "Firms should consider assigning the following key responsibilities to the Chief Risk Officer (CRO)."[13] A list of seven bullet points then follows, which essentially answers the question: "What should the Chief Risk Officer do?" Recall that by 2008 a small number of major institutions had a CRO, but their jobs were all different, and nobody really knew what the job description should be; here suddenly there was group of industry leaders saying what the CRO should do. I believe that the decision of industry representatives to come together during the crisis, share different approaches and lessons learned and then unite behind a set of consensus principles and specific recommendations for managing risks effectively was a pivotal development for the evolution of the discipline. That spirit of knowledge sharing about risk management approaches has subsequently continued and deepened across the industry.

I guess the point I'm trying to make is that today, there is a widespread general acceptance that senior risk management practitioners should come together occasionally to share their experiences and insights and try collectively to make recommendations about what works, so as to improve risk management practices across the industry. That's a big change from the more secretive, risk-management-as-a-competitive-weapon philosophy which held sway prior to the crisis.

Frances: *Do you think that is a good thing or a bad thing? For example, if an organisation regards its risk management as a competitive advantage, then is it not more likely to take it seriously than if they are doing it because they think they have to?*

Mark: I am saying that the banks that survived the crisis recognised that they need to make sure that their end-to-end risk management capabilities, including things like databases and technology, as well as risk management processes and skills in the front line, are not lagging, they conform to some sufficiently strong standard.

The question now becomes: How sustainable is that? How can you maintain the focus on ensuring risk management is strong, after memories of the crisis fade? To me, that is the culture point. It's one thing when the regulator is on your case about this or that. But when the regulator goes away, what drives your priority towards risk management? As we discussed, in recent years it is the regulators that have driven the agenda. Today there is obviously a heck of a pipeline of regulatory "To Dos" for big institutions in the main jurisdictions. Now, the real challenge for many is not writing big cheques and engaging phalanxes of consultants. The real challenge is how to keep the focus on the institution's risk profile, and how that is changing, amidst such a crowded agenda.

And that goes back to the core risk management principles: keep the focus on ensuring there are regular, effective conversations happening about what's new, what's growing rapidly, what don't we understand, stress testing and so on. We must not let the current big infrastructure and capability build in response to the Basel regulatory imperatives crowd out the room for the old "Dan Napoli dialogue" about risks – this is hard.

Frances: *One way to do it might be to regard risk management as a potential source of competitive advantage, which is perhaps a good reason for organisations to keep mum about their risk management processes. They're more likely to be serious about managing risk if they think it contributes to revenues than if it's something they do just because they have to.*

Mark: Yes, I think you are right. During my time as CRO at ANZ, I made this point in speeches, that we wanted our risk management to become a source of real strength for us, a competitive advantage at least domestically, if not more broadly. That was a cultural strength at the time, because it meant there was a genuine willingness by the bank leadership, in the absence of a regulatory imperative, to build a strong risk management capability. The genesis of this objective was partly out of a desire to avoid a repetition of the recent risk management mistakes from the past, but this evolved into a clear commitment to build and position our risk management capability as a source of commercial advantage. In practice that included a conscious strategy to look outwards and find some way to get "in the loop" to learn as much as possible about the details of industry best practices in risk management. This was a fairly novel concept and wasn't easy to do back then, because at that time it was not easy to know where to go, who to talk to, and how to learn as much as possible about the risk management practices of others in the industry.

By contrast, amidst the demands associated with digesting and implementing all of the current major regulatory changes, I don't hear many firms talking about risk management as a source of competitive advantage today. However, I believe this will change, once the new regulatory framework is bedded down. Importantly, I don't believe that there is any conflict between openly sharing risk management approaches in order to support continued strengthening of industry best practices in this area (… from which everyone benefits), and positioning risk management internally as a source of commercial competitive advantage. This is because doing risk management well is hard – the devil is in the details, it takes a very long time to build superior capability through sustained commitment to doing so, and culture has a crucial role to play.

Matthew: *So how is the front office taking all this, do you think?*

Mark: I think again it's cultural. This is another change that I've seen in the last two to three years. In the midst of all the regulatory changes and conduct issues, in many institutions we are seeing the emergence of business unit heads/front office leaders, who are also risk managers in a day-to-day sense and care deeply about risk. Probably the most important feature of a strong risk culture is front-line, business unit ownership of risks. Even three years ago it was often difficult to convince some business unit heads that risk was part of their responsibility. Today I think that's shifted, and that is a very positive development.

Frances: *Why do you think that shift has happened, where suddenly front office people are accepting ownership of risk? Do you think it's a function of their career progression? Or is it some external development? Or does it come from management?*

Mark: I think there are several different contributing factors, including all of those you've mentioned. While it's hard to generalise, in the institutions that I'm familiar with, a lot of this has come about as a result of initiatives in the area of risk culture. Over the last couple of years, most major banks have done some work in the area of risk culture, and inevitably, this work seems to reinforce the front-line ownership of risk.

As part of the risk culture diagnostic process, it is hard to avoid, one way or another, attempting some kind of assessment of how well risk is understood and owned in the business. It frequently used to be the case that when you started doing that work as a consultant, staff would tell you: "Oh risk is not discussed in our business, we are focused on revenue", or any one of half a dozen other typical reasons why risk is either not discussed or not prioritised in the business. You only have to go back one time to the executive committee with that kind of feedback, before the savvy business unit leader says: "You know, that's probably not where we want to be 12 months from now…" In my experience, that realisation can be the catalyst that makes the necessary culture shift possible.

Additionally, many major institutions now directly link their periodic risk appetite review process with their long-standing process of approving business operating plans and revenue targets. For the business leader, that means there is no way to get away from conversations that are increasingly embedded within the business planning process about the risk implications and consequences of your growth aspirations and plans for your business. Some of this change comes ultimately from taxpayers, who took the hit in the crisis. One of the most important lessons from the crisis was that you do not want business unit leaders aggressively pursuing ambitious revenue growth targets – often in pursuit of lavish personal performance bonuses – unconsciously, without regard for the risk implications of their actions and the consequences for the aggregate risk profile of the organisation. Instead, you want the commercial folks to get into the habit of thinking: If I do implement all my business plans and specific revenue growth initiatives, in order to achieve my targets, what are the likely consequences for our risk profile of those plans and initiatives under a variety of economic scenarios? How comfortable am I, and how comfortable is the larger organisation, with those risks – what could go wrong, and how could we deal successfully with an extreme downside scenario?

Indeed, that's one of the most important specific conversations that is really at the heart of doing risk appetite. Leading banks are now having those conversations with all the business units at least annually, if not two or three times a year. I think it is almost impossible to be a business unit leader in the middle of that process, and *not* become, over time, both more thoughtful and articulate about your risks, and also a stronger owner of them.

Importantly, I think boards are also beginning to have higher expectations of the extent to which business leaders should be articulate about their risks and able (at least in the boardroom) to clearly demonstrate ownership of those risks. This directly impacts prospects for career progression, and is a very welcome development.

Finally, at least in some jurisdictions, supervisors now want to meet periodically with business unit heads and discuss the risks in the business directly with them. Effectively, they are increasingly talking to the actual risk takers, rather than just to the senior risk management staff.

So I think all of these developments are having an impact on the increasing front-line ownership of risks.

Frances: *One of the things that has changed since the crisis is that a lot of proprietary risk taking has moved from the banks into what might broadly be termed shadow banking, in particular into non-bank entities such as hedge funds. The response has been to try and regulate things like hedge funds. Are they just closing the gate after the horse has bolted? Are the new regulations on hedge funds going to go any way toward capturing the risk that is migrating from the banks, or are they going to be worthless?*

Mark: There are two questions there. To the second question about new regulations on hedge funds, the honest answer is that I don't know. I think it is an important question; but frankly, we probably just don't know enough yet about the broader consequences of the wide diversity of risk-taking activities in hedge funds to be able to answer your question with confidence.

More generally, shadow banking is a generic term that means different things in different jurisdictions. It means a very different thing in China from what it does in the US, for example. I have been involved in a few academic conferences about this over the last couple of years, and I sense that we are still closer to the beginning of the journey than the end. It seems we are still trying to nail down what exactly is the concern that needs to be addressed. For example: what kind of strengthened regulation should be imposed on the asset management industry?

There are concerns about potential contagion and systemic risks. What if a problem occurs at BlackRock, for example – what might the consequences be? To answer that question we have to consider carefully: what is the event and what specific risks are we worried about? Are they financial stability risks, or material risks to the regulated banking system and depositors, possibly transmitted via impacts on fragile, illiquid markets? Are we concerned about risks to the taxpayer? Or are we talking about risks to fund investors?

Following the crisis, we moved very quickly to tighten regulation on the banking side of things. However, I think it is prudent now to slow down somewhat on the shadow banking side, and not rush to regulate further, before allowing for deeper consideration of the broader consequences of the shift of proprietary risk taking out of the banking system into the much less transparent shadow banking system. This would allow for a more thorough analysis of the impacts of this shift on the depth and liquidity of key markets, and a deeper understanding of the broader consequences of this shift for financial stability. This is not a very sexy answer, but it is the best answer that I can give at this time.

Coming back to the first part of the question, are we "closing the gate after the horse has bolted", through the avalanche of new banking regulations – Basel 2.5 and Basel III, Dodd-Frank etc.? Perhaps, at least with respect to the last crisis …

Nevertheless, doing nothing was not an option, because we do have an obligation to society to do everything possible to prevent a repeat of the financial crisis, given the huge damage it did to the global economy. Even today, growth is very weak in Europe and this has a real, tangible impact on the lives of people. I think the key regulatory changes contained in Basel III, on both the capital side and the liquidity side, are both in the right direction. Who knows yet if the calibration is right – this will need to be monitored over the coming years, with adjustments, if necessary.

However, I do worry about the unintended consequences of the cumulative effects of so many new regulations – each of which may look sensible in isolation – especially in emerging markets, where in general there's less capability to effectively implement them, both on the industry side and on the supervisory side.

However, I worry even more about the potential negative consequences of some recent proposals to change the design of the Basel regulatory capital framework in a very fundamental way.

At the centre of the debate is an important question around the proper role that banks' internal risk models – which are at the heart of the advanced approaches under Basel II and Basel III – should continue to play within the future global regulatory framework. The central question, which is currently the subject of fierce debate, is: Should we abandon internal models altogether, and design a completely new regulatory capital framework, which would be based on three elements – (1) high minimum capital floors calculated from newly revised standardised approaches to credit, market and operational risk, (2) a simple leverage ratio that "bites" (no longer just a "backstop" measure) and (3) a regular, rigorous, system-wide stress-testing process? Some senior regulators, including several from the USA, are advocating such a shift. Others are less convinced of the wisdom of making such a major shift, especially at such a late stage in the post-crisis regulatory reform journey.

In my view it will be very important to watch how this debate unfolds. I expect that the way this particular debate is resolved, and the decisions that will be taken regarding "next steps" in the further evolution of the regulatory framework, will have profound impacts on future banking business models, the allocation of credit to the real economy, and the effectiveness of banks' internal risk management processes.

Stepping back, much of the new regulation that has been adopted can be thought of as being like tightening speed limits and putting bigger and better airbags in cars. These developments are certainly prudent and sensible steps. However, at the end of the day I believe the most important issue is still about how we drive the cars. That's really about the way banks are managed and governed, and about the standard of typical, mainstream industry risk management practices, which in my view must be substantially improved and strengthened in many jurisdictions.

Indeed, that's the main motivation for why I've spent so much time over the last 15 years working with various industry committees and working groups around the world to identify, articulate, disseminate and promote good risk management practices – as best we are able to discern these in different areas. This is a multi-year process of continuous learning, which tries to incorporate the key lessons learned from the many risk management successes and failures in different institutions.

Matthew: *What do you think you have learned from all of your work with industry committees and working groups over many years?*

Mark: The most important realisation for me is that risk is *fundamentally opaque*, and successful, experienced professionals do not always agree about how it should be managed. In particular, the aggregate, integrated risk profile of a large financial institution is extremely challenging to understand and manage well, especially at times of crisis when things change rapidly. This is a core truth, which I believe is too often forgotten, and which should cause all of us to remain very humble.

I've also learned that it is very difficult in practice for banks to correctly anticipate the likely impacts of commercial growth aspirations on their forward-looking risk profile, and to consciously ensure that the aggregate level of risks will remain within acceptable levels, over the future period considered. That's the key idea behind risk appetite, and it didn't happen prior to the crisis. Some banks are beginning to do it now, and those that are doing it relatively well are demonstrating that (a) it is valuable and (b) it is really hard. So we have to keep helping everybody to get onto that path and to do it better. I believe that the industry has an obligation to society to do these things as well as possible, and that stronger regulation is not the sole answer to avoiding a repeat of the crisis.

Matthew: *In the 2000s everybody was trying to come up with economic capital, but at a time when risk appetite was so difficult to determine, do you think the risk numbers just became the regulatory capital numbers?*

Mark: There's no question that today, the world runs on regulatory capital. Pre-crisis, having a strong credit rating was a stated objective of many banks, and the economic capital numbers that were produced by increasingly sophisticated capital models in support of the targeted credit rating were often higher than the minimum regulatory capital requirements, so economic capital was often the dominant constraint internally at that time. However, with the large, post-crisis increase in minimum regulatory capital requirements under Basel III, regulatory capital requirements are now typically much higher than the corresponding economic capital numbers. So for many banks, the economic capital calculations are currently of somewhat lower significance in many banks. Nevertheless, these economic capital calculations are still important for various reasons, including capital adequacy and risk-based pricing. This is because they capture important dimensions of risk, which must be understood and managed, but which are not reflected in the Basel regulatory capital calculations, such as credit risk concentrations and correlations, correlations between different risk types, and other risk aggregation effects.

The industry work done on risk appetite showed that risk appetite and economic capital are not the same – there is a big difference between them. The 2011 IIF report on risk appetite contains a detailed section on the relationship between the two concepts.[14] Risk appetite is ultimately about what we are willing to do, what we are not willing to do, and how we can link our appetite and our risk capacity to our strategy and growth objectives.

It was very fashionable, pre-crisis, for CEOs, board chairmen and senior bank executives to say: "We are going to target X% growth at low risk." Unfortunately, there was a (usually hidden) potential structural disconnect between what was said about the growth objective and risk; and there was in fact no mechanism to align the two. The crisis showed us, ex-post, that many of the largest banks took far more risk than they realised and much more risk than they could handle, in pursuit of their growth objectives. The key point of risk appetite is to properly align the institution's growth objectives with the desired risk levels and to ensure consistency between the two; this enables the institution to grow with conscious regard for risk. This goes far beyond the simple concept of capital, which is nevertheless a constraint in the risk appetite process. As mentioned previously, a number of banks have succeeded in a very thoughtful way to articulate their desired risk profile and align their risk appetite boundaries with their business plans and growth objectives.

Matthew: *How often do they do that?*

Mark: At least annually. Some Australian banks do it two or three times a year. As you are growing in different parts of your business, you need to be sure that you are not unconsciously taking unacceptable levels of risk, or unnecessarily constraining your ability to respond in an agile way to new commercial opportunities. So you need to think about what kind of risk appetite conversations to have, and when you need to have them. I think the evolution of risk appetite frameworks and processes in the largest banks is one of the most significant post-crisis developments in risk management.

Matthew: *How do you align risk appetite when regulatory capital dominates?*

Mark: That's a good question. It turns out that in many banks, risk appetite is *not* mainly about capital; rather, it's about their capability to successfully manage particular risks and their preferences for certain risks over others in pursuit of their commercial and strategic objectives. For example, most emerging market banks have plenty of capital, in the sense that their actual capital levels far exceed minimum regulatory requirements. In theory, they could allocate some of that excess capital to exotic derivatives trading, or to junk bonds (say), but typically you don't see them doing that. Why not? Because management may not have the relevant skills, experience and expertise necessary to understand and successfully manage the risks associated with those activities; consequently, there is not sufficient comfort at the senior management or board level to support undertaking such activities. As in this example, your risk appetite, how much risk you *choose* to take, is typically far less than the amount of risk you *could* take, if all that mattered was capital and liquidity; risk management capability constraints play an important role.

One good outcome is that thinking about risk appetite has now mostly moved beyond simple numerical measures like capital and liquidity. It is now more about knowing your core businesses and points of relative strength and competitive advantage, where the excess returns are, and choosing to grow preferentially in specific parts of the business rather than in other areas, while all the time trying to ensure that the likely cumulative impacts of all of your specific growth initiatives, taken together, will create an aggregate, forward-looking risk profile that will remain within acceptable levels across all reasonably foreseeable future scenarios, including scenarios of significant stress. This is quite difficult to do, and is essentially an iterative, learn-by-doing process.

Finally, in some leading banks, risk appetite is now being determined for individual businesses, not merely for the group as a whole, which takes the risk appetite discipline of assessing the risk implications of growth initiatives, and determining the boundaries of acceptable risks, down to a much more granular level in the organisation. It also substantially strengthens business unit ownership of risks. This is a very welcome development.

Matthew: *One impression I have is that, even though everybody thought they had their own proprietary way of adding value, in practice they pretty much copied one another. For example: We are going to do CDOs because so and so is doing CDOs. This can lead to crowded trades[15] with hard-to-predict revenue and risk outcomes. How do you link that back to appetite?*

Mark: Before the crisis, hardly anyone thought about that. Now I think everyone is aware of the potential for crowded markets. Crowded trades are one worrying consequence of the significant decline in market liquidity for many products, which has resulted from the new regulations affecting Wall Street, particularly Dodd-Frank and the Volcker Rule. Consequently the risk of everybody running for the exit at the same time is now significantly higher than it was around the time of the crisis. I think there is much more awareness of this risk now.

In any case, a proper risk appetite process requires that all risks associated with any new initiative or product should be carefully examined and thoroughly assessed, together with management's capabilities to successfully identify, control and manage those risks, *before* the product is approved. Given uncertainties about the potential for crowded trades and hard-to-predict revenue and risk outcomes that you mentioned, a robust risk appetite process would almost certainly approve relatively modest exposure limits for such products, at least initially, in order to constrain the downside risks to acceptable levels, even under severely adverse scenarios.

Matthew: *What about pro-cyclicality? It seems to have almost been reinforced by the way margins are called. Even with a lot of government intervention, we still have a pro-cyclical system that can disrupt. It is almost inevitable that you need somebody to step in and calm everybody down. Hitherto it has been governments that have done that. But I wonder whether there isn't a role for insurance, the pension funds or other long-term investors. Some of that was going on in 2008, where investors took advantage of bargain basement prices. But it was so piecemeal that* *you still needed the government to quieten everything down. How do you ensure that the pro-cyclical reaction is disrupted when it needs to be? Particularly when the world is in a crowded trade.*

Mark: Here I understand you are principally referring to excessive swings in asset prices, which are one highly visible and challenging aspect of pro-cyclicality; the supply of credit is another. Pro-cyclicality is a hard topic that has received much attention since the crisis – as part of the broader, heightened focus on financial system stability, which has included extensive discussion and formalisation of the goals of macro-prudential supervision. An important element of the Basel III framework is the new Countercyclical Capital Buffer, a tool that allows supervisors to boost minimum regulatory capital levels of banks during boom times, whenever they perceive that excess credit growth is associated with an unacceptable build-up of system-wide risks. However, this supervisory tool is new and currently untested. In the meantime, we've already witnessed reductions in liquidity in some key securities markets, as banks have scaled back or eliminated entirely their market-making activities in response to regulatory pressures. Hence, I think it is likely that we'll have to continue to deal with periodic bouts of price volatility, going forward.

In partial response, governments and market regulators can look at things like ensuring that market participants and central clearing counterparties are adequately capitalised, and that strengthened margining processes work in a timely and effective manner, and perhaps placing certain restrictions on specific activities such as short selling and algorithmic trading.

Nevertheless I expect we'll need to be prepared for occasional steep declines in asset prices going forward, especially in times of market stress and crowded trades, when liquidity for some products can disappear quickly. Therefore, market participants will need to factor these risks into their risk management processes, including risk appetite and limit-setting.

Of course, it is challenging to do this well, because traders have short memories and human nature is fundamentally cyclical: when things are going well, you want to double up, you want to do more and it is difficult to see the risks emerging. And during the really difficult times, when you have taken losses and pessimism abounds, you want to tighten and close everything and it's difficult to see the opportunities clearly. The old saying is that the bad loans get written in the good times … So it's very difficult to get these things right.

As mentioned earlier, the difficulty is compounded by the structural limitations of risk models, notably their dependence on history – which means the risk numbers can at times be misleading, especially at those crucial moments when the cycle is turning or there is a sudden spike in volatility, and the immediate future looks pretty different from the past. Under these circumstances the historical conditions and relationships between the key variables which are reflected in particular risk models, might no longer continue to hold true, and the forward-looking risk estimates from those models should be viewed with a very sceptical eye.

In these situations, it is really up to boards to exercise judgement about when management is getting over-confident following a run of success, and to step in and intervene by "tapping the brakes" when necessary. This is also very difficult to do. This underscores the importance of governance, and especially the crucial role of boards in dealing with these kinds of issues. Boards would be well advised to allocate more of their time to this kind of challenge.

If all else fails, supervisors need to step in. But it's hard: they didn't do it successfully in places like the US and Europe in the run-up to the crisis, because they are human beings too and everybody always has an argument about why "this time is different".

Matthew: *Imagine a "Dan Napoli dialogue" about risks and the dutiful risk officer says: Look at this position, it looks fairly big, it looks like it will take more than a week to clear. Then the front office guy says: Well actually I have got this client who is going to come in in the next couple of days, so we are going to stick to the position. Is there enough being done to estimate the distribution and how the liquidity impacts the inventory of positions? Can a risk manager really challenge the front office when the front office inevitably has the best view of the liquidity of the thing they are trading?*

Mark: Actually, all those years ago market risk was very well managed under Dan Napoli, long before anybody invented Value-at-Risk. The question was simply: Do you understand your exposures or not, and are we comfortable with those? A discussion of liquidity in the market for the particular instrument in question would certainly be an important part of the conversation. Specifically, it would be important to talk about the length of time that it would likely take the trader to successfully liquidate the position without unacceptably moving the market, both under normal and stressed conditions, and to look at historical data about daily turnover volume and extreme values of daily price changes for the security, since this information could be used to infer a ballpark estimate for how much could be lost by continuing to hold the position.

Matthew: But what would have happened if Napoli thought that the guy didn't understand his risk?

Mark: Then he would say "I want you out of that position by the end of tomorrow."

Matthew: So he had that call.

Mark: Yes, Napoli had that call and he had the unambiguous authority (directly reporting to the president) to say: "We have had a chat and I want you out of that position by the end of tomorrow." He wouldn't do that very often, by the way ...

Frances: He wanted to keep his powder dry.

Mark: Yes. When the risk manager has that authority, nobody misses meetings and everybody returns your phone calls. But if you have to play that card too often, then you probably have a culture problem. If the culture is working well, the conversation might go like this: "I see the average daily volume in the security is X and your position is twice X. Realistically how long do you think it would take you to work out of this if you wanted to, without having a problem?" And the trader says: "Realistically, probably a couple of weeks..." And then you say: "How comfortable are we about that?" In an organisation with a strong risk culture, you may not have to say anything else – tomorrow you come into the office and you see that 15% of the position is already gone. It comes down to influencing and persuasion, so you really want to use the "big club" (of instructing someone to liquidate a position, or perhaps vetoing a proposed transaction) as little as possible. The job of the risk manager is not to have all of the answers, since the trader will typically have superior information about the liquidity of his or her positions, but rather to ask the right questions, to ensure that the right conversations are happening and that decisions are being made in a timely way.

But if the original question is: Do people sufficiently take into account the volume, turnover and liquidity characteristics of positions? I would say: No, not always. But good ones do. And you can take that into account when you set limits for highly illiquid products.

Matthew: *What is it going to look like in 10 years' time?*

Mark: I'm not sure if by "it", you mean banking in general, or risk management, so I'll discuss each one in turn.

Ten years from now, I predict that – among other things – we will see a world in which the largest banks will be smaller, less complex and generally lower risk than today, in part because of simplified business models, increased capital levels and strengthened risk management practices; shareholders will have come to accept generally lower returns from these more utility-like banks; "shadow banking" activities will be mostly out of the shadows and the risks associated with these activities will be much better understood, including the risks to the regulated banking system and to financial stability; bank failures will be much better managed and agreed frameworks and processes for cross-border resolution between major jurisdictions will be in place; approaches to macro-prudential supervision will be tested and further refined; the industry will (still!) be working to strengthen risk management practices and proceeding with the implementation of Basel V; the level of supervisory resources and skills will be significantly increased in all major jurisdictions; and there will be general agreement, both internally amongst the individual members of the Basel Committee, and also between regulators and industry about the proper role of internal risk models in the regulatory capital framework (just kidding about the last point!) …

In the meantime, from a specific risk management perspective I think we've still got a great deal more work to do over the coming decade to strengthen typical industry risk management practices in many areas, including risk data aggregation, operational risk and cyber risks. We also still have years of work to do to further strengthen liquidity risk management practices. The good news here is that the Basel Liquidity Coverage Ratio and the Net Stable Funding Ratio will force banks to pay attention to that. The regulators are the forcing agent there, and I think that's good.

But the two main areas in risk where I expect we will continue to see particularly intense focus over the next 10 years will be strengthening risk governance (especially at the board level, which I've already mentioned) and strengthening risk culture. Risk culture is currently at the forefront of banking; I fully expect that focus to remain, and be augmented by a major focus specifically on "conduct risk". I think the developments that we will see in the area of risk culture over the next decade will be substantial.

To approach the topic of risk culture, a good place to start is with the fact that risk is fundamentally opaque: it's best understood and most effectively managed through conversation and dialogue with others. This internal dialogue about risks is the key enabler of effective risk management – akin to the "software" that makes the risk management decision processes work ... The quality of those conversations about risks is a central element, and also a strong indicator, of the risk culture.

When attempting to assess risk culture, it might be relatively easy to tick any number of easily observable, high-level culture indicators, like "tone from the top", but at the end of the day you'll only be able to make consistently good (or best-possible) decisions about risks, if the dialogue about risks is effective at every level: in the boardroom, at the executive table and in each business, through middle management, right down to the front line and even to the most junior people. Consequently, a crucial step, which is essential for understanding and evaluating a firm's risk culture, is to assess whether or not that dialogue about risks exists and is effective at every level.

If risk is not being discussed every day, or if the risk dialogue is not effective, then it is hugely important to find out: why not? It could be that when you talk to people, they tell you that risk is not part of their job: "I'm in the business line and the risk people do risk, so I don't bother with that." Or it could be: "We don't have time, we've had our budget cut and we are working 'until nine o'clock at night and we just don't have time for these conversations." It could be: "I am worried about risk, but I haven't had any training and I don't really know how to talk about it. I know duration is important, but I don't really understand it." Or: "I am worried about our suitability processes in the private bank, but I don't really know how all that works, therefore I don't want to embarrass myself and so I don't raise the question." Or it could be: "I have asked risk questions, and been told to go back to my desk, sit down and go back to my job ..."

Actually, in my experience there could be up to 15 or 20 different reasons why there isn't an effective internal dialogue about risks occurring every day, alongside other routine daily conversations about customers, products, pricing and revenue. These blockages or impediments to the risk dialogue are analogous to cultural "blind spots" in a particular business line; however, while they are often difficult for insiders to see, they are usually not too difficult for an outsider to detect if the right approach is taken. For example, an almost universal problem is that junior employees are frequently too afraid to speak up with their questions and concerns about risks.

Importantly, once you've detected these impediments, the natural next step is to create a targeted action plan to directly address the particular issues identified. Specific objectives can be developed, for example: to identify behavioural changes that senior management need to undertake, both individually and collectively, in order to strengthen the quality of their own discussions about risks and to provide role modelling of desired behaviors for staff; to clarify for line staff their specific responsibilities for risks, and (over time) to adjust job descriptions and compensation frameworks to incorporate these responsibilities; to provide risk training to staff; to improve the quality of forward-looking risk reports to provide increased levels of transparency about risks in a particular business, in order to facilitate and support regular conversations about those risks; to clarify for staff the boundaries of acceptable risks; to create a forum for regular risk discussions and/or to make risk a standing agenda item at team meetings (with allocation of sufficient time for those discussions); and, almost universally, to encourage and empower junior people to participate and speak up in risk discussions with their questions or concerns, listen to them with respect when they do, and then visibly reward this behaviour. Actions such as these send powerful signals to staff regarding the increased weight that management attaches to risk considerations within business decision-making processes, and they combine to strengthen the internal dialogue about risks and drive culture change over time.

Importantly, when targeted actions such as these are explained and driven by the business leadership, they are typically understood and embraced by employees as being beneficial to the business; experience indicates that business leadership of these changes is a key driver of impact.

In summary, the key point is that senior management and boards need to understand if the internal dialogue about risks is not happening reliably and routinely, or if it is not effective, or of sufficiently high quality, then why not – what's blocking it? Such understanding can lead directly to practical, targeted actions to "unblock" the risk dialogue in specific business lines and thereby substantially increase the quality of the firm's internal risk management discussions and strengthen its risk management decision processes. This is the essential outcome and also the substantial, tangible, commercial benefit of strengthening risk culture.

I think the skills needed to assess and shift risk culture are in many cases very different from bankers' and supervisors' traditional skills. Indeed, one of the main conclusions from the 2013 APEC training programme on risk appetite and risk culture was that most supervisors are currently not able to effectively assess the culture in large financial institutions and will need different skills from those they typically have now, in order to do so. They will need training and upskilling, and I believe it will take a while to build this kind of supervisory capability.

Finally, when thinking about the future 10 years from now, an important factor that I see is the very big divergence of skills and capability with respect to all aspects of risk management, both across the industry and, on the supervisory side, across different jurisdictions. What worries me is that we don't talk enough about this phenomenon, or acknowledge it widely. The Basel Committee and the FSB write many documents where some of the contents are, frankly, somewhat aspirational and not very realistic. I don't think any institution in the world meets all of these requirements today. More importantly, many weaker institutions and supervisors have a great deal of work to do to build needed capabilities with regard to risk management; this takes resources and time. We should acknowledge this fact more openly and discuss what is needed to effectively address the issue.

Matthew: *So why doesn't anybody point out that the system is too complex? If the gulf is as wide as you are saying, the pragmatist in me says: Simplify it.*

Mark: This is a hugely important question that you are asking. Actually, several people have pointed this out. For example, Thomas Hoenig of the FDIC[16] in his speech "Back to Basics"[17] said essentially that "the regulatory system is way too complex, and a simpler approach is needed".

The risk-based regulatory capital framework that is Basel III – including Basel II and Basel 2.5 and the liquidity aspects and everything else – is certainly complicated. It is also untested. We certainly hope it's better than what we had before, but we still have to see it work for a few years to be able to judge. Ask me again in 10 years how effective all these reforms were … I think we have done the best job we can to learn the key lessons and put difficult, sensible and thoughtful reforms in place, but it's all untested.

Regarding the complexity of the framework, I would make a couple of points. Firstly, every experienced banker would acknowledge the complexity of the aggregate risk profile of a large financial institution, operating in multiple business lines and multiple geographic regions. Consequently, the design of the internal risk management framework inside the organisation, including the risk policies, metrics, limits and reports, delegated decision-making authorities and day-to-day risk management processes and controls, is also necessarily highly complex, and would probably run to several thousands of pages of detail if expressed in a single document.

So it seems to me that the over-arching choice is whether the regulatory framework for the largest and most complex banks should mirror and capture at least the most important aspects of that complexity, including a close examination and treatment of the measurement and management of all of the most material dimensions of risk inside the bank, or whether it should do something different.

The former approach is embodied in the current Basel framework, albeit imperfectly; the result is a framework that is necessarily very complex, as it includes an extensive list of detailed and rigorous requirements regarding the components and operation of banks' internal risk management and governance processes, including requirements relating to the design, use and effectiveness of banks' internal risk models.

From my perspective, the advantages of the current approach include its risk sensitivity, as well as its designed, close proximity to the complex internal risk management measures and processes that banks typically use in their day-to-day risk management. This close proximity, which is clearly observable to bank employees and supervisors, leads quite directly to many important benefits. One of these benefits is the supervisory review process relating to Basel compliance, which typically consists of supervisory examinations and extensive dialogue between bank staff and supervisors about how particular elements of the bank's risk management systems and processes either do or don't meet the detailed Basel requirements; this supervisory review process is typically very impactful and eventually leads to a strengthening of those systems and processes. In this way, over the past decade the Basel requirements have often acted as a catalyst and detailed roadmap for building and strengthening specific elements of the risk management systems and processes of many in the industry, especially emerging market participants.

However, an obvious disadvantage of the current approach is that the volume and complexity of the Basel regulatory framework can make it just too difficult for bank staff to fully understand in its entirety and for supervisors to administer in

practice, through the process just discussed – leading to the risk
that material weaknesses in a bank's internal risk management
capabilities might be missed, amongst all of the detailed regulatory
"trees". Another disadvantage is that the volume and technical
complexity of the Basel requirements can have the unintended
effect of making it quite difficult for bank senior management
and board directors to participate in conversations about these
matters and to contribute to those discussions in a meaningful
way, which provides a difficult challenge for effective risk
governance.

As mentioned, some people believe that the current
framework has indeed become far too complex and we'd be
better off to take a simpler approach. For example, an important
contribution to this line of thinking came from Andy Haldane in
his 2012 speech "The Dog and Frisbee".[18]

Haldane makes some very important points and he makes
them well: how does a dog catch a Frisbee nine times out of ten,
every Tuesday in the park? It does not have a PhD in
aerodynamics. It's using some relatively simple rules to catch the
Frisbee, which has very complex motion properties. As I
understand it, Haldane's main point, demonstrated in the paper
through several examples unrelated to banking, seems to be that
in environments characterised by high levels of complexity,
simple indicators often outperform more complex ones.

Notwithstanding all the work that's been done to strengthen
the Basel framework since the crisis, a further, fundamental
redesign of that framework is now under serious consideration,
which would either reduce or eliminate the role of internal
models in the framework. There has been extensive debate about
this suggestion over the past year or so; impetus was given to this
idea by Daniel Tarullo, Head of Supervision at the Federal
Reserve Board in the US, in a speech in May 2014, where he
recommended that consideration be given to "… discarding the
IRB approach to risk-weighted capital requirements".

In a related development noted by Wayne Byres, current
Head of APRA and former Secretary General of the Basel
Committee, in his September 2014 speech,[19] there is diminishing
faith in the use of internal models by banks to calculate

risk-weighted assets for the purpose of determining minimum regulatory capital requirements within the Basel framework.

To put this development in context, in the early part of the last decade Basel II was designed to use specific, designated outputs from banks' internal risk models for different risk types – under tightly prescribed conditions, including a "use test" and supervisory examination and approval of the relevant internal models – as a partial driver for calculating risk-weighted assets (RWAs) and minimum regulatory capital requirements under the advanced approaches within Basel II. The rationale for this design feature is that the priority objective was to make Basel II more risk-sensitive than its predecessor, Basel I. Importantly, banks' internal models remain at the heart of the advanced approaches within Basel III; this is a core design feature of the current, post-crisis Basel regime.

To address questions about the consistency of Basel II implementation, the Basel Committee published several studies in 2013 that compared the calculations of RWAs by different banks for identical, hypothetical portfolios. These studies showed excessive levels of variability in banks' RWA calculations, for both credit risk and market risk. While there are multiple factors contributing to this variability, these studies have nevertheless been cited as a key reason for the declining level of support from some national regulators for the continued use of outputs from banks' internal risk models as a partial driver for determining RWAs and minimum regulatory capital requirements under the Basel regime. Since banks' internal models remain at the heart of the current Basel III regulatory framework, it is the wisdom of this design feature that is now being questioned. My own sense is that the complexity of the Basel framework is not helping here.

In this context, the Basel Committee published a five-page report to the G20 in November 2014 describing all the technical initiatives under way to reduce the level of RWA variation between banks.[20] The penultimate paragraph of the paper also describes the longer-term review of the design of the regulatory capital framework that is under way, and makes clear that the review will consider "alternative approaches for determining regulatory capital that reduce or remove reliance on bank-internal models".

What should we do? Should we abandon the use of banks' internal models in the regulatory framework altogether, and undertake a radical redesign of that framework to reduce complexity, or should we retain the design of the current, risk-sensitive Basel framework, and "fix" the internal models that are at its heart? A wide divergence of views is evident regarding this fundamental question, which is now being actively discussed.

Interestingly, there is no clear consensus amongst national regulators about what is the best way to proceed. For example, in his 2014 speech, Wayne Byres stated that "APRA's preference is to find ways to strengthen the current risk-based regime: there are many benefits from a risk-based capital system and we don't want to see the baby thrown out with the bathwater".

Generally, the industry is also not in favour of removing internal models from the regulatory framework, and would rather "fix" them. If the primary goal is simply to increase the comparability of banks' RWA calculations (and I'm not personally convinced this should be the primary goal!), then besides tightening up the use of national discretion by regulators in their various implementations of the Basel regulations (which is another contributing factor to the variability in banks' RWA calculations), we could possibly look to reduce the degrees of freedom that banks have with respect to their choices of historical data samples that are used in risk modelling. However, in light of the primacy of the internal uses by management of these risk models, as described earlier, this should be done very carefully. In late 2014 the IIF made some specific, detailed recommendations to the Basel Committee in this regard.

My personal view is that there are very significant risks that would arise from any decision to move away from the current risk-based Basel framework to a new regulatory capital framework, presumably with either minimal or zero reliance on internal models. My concern is that such a move could destroy the very close proximity of the regulatory framework to the complex internal risk management framework that I spoke about earlier, with the chance of severe, adverse, unintended consequences, which may be impossible to foresee.

In particular, I worry about the consequences for the future stability and effectiveness of banks' internal risk management processes if and when the strong (albeit, very complex) "guard rail" of the current, prescriptive Basel requirements – including detailed supervisory examinations of banks' risk management systems, processes and models under the advanced approaches – is removed, and replaced with other, presumably simpler regulatory requirements. I believe that the requirements of the current Basel regime force banks to be disciplined about making improvements to the details of risk management, in a way that many probably wouldn't, in its absence. I also worry about the chance for negative, unintended consequences for the future development of banks' internal risk management processes, especially in emerging markets, of such a move away from the current Basel framework.

I think this could be quite dangerous. Consequently I'd urge the Basel Committee to proceed with caution and great care in conducting its longer-term review of the design of the regulatory capital framework.

Notes

1 0.50%.
2 The change in the duration of a bond for a small change in the interest rate.
3 The size of the loss was later increased to $337 million.
4 Served for 27 years in a variety of roles in the Investment Banking industry before retiring in 1998. For the last 20 years of his career, he distinguished himself with Merrill Lynch & Co. by serving in a variety of senior management roles (Bloomberg.com).
5 Held various positions at Merrill Lynch, including serving as its global head of health care equity capital markets. He was previously a member of Merrill Lynch's Private Equity and Investment Banking groups (Bloomberg.com).
6 Risk Management Lessons from the Global Banking Crisis of 2008, Senior Supervisors Group, 2009.

7 Asia–Pacific Economic Cooperation.
8 Asset-Liability Committee.
9 Implementing Robust Risk Appetite Frameworks to Strengthen Financial Institutions, IIF, June 2011.
10 Reform in the Financial Services Industry: Strengthening Practices for a More Stable System, Report, IIF Steering Committee on Implementation, December 2009.
11 Final Report, Committee on Market Best Practices, IIF, July 2008.
12 Guidelines – Corporate Governance Principles for Banks, *Basel Committee on Banking Supervision*, Basel, 9 January 2015.
13 Final Report, Committee on Market Best Practices (n 11).
14 Implementing Robust Risk Appetite Frameworks to Strengthen Financial Institutions (n 9).
15 Where a large number of market participants hold similar positions in a security or type of security.
16 Federal Deposit Insurance Corporation.
17 Hoenig, T.M., Back to Basics: A Better Alternative to Basel Capital Rules, American Banker Regulatory Symposium, Washington DC, 14 September 2012. Director Hoenig addressed: (1) the evolution of the Basel proposal; (2) capital, the safety net and markets; (3) an alternative to Basel; (4) whether a simple measure with a relatively stronger minimum capital level would reduce liquidity in the market, constrain loan growth and undermine the economy.
18 Haldane, A., The Dog and the Frisbee, Jackson Hole, The Federal Reserve Bank of Kansas City 36th Symposium, 31 August 2012.
19 Byres, W., Perspectives on the Global Regulatory Agenda, RMA Australia CRO Forum, Sydney, 16 September 2014.
20 Reducing Excessive Variability in Banks' Regulatory Capital Ratios – Report to the G20, Basel Committee on Banking Supervision, November 2014.

9 | Paul Bostok

London, 24 November 2014

Understanding the objectives, appetite and tolerance for risk drives good risk management. That message sometimes gets lost.

Before he retired, Paul Bostok was a partner of GMO and Managing Director of their London office. Prior to that, he was portfolio manager at GMO Woolley.

He explains why the usual risk measures often miss the point.

Paul Bostok: Having done a PhD in particle physics at Oxford, I suppose I became one of the early quants. When, in 1985, I finished my doctorate, the investment management part of Baring Brothers was looking for somebody to do financial calculations on a new-fangled gadget called a personal computer. This entailed putting Lotus 123 into one of the floppy disc drives and our data into the other. There was also a mainframe computer, but that held all the client records and other big stuff, it wasn't set up to do things like financial analysis. I was one of the first people to do that sort of thing.

For two years I worked with Paul Woolley[1] and Robert Rice[2] on optimisation problems as well as running a protected equity fund.[3] At the time, some specialist firms in Chicago had launched portfolio insurance products. But as a junior analyst at the time, you also tended to work a bit on everything.

Frances: *Leland-Rubinstein[4] was the best-known one, I think.*

Paul: Yes there were three of them: Leland, O'Brien and Rubinstein, and they had their own firm. But of course when October 1987 happened it kind of knocked the wind out of those particular sails because they were hit with a lot of one-day volatility.

So two people who influenced me about that time were Paul Woolley, who started the London office of GMO (with whom I worked for nearly 20 years), and Robert Rice, who, as I have mentioned, was at Barings, but then went on to found Occam, which specialises in optimisation-type technology. They are both strong characters and well known in the industry.

Matthew: *Why did you choose finance out of university?*

Paul: I kind of had enough of my subject really, or I thought that I did. Also, the range of opportunities were rapidly shrinking in the UK at the time. The Thatcher reforms had put an end to tenure, lectureships and that sort of thing. This meant that the best you could aspire to in academia was probably three years as the most junior person in the department while hoping that someone else would take you at the end of that time. So it was really not very reassuring or promising,

I looked at some of the big consulting firms that were quite popular in the 1980s, such as Bain and Andersen, because I was attracted to something with a broad mandate, with business and economics. After looking at a couple of them I saw an ad for a merchant bank in investment and I thought that might fit.

Frances: *Computers were entering into that really rapid development phase and data became more reliable and easier to transmit. This allowed us to take advantage for the first time of the innovations of Harry Markowitz, Bill Sharpe and Fischer Black. So your skills would have been very much in demand.*

Paul: Yes. I can give you two examples. My first task at Barings was to build a database. Salomon Brothers had built a government bond index and MSCI, which then was Morgan Stanley, was doing the same with shares. So we tied them all in, and after about six months we were able to do some analysis on the data. The other example is that, when we started GMO, all the UK company data were on Extel cards, which were literally folding out paper sheets that were kept in a big filing cabinet: one sheet for each company. It was probably 15 years ago that they were replaced by one compact disc that came once a month or every other month. Now, of course, it is all downloadable. So, yes, lots has changed.

Analysis 1980s style was far from easy and, as you say, you had to get your hands on something to analyse, which of course nowadays you would take for granted.

So after those two years, in 1987, Paul Woolley wanted to leave and start GMO UK. Within Barings, the quant unit was competing with a much bigger team of traditional, active managers, who didn't really want us to go out and talk to anybody because we sent a different message to the one they were selling. So it made sense to do our own thing. GMO were not looking to expand, but they saw it as an opportunity and helped us get set up. I was there for 22 years and left in 2009.

Frances: *It's quite unusual in this industry to stay in one position for so long.*

Paul: It is quite unusual, though it is not terribly unusual in GMO, especially not for that generation because I suppose, having starting it, you want to see it make a success. Of the other people who influenced me at the time, the most important would be Jeremy Grantham,[5] who had over 20 years' experience before I got there. On my first visit to GMO in Boston, he explained in detail how company earnings and prices were related in US equities. I went to do the same for the UK and then worked on an international version. So one conversation generated literally a year's worth of work.

Frances: *Yes he is very well known.*

Paul: At GMO obviously I helped set up the initial equity quant-style portfolio and then a bit later managed the UK equity specialist funds at the same time. There was a strong focus on risk positioning. I am sure it will make you smile, but I was also the compliance officer. That is how it goes when you have such a small team. We started with four people and that grew to nine I think.

But as soon as we started growing risk became a more specialist activity and of course the culture changed completely post Nick Leeson.[6] He had two jobs in one within Barings Bank and, as we now all know, used it to dangerous and spectacular effect.

And then the risk role kind of moved on. I don't think it was making the best use of my abilities as a portfolio manager and I think I wasn't necessarily the best person at it either. So I carried on doing research, mostly on valuation and risk and asset allocation type things and then later on became notionally the chief executive, although I was really only looking after investment people. The business people were looked after by the Head of European Sales. But it did mean I set up a risk initiative.

In investment management firms, at the micro level there are at least two sorts of risks that we think about. One is the client risk, which is traditionally about volatility and portfolio risk management tools and stuff like that, which you may or may not think are any good. The other includes the risk of a trader doing something horrendous, which I kind of think of as more business risk. Business risk is a whole lot of other things that may or may not affect clients but may do damage to the business in some way.

Frances: *That would cover operations risk and stuff like that, including rogue traders and fraud.*

Matthew: *Why do you think it keeps on happening? For example, why wasn't Barings the last? Yet you had that Société Générale trading loss in 2008 and lots of others. What is the culture that you need to get in that respect, so that the risk manager is in a position to challenge portfolio managers and traders?*

Paul: Unlike in banking, in investment management, trader risk, rightly or wrongly, is relatively straightforward, especially in a quant fund like ours, where dealers are nowadays separate from portfolio managers. Initially, when we were smaller, it was the case that the fund managers would place orders and execute trades themselves. But as we grew, we got a specialist trading team. So you have quite nice boundaries of accountability.

With a quantitative strategy, buy and sell orders are generated according to pre-defined decision rules. If you run, say, a monthly update, there will be a buy and sell list that can be audited to see why each buy or sell order was given. Even a year later, if somebody wanted to know why you bought so and so, you could recreate, from the records of the market conditions at the time, the decision itself and you could say why it was done the way it was. In this process, the buy and sell list is handed to the trader and then, in my experience, there are two things that can go wrong. One is very simple and does happen from time to time because people are human and it's pure and simple error. I did one once, though I don't know if it counts now. There were two companies in Britain, one called Waste International, as in recycling kind of stuff; and one called Wace, which was someone's name. It was a telephone order to a broker and I meant one and he heard the other. That was sorted out when he phoned back to confirm that the order had been executed. He said he was very sorry, he must have misheard, and replaced the shares with the ones that we wanted. Those were the old days of telephone orders, when people knew you and it was very simple. We also had one where somebody ordered too many shares – got just the wrong number: not huge fat fingers. It was after trading hours when we realised, so we phoned up the broker and told him we'd ordered too many, and they just amended the order and sent it back through just like that.[7]

The great thing about that was that the culture of the organisation was such that the fund manager who found the mistake, the first thing he did was to come and tell me, as opposed to burying it. He wasn't worried that he was going to get blamed for it or lose his job. His first thought was: I will go and tell one of the partners and hopefully they will know what to do. I think this is very important and one of the reasons that you keep out of trouble. I don't know what you can do about that if you have a culture where it doesn't work that way but fortunately if it does work like that it is self-perpetuating. People see that problems go away, and they know that they don't go away if you bury them.

And they see that everything is fine and that nobody got cross and nobody got fired or told off. It makes it more likely that if it happens again you get a good result.

Frances: *It can be hard to build up that environment, but it's very easy to destroy it.*

Paul: The other thing that can happen is that the trader deliberately does something wrong, sometimes for personal gain: add a few on each time, front-running or favouring a broker who's going to give them a motorbike at the end of the year. I also heard of a case where somebody did it just because they felt like it, but that is very rare in investment management. Both the portfolio manager and the compliance manager are in positions to spot that kind of thing. For example, if the trader is not buying the shares that were on the sheet, it will show up when the fund manager compares what he thought his portfolio was going to look like with what it actually does look like. If somebody is determined to throw a spanner in the works they can do so, but usually not for very long and not for very much. Trading in an investment management organisation is such a clear responsibility and a clear function it's probably easier to manage than most other sources of risk.

Matthew: *What about the culture in the trading room. What would the head of dealing be like, and what standards do you think he would hold his team to?*

Paul: The culture at GMO generally was to try and be industry leaders, squeaky clean – even if it was a pain. The head of dealing had to fit in with that. The dealing team was in Boston because in London we only ever had enough dealing to keep one dealer busy in UK equities, who therefore could be closely supervised by the UK investment team. But in Boston the head of dealing became a partner, which carried a level of reward and trust. That helped because the investment people are seen as being senior to everybody else, which I think is healthy, but elevating the head of dealing to partner level was good because otherwise it could have been a bit of "us versus them".

Matthew: *How did you deal with issues to do with liquidity and the time horizon?*

Paul: In our first year at GMO there was no money to be managed. We spent our time writing articles in the hope of interesting investors in what we were doing. One of the things I wrote about was liability-driven benchmarks for pension funds. In particular, we used a kind of asset-liability matching, which I think is familiar today. I think Salomon Bros has written a lot about it. Martin Leibowitz[8] invented it, I think, but he was trying to convince everybody that equities were short duration, and we rewrote everything with the opposite proposition. He'd done some correlation analysis of what happens to equities when interest rates go up and down, whereas we estimated the duration by taking account of when you get your money back.

Thinking of equities as being long duration made it lot more obvious that a mature pension fund with lots of retired people would prefer to have bonds. But for a startup, if you were doing a pension fund for Google, for example, you have a much longer horizon, so you don't need a huge amount of income for quite a while. This means that you put more in equities, which seems pretty common sense. But when you think about it, even if you have a lot of retired people in your fund, they are going to live on average probably 25 years or so: they have still got relatively long time horizons. The quandary of the pension industry is that nobody behaves like that, and I don't think anybody has really figured it out. But I think the answer is to do everything you can to persuade investors to be as long term as they comfortably can be.

Even so, even with long investment horizons, they are barraged with quarterly investment reports and annual reports, which managers are required to generate. Whatever you try and do about it, people are under constant pressure to think about making adjustments in the short term, especially after something that dents their confidence, such as a year of disappointing investment performance.

Frances: *It sometimes seems that there is pressure on funds to act against the interests of their investors, and that is squarely against the intention of having pension funds in the first place.*

Paul: Ideally risk should be client-specific. This is a question that is more for consultants and actuaries than for fund managers: What are your objectives here and what would trigger some kind of failure? These are the real risk questions.

Pension fund sponsors are understandably quite sensitive about whether their contribution rates are going to have to go up. And that seems to me to be a real risk issue. It gives you something that you can grab hold of so you can start constructing a financial strategy with that risk in mind to address it. The kind of standard approach of just looking at volatilities or default probabilities or other industry-wide things doesn't really do it for me as much as that very tailored approach would. A question I often ask is: What would I do if it were my money? I think if you think about that in the context of home finance, for example, it does become quite clear that there is an amount of money that you don't care about and there is an amount of money that it would be tragic if you lost it. I think funds have similar concepts but they are not usually aired in the discussion of risk.

Frances: *It helps nail down their risk tolerance.*

Matthew: *Or the contribution rate thing: we will tolerate some losses but if it goes further than that it is not a good outcome.*

Paul: If the fund sponsor has to bung £50 million or £100 million over the fence or, as you say, increase the contribution rate so that the pension becomes, say, 20% of payroll instead of 15%; I always felt that if those risks could be articulated the industry would be better able to do something about them.

And that brings me to time horizon because if you are talking about contribution being 15% to 20% of payroll you might be saying I don't want that to happen in three years' time, which is fine. You now know that you have a three-year time horizon. You can work with it.

Frances: *Three-year horizons aren't unusual in investment management-land. And yet there is a move, often led by the regulators, to measure risk over daily investment horizons and then extrapolate that measure to get an annualised number. Personally I think it is dangerous and from what you said I think you would too.*

Paul: Yes. Most people at GMO would agree very strongly with Keynes' analysis. In the famous chapter of his *General Theory of Employment*, which deals with investment theory,[9] he is very anti-liquidity and anti-short term. He would definitely not be in favour of any kind of taking daily movements and extrapolating to longer time horizons. At least if you are going to do that, you shouldn't just multiply by the square root of 252^{10} or whatever the back-of-the-envelope number is. Instead you should say: There are serial correlations, so if we get a minus 5% today it doesn't necessarily mean we will have 300% volatility for the year because that minus 5% will probably correct in the next day or so, and the annual volatility will turn out to be much lower. I don't have a problem with using daily observations to measure risk if you take into account the serial correlations.

But when industry standards get made they don't tend to be terribly sophisticated because they need to be transparent and easy to implement, so nobody is going to get it wrong. In that case I think a daily measure is going to be misleading and not useful. And all of the financial instruments that are traded on a daily basis that you can think of have all got a big enough history that we know what that risks are without doing that; we can take observations at longer intervals that are more relevant to the way the investments are managed. The instruments that are more difficult, such as venture capital and things that are not traded daily, well you are not going to be able to do anything fancy with them such as daily pricing anyway. So I am not sure how using daily data observations is helping anything. Even with simple models, you have really got to be on top of what it is you're doing.

Frances: *One of the biggest mistakes is using the wrong kind of history. All of these models rely on some kind of price history and one of the things that caused them to understate risk was that they were using data samples from history that were both too short and with observations that were too frequent for the investment horizon. And that's without even taking into account serial correlations and changes in correlations when turbulent markets hit. I think it's pertinent to that exercise in asset-liability management involving Salomons that you mentioned earlier. You said they used correlation analysis and I'm guessing that they probably used history that was too short. If you use the wrong history you'll get the wrong answer. It's a common mistake.*

Paul: But it was also the fact that they were Salomons: bonds were their strong suit. I would guess they may have used daily as well, mainly because they had it, and they could, and there was more data.

Frances: Everybody assumes that more frequent data points must be more thorough and it is not necessarily the case.

Paul: Well, in equities it would get you the wrong way because of course there are several elements of equity pricing and the current interest rate is only one of them. So on any given day that might not be one of the important things and you don't know, at least until you have done more analysis. That is why you have to have experience as well, which can be a problem in the quant firms if they just go for fancy maths. At GMO if you have a new idea and you run some analyses, with experience you get to know the data so well you can tell straight away whether it will work only in the recession years or only in the down years. It's hard to do that without the perspective of experience.

Frances: Exactly. It is using in-sample as opposed to using out-of-sample data to test your ideas.

Matthew: Was there a point when models became too complicated? Is there the control of hubris that you don't continue expanding or you don't try new strategies?

Paul: Neural networks[11] might be a good example of that. Quite often you can't tell why they made the decision they've made, which for a fund manager is a no-no. "Why did you buy it?" … "The black box said so and that is all I can say or tell you." I think that is not a possibility. If you construct some very fancy advanced mathematics, if there is only one person in the office who understands it, that is another no-no. They could just be pulling you along and they'd be the only person who'd know either way. So are you going to assume that they are right or they are wrong? I'm afraid you have to assume they are wrong unless a second person can look in and say: Wow, that is a fantastic thing they have done there. So I think that is a problem. At GMO we mostly thought that complication was to be avoided, although there were some really fancy maths people in the industry, and they seemed to be mostly interested in option-pricing.

Matthew: Do you remember in 2004, there seemed to be a huge switch out of equities into fixed income? Do you remember the reason for it?

Paul: Around that time there was some kind of misapplication of a standard when pensions started doing asset liability management.

They tended to do that by forecasting a bunch of cash flows and then discounting them, bonds, particularly inflation-linked bonds as it happened. That by itself is no bad thing, but bonds more generally were taken to be the risk-free asset for pension funds and because of the cost and risk, some of the firms decided to sell the pension assets to insurance companies in exchange for the liability of paying the pensions. The insurance companies were happy to do that, because it was on a bond basis and they felt it was a risk that they could hedge and manage in the usual way. That may have been partly what was going on around that time.

Frances: I remember talking to people about asset-liability matching about that time. It was all the rage: if you were not doing that you were considered in some way negligent.

Matthew: To a distant observer, it seemed an interesting conclusion to reduce exposure to equities in favour of fixed income so demonstrably. And to then include hybrids[12] in the fixed income mix.

Paul: Although it is partly invisible, because these were private insurance arrangements, I think that the firms that did it would have found it was extremely expensive. But you can't really be sure because you don't have the alternative pathway of actually waiting for 40 years and paying everybody off. But I am sure it would have been at the high end of their actuarial forecasts for liabilities, because an insurance company wasn't giving you a 50/50 guarantee, it was giving you a 100% guarantee. You're really eliminating risk but you are doing so at pretty close to the maximum cost. I'm sure that was an unintended consequence of going over to what amounts to an interest rate-driven benchmark for equities.

Frances: It seemed over-conservative to try to match liabilities over a long horizon.

Paul: Apart from disasters and crashes and everything else, I think the central question that fund managers try to answer is how to evaluate how much risk is being taken in the normal run of events. Too many just accept volatility because they have got the tool box that goes with it. But I'm not sure that is terribly useful for the longer term because you know that equities are volatile anyway.

Matthew: It seems that people are using the wrong tools and there is not enough discussion about the tools. There also seems to be a misperception of how sophisticated they really are.

Paul: If you think of a young person and you are saving up for your first house, you might want in two years' time to have enough for a deposit. In that time, equities could be up 20% or down 10% or pretty much anywhere in between. That's not really satisfactory for such a short horizon. In that case equities would be the wrong thing because of the volatility. But if you are saving for retirement, you can look beyond that horizon. A minus 10% result after two years may be tolerable if you don't have to sell your equities. You can just sit on them and collect the income and wait for the plus 10% year, which won't be too far away precisely because equities are volatile: you're probably going to get one of those in the following two or three years. Where you don't have a definite cut-off date or if you have a very long investment horizon, the volatility really doesn't tell you much about your risk. Volatility is a popular measure because you have tools to calculate it. And Markowitz analysis, which gives you a volatility measure, has huge credibility because not very many bits of finance have Nobel prizes attached to them.

Frances: If it doesn't take into account what the objectives of the investments are, then it is one hand clapping.

Paul: Yes, so returning to the case of a pension fund, the Google fund is less interested in income because it would have to reinvest it anyway, which exposes it to reinvestment risk. That is, when you come to reinvest accumulated income in six months' or a year's time, the market may be rather expensive. The volatility measure does tell you a little bit about that, but it relates only to the income bit. Your main interest is in what happens over a very long horizon.

On the other hand, if you're the post office fund, say, your members are likely to be older, with some already retired. Your investment horizon is therefore much shorter and your current income requirements are relatively high. So your aim is to achieve a high income yield. If the income yield on your investments is less than your current income requirements, you have to sell assets to make up the shortfall and to meet redemptions.

So in either case the current yield versus whether you are cash positive or cash negative is more informative than the volatility. Plus, it is a very basic indicator and hard to get wrong, so it makes sense to take a look at that one first. But to be fair, that is what funds do. Presumably that is what the actuarial analysis is for that determines the fund strategy, when it chooses how much should be allocated to cash, bonds or equities. But it does rather beg the question of, once you have done that, why are you are still measuring volatility when you have now decided that 50% in equities is the right amount for your risk profile? Why don't you do something else, like put more effort into whether the fund manager is still any good?

Many investors seem quite sensitive to leading, or star, fund managers and the big names leaving organisations, and I think that is one of the practices that makes relative sense. Yet there are limits to that too. In some organisations the culture of the fund manager really is more important than individuals in driving the investments, whereas in others individual portfolio managers are more important. In quant firms, the culture of the firm dominates, for example.

But if it really is a Warren Buffett himself who wanders off to go to a different firm then that must be taken seriously and monitored in my opinion because in such firms, it's the expertise of the individual that you're paying for.

Frances: *The assets walk out the door every night in some organisations. This links back to the point you made at the start where with a quant strategy you can, at least in principle, audit a decision back 10 years taking into account the conditions at the time and what was known then, asking whether that decision made sense. With a traditional fund manager, that is not the case. Because of the difficulty of auditing buy and sell decisions, those funds can be much more susceptible to churning, which can be extremely expensive for the investor.*

Do you think there is pressure on the investment manager to be seen to be doing something, to trade for the sake of trading, even if buy and hold might be the most logical thing to do?

Paul: Industry-wide I think it does without any doubt at all. Jeremy Grantham worked with one of the big endowment funds, I think it was one of the universities; it asked the best investment managers for a ten-year investment strategy. This they bought and held for ten years. That was very unusual, and was possible only because of that discipline of specifically setting it up and earmarking it that way. Even so, it was probably quite a small amount of the total fund. I don't know of anyone else that has done something similar, mostly they trade portfolios much more frequently.

In fact I think fund managers would find it embarrassing to charge a fee and not do something, even if they had analysis on paper that convinced them that the best thing to do would be to buy and hold for ten years – or even one year.

I think fewer and fewer fund managers are now paying themselves to do turnover, because it is a big cost to the portfolio, but it is still in the background. If we don't trade the portfolio, people will say: Why I am paying you a fee when you have not made a single change in the portfolio?

In the quant process, trading followed decision rules. We were running Value[13] strategies most of the time, but then added some Momentum[14] strategies, which had the effect of improving returns and diversifying risk, but it also pushed up turnover. I remember turnover as low as 20% in equities, which is quite low.

Frances: *Value strategies do tend to be low turnover.*

Paul: The mixture of Value and Momentums is probably up to 30% or 40%.

Frances: *Which still isn't high.*

Paul: So we never felt any additional pressure. But it is a very interesting question, because if you could have devised a Value strategy that needed even less turnover, it might have caused eyebrows to be raised, so I'm not sure whether we could have ever put it into practice.

Frances: *Some consultants seem to feel that they need to turn over managers to show that they are doing something.*

Paul: Changing managers is definitely an expense, and there is no guarantee that it will pay off. Changing managers tends to be really seriously expensive because the incoming manager can say: Who bought that lot? And end up selling half of the portfolio all in one go. Even if you are a small fund that costs a lot in terms of market impact. But if you are a big fund, and you move the market a bit at the same time, it will cost you even more. But to say: Don't fire managers; from our perspective that is pretty neutral, because if the other managers don't get fired then we don't get to go to any beauty parades. So I don't think I have got a vested interest in saying that. But it does tend to be that you get fired at the wrong time. For example, pure Value and Growth[15] are somewhat cyclical things and if the investor hops from one to the other counter-cyclically they can lose a lot. And of course it is difficult to fire a manager after a really good year. So managers tend to get fired at the wrong time because it was their portfolio type that didn't do well, not necessarily the way they managed it.

This is where benchmarks that are specific to the fund type[16] can be helpful to investors. They allow performance to be understood in terms of how much value the manager has added relative to other managers of the same type of fund. You can say: all Value portfolios were down this year. That way all the touchy-feely questions can be asked separately: Do these people know what they are doing? Are they competent? Are they professional? Are they responsible?

Frances: *Smart beta indices are becoming very popular for that reason.*

Matthew: *How did you go about crisis management?*

Paul: Early on in GMO, to look at business risk, we gathered the heads of different units like sales, computing, IT, compliance obviously, client relations (I don't like "back office" as it is a rather demeaning term), legal, HR and so on. We met two or three times and the first task was just to think of things that could go wrong that could seriously mess up your life. And then we went through them all and attached two numbers. Firstly, we asked how likely the event was – three indicated something that probably *was* going to happen and one meant really, really not likely, but you never know. Then we asked how serious it would be – three for very serious, one for not much impact. Then all we had to do was start with the high risk and high impact cases – "three/three" risks – and work our way through one at a time. The three/three possibilities had to be sorted if they were there – and there weren't very many. They meant you had missed something, but at least you hadn't missed it any more. And the others, you just have to do what you can. Some of them were attached to stuff you already knew about, like having an offsite plan if the local phone exchange goes down or the building catches fire. I can't think what that is called now.

Frances: *DRP.*

Paul: Yes, Disaster Recovery Plan. So one or two of the risks plug straight into that. I thought that was a good way of engaging everybody in the process. Surprisingly for risk management it turned out to be fun. Because if you ask people what is the worst thing that could possibly go wrong and how bad would it be for you, they start thinking of things and start cringing and it is quite funny. It is a bit like trying to write a murder mystery or something, to try and think of the worst possible things that can happen and making a story around it. And that is what we really wanted. Then we just set up regular monitoring. Then, when senior management took it on, they embedded it more into the general management process. My version of it was essentially a one-off to get to a point where you made sure that you had covered all the bases and you still are covering them. It was soon integrated into regular management meetings as being one of the items for everybody to keep an eye on.

Frances: *I think that kind of approach to business risk management has become quite widespread. It sounds like you were a pioneer.*

Paul: Related to business risk management is regulation. I don't think it's terribly controversial to suggest that regulation has largely failed, hasn't it? If you think about different levels in the last crisis, I think the Treasury had some responsibilities that they seemed largely unaware of. The Bank of England specifically was supposed to be in charge of the banks, but it wasn't monitoring any things that were to do with the crisis, even though with hindsight some of them must have been fairly obvious. I'm thinking of the massive increases in leverage that they were taking on and so on. And the FSA[17] wasn't really successfully managing the fund managers. The obvious criticism is that it looked like a kind of box ticking, form completion exercise more than digging into what people were doing and why they were doing it.

Frances: *Many people have observed that the risk management requirements by regulators are becoming so onerous that medium-sized firms in* *particular – and even quite large ones – are struggling to muster the resources to meet regulatory box-ticking and it's leaving not enough resources for real management of risk.*

Paul: A related point is that there are nowadays some quite huge barriers to entry of actually starting a new investment management firm, which I don't think is very healthy. I guess it must help big established firms who aren't perhaps as good as they could be, especially in a situation where in the past some of the top fund managers working in an otherwise mediocre firm might have gone and started their own thing. I think now they wouldn't be able to afford it, or they wouldn't want to, given all the risk and hassle of complying with misguided regulations.

Obviously that wasn't true when we started GMO in London. Our first compliance visit was actually from the Department of Trade and Industry (DTI) before IMRO[18] even existed. They came to see what we looked like and in many ways I think that is a better way of controlling things than sending us a form and never setting foot in the door. Because when you meet people you form an opinion of whether they're honest, doing what they say they're doing and whether they're the kind of people you would trust or not. Clearly there is no ideal way of doing that, but I don't know how many pages of forms would give you the information that you get from meeting somebody face to face and asking some pertinent questions.

When we started, we had to go and get our fingerprints taken at Bishopsgate Police Station. That makes you take your responsibility seriously!

It would be interesting to know what would happen if they now came into some of the investment firms and had a chat about stuff generally. A lot of people were saying that the sub-prime loan market was a worry, but of course that really never got beyond the walls because there was no forum for people on the banking side to pick that up.

Frances: *It wasn't a box to tick so it didn't get ticked.*

Matthew: *The firm I was working for at the time got a call from Goldman at about the beginning of 2007 to have a look at their portfolio and ask whether they had any of these things in their portfolio. Before people started to wake up, when some people were busy generating more of this* *stuff, there were other people, who were working out how they could extricate themselves from it.*

Paul: I went to a presentation, where one of the brokers talked us through sub-prime investments. I decided I wasn't interested on two grounds that I think are worth bearing in mind from a risk point of view. One was that I didn't really understand it. The other is never buy anything that is too good to be true, for the same reason. As far as I could see they had parcelled up all the obvious bits of the bond, such as the coupons, and they were trying to sell me something that was basically everything that was left over. I remember thinking that what's left over from a bond is usually not worth very much, yet they have managed to put this value on it. I couldn't understand how they could have done that and I thought it was too good to be true. It was really beyond what our investors would have bought anyway, which was fortunate. But I think those rules of thumb are not bad. Never let somebody talk you into buying something you don't "get". Shares and bonds are very gettable things. Commodities and things: I would be interested to hear somebody convince me. I think that it would have to be more of a tactical case because in the long term, I guess that they follow inflation, no more no less.

Frances: *Not even that, because you have substitution effects. And also each commodity market works differently, so you have structural inefficiencies, some markets are driven on the spot, and some are driven on longer-term contracts, for example.*

Paul: Whereas with equities, you can make a quite convincing case for them to give you a positive long-term real return. Likewise with bonds, nominal or real, whichever you're in, you can have a definite view of what the possible outcomes might be. So it's very important that you know what you're getting, what is likely to add value and what the possible outcomes could be.

Frances: *When I was risk manager at Aviva a couple of the portfolio managers wanted to buy index CDS.[19] Now that is not a very complex instrument, really, but I wanted to know what was in the index itself. I asked them to give me a list of the bonds that made up the index, what the optionality terms of the swap were and so on, and then I'd be fine with it. But they said they couldn't do that. When I asked why, they told me that it was because they didn't know what was in it. Of course I* *didn't sign off and asked why they wanted to invest in something even though they didn't know what was in it.*

Paul: There were huge concentrations of risk in those instruments and some people had done quite well out of them. But that begs the question you see asked a bit too seldom for my comfort. It is when investments perform better than expected, do we ask why that happened? It's human nature in investment management to assume that a very good outcome is great management but a bad outcome is bad luck. It's a natural human reaction, but it is irrational.

Frances: *The only way to counterbalance that is to have the discipline to say: Anything that wasn't within our range of expectations has to be questioned, whether it is good or bad. I don't think many people do that. I know some people do but not as many as you would like.*

Paul: Yes, a depressing thing of being on the fund management side of the fence is that clients take the other view. If you are up a lot in performance, they say things moved in your favour but if they're down it is specifically you're the idiot, you lost the money. But you're absolutely right, there is an asymmetry on both sides.

Matthew: *The thing now is they have done the bail-out, and they have sold the equity at a profit and they think they worked that out. But of course the only reason they could sell at a profit is because of the quantitative easing, which made the equity market a one-way bet.*

Paul: I don't think very much has been achieved in addressing the question of how we stop this happening next time. There are two aspects I can think of immediately. One is the kind of agency problem and the other is the "too big to fail", which I think originated with Long Term Capital Management, and what you are left with at the end is that definite feeling that bailing out four or five of the biggest Wall Street firms was a big mistake. It gave people in those firms a skewed view of what might happen: heads we win and tails you keep us afloat.

Matthew: *It's one of the dangers of regulation: what makes sense in one culture doesn't make any sense in another. For example, the fund management industry should have the wherewithal to fix itself. The trustees, the investors should be able to say: No. They don't need government to tell them that. But banks are considered special because they are needed (although I sometimes wonder if they are needed), it is assumed*

that everything will stop if these people go away. There doesn't seem a
way of corralling a group of interested parties to say: Your compensation
structures are wrong. The shareholders don't do it, so governments are
trying to do it.

The corollary of the "too big to fail" institution is that a bank is
effectively a utility, and so therefore bankers' pay should be at the same
level as utilities – they should be paid like post office or electricity workers.
But that's not going to happen I think. The other thing is that regulations
may be getting too complicated – their fingers are in so many pies that
nobody can govern them.

Paul: There has been a lot of talk about compensation in financial
services. It is quite interesting that Europe was against paying high
bonuses to bankers. It's a real difficulty, because if you have a
proprietary trading desk profit related pay is a problem because it
is effectively giving the traders a free option. If they take an
enormous amount of risk they are quite likely to make an
enormous amount of money, but in the odd year when they fail,
they don't take any loss personally. Of course they might lose
their job, but by now they have £5 million in their bank account,
so what do they care if it takes another year to find a job? At
GMO we had the opposite culture. Nobody as far as I know, at
least the culture was that nobody had a big salary. Nobody was
going to get paid merely because they were gracious enough to
turn up and walk through the door every morning. You were
paid because you had done a good job that year, and so the bonus
would reflect that. So actually in terms of the European rule[20] we
were completely the wrong way round. But still I think there
might be good reasons, cultural reasons for doing it, especially as I
think in most of these organisations the salary bill is probably the
biggest expense.

I think there are sensible things you can do. For example, your
big success payout accumulates over, say, four years, so you get a
quarter of it every year. If you make a tragic loss some of it
vanishes and it nets out and you get an amount that is more
representative of the whole cycle.

Frances: *The other issue is that when an investment manager has a*
compensation structure like at GMO, a smallish salary with a fairly large
incentive payment, the incentive payment often isn't purely investment

return related. It is usually related to a much broader range of a person's activity because only a small percentage of the firm's employees are actually engaged in making investment decisions. For example, the firm can't work without the operations people. I think that is another reason why the European rule of capping bonuses is inappropriate and probably counterproductive.

Paul: I think your earlier point about banking being like a utility is a good one. One way of thinking about it is that the utility bit has to be separated. As you say, if you have a societally necessary function of matching buyers and sellers, in cash markets of liquidity, or whatever it is they do, then that should be separate from the profit-making areas like trading and brokerage. The one-stop-shop thing and the fund management house and everything else can be taken away. They can have whatever salary structure they like, but the bit that's left that looks like a utility does have to have a very different pay culture, because we can't have it fall over again and cost everybody a ton of money. It could be that those people can be very highly rewarded because utility functions can probably largely be automated, so you need only a relatively small number of people, who could probably be quite well paid. But they would be paid the same amount every year for doing what they do.

Frances: *By contrast, if an investment manager or a broker fails it is not a big deal because, so long as client money is segregated, clients need not lose any money at all. For example, if, say, Threadneedle goes under, the portfolio doesn't even need to be liquidated because another fund manager will take it over. That is quite different from a banking utility, which has to be kept functioning and therefore may need to be saved with public funds, like the electricity grid.*

Paul: Yes it is not a problem for the clients if an investment manager fails. It was quite interesting when Barings went bust. The fact that struck me with some force at the time was that the people who were most at risk were the people who had cash deposits at Barings Bank. You think of cash as the risk-free asset, well of course all the institutional clients with all their shares registered at the registrar weren't at risk at all. But people with cash in Barings Bank suddenly had a big hole in their accounts. Quite amazing!

Frances: *I wonder if you would be able to summarise for us?*

Paul: Yes, in reviewing all these things, it has reminded me how important the human side is. Ultimately it is all about that. The regulators really need to get to know – personally – the people they are regulating. If you are a trustee, say, then get to know your fund managers – what are they good at and not so good at, what do they tell you and what do they leave out, that kind of thing. Of course the consultants can help a lot with that. If you are in fund management, it's important to really know your colleagues, like are they part of the team or is there a danger they will manage the fund their own way – and what would they do if something went badly?

Secondly, on the technical side, I guess you have to keep questioning the consensus. Short-term price volatility is the most widely used risk measure – so I'd say "OK, but how is that relevant to me in this particular situation?" Or you can start from a blank piece of paper and say, "What outcome do I most worry about?" and then figure out a measurement to capture as much of that as you can.

Lastly, I'd really make a special plea for common sense and, to make that work, as much simplicity as possible. One way to put that to work would be to ask investment people what they are doing, and not to stop until you really understand it yourself. If they can't explain in simple terms, maybe they are not fully on top of it.

It's funny really that we started talking about particle physics, computers and quant firms, but in conclusion really I do believe that the best risk tools are common sense and understanding other people.

Notes

1   A British economist who worked for the fund management firm GMO, retiring as Chairman of GMO Europe in 2006. He then founded the Paul Woolley Centre for the Study of Capital Market Dysfunctionality at the London School of Economics in 2007.

2 Chief Executive of OCCAM Financial Technology. From 1987 to 1989 he was Managing Director of Baring Quantitative Management.

3 Capital protected or guaranteed minimum return.

4 Mark Rubinstein, John O'Brien and Hayne E. Leland. Rubenstein developed the portfolio insurance financial product in 1976.

5 A British investor and co-founder and chief investment strategist of Grantham Mayo van Otterloo (GMO), a Boston-based asset management firm.

6 A former derivatives broker whose fraudulent, unauthorised speculative trading caused the spectacular collapse of Barings Bank in 1996.

7 In stable market conditions, any losses incurred as a result typically are small and are absorbed either by the broker or by the asset manager, who usually agree between them how it should be allocated.

8 A financial researcher, business leader and a managing director of Morgan Stanley. His most well-known work (co-authored with Sidney Homer) is *Inside the Yield Book*, first published in 1972 and reissued in 2004, a work that, according to Frank Fabozzi, "transformed the markets' understanding of bonds". He was instrumental in developing the Dedicated Portfolio theory in the 1980s.

9 The Marginal Efficiency of Capital, Chapter 11 of Keynes, J.M., *The General Theory of Employment, Interest and Money* (New York: Harcourt Brace, 1936).

10 Trading days in a year.

11 A family of statistical learning algorithms inspired by biological neural networks (the central nervous systems of animals, in particular the brain) and used to estimate or approximate functions that can depend on a large number of inputs and are generally unknown.

12 Hybrids, usually of bonds and equities. The best-known example is the convertible bond, a corporate bond that converts to equity in the issuing firm when some pre-specified conditions are met.

13 Value investing generally entails buying securities that appear underpriced according to some form of fundamental analysis, typically those that trade at discounts to book value or tangible book value, have high dividend yields, low price-to-earnings multiples or have low price-to-book ratios.

14 Momentum investing generally entails buying securities that have had high returns over the past three to 12 months, and selling those that have had poor returns over the same period. While no consensus exists about the validity of this strategy, economists have trouble reconciling this phenomenon with the efficient-market hypothesis.

15 Growth investing generally entails buying securities that exhibit signs of above-average capital appreciation, even if the share price appears expensive in terms of metrics such as price-to-earnings or price-to-book ratios.

16 Smart beta indexes, provided by a number of independent organisations, are rules-based indices that reflect exposure to specific factors, market segments or investment strategies, typically not weighted by market capitalisation.

17 UK Financial Services Authority, now the Financial Conduct Authority.

18 UK Investment Management Regulatory Organisation. A predecessor of the Financial Services Authority.

19 Credit Default Swap.

20 Of limiting the scale of bonuses relative to base salary.

10

Todd Groome

Washington DC, 18 November 2014

Regulations are mostly about containing the risk in asset portfolios. That could be the wrong way to do it.

Todd Groome is a Washington DC-based adviser to hedge funds and other financial services firms, as well as public policy organisations regarding financial regulatory issues, and he is a visiting scholar at The Wharton School of the University of Pennsylvania. Before that he served as Chairman of AIMA, was an adviser at the IMF on financial market and stability issues for the G7, and was an investment banker in London for more than 13 years.

He describes some of the thinking behind recent regulations.

Todd Groome: I'm a lawyer by training, I attended the University of Virginia School of Law, worked with Hogan & Hartson, in a deal-oriented law practice, in Washington DC, focused on financial institutions, particularly distressed banks and savings banks in the 1990s.

I came out of school in 1984, about the time of the S&L[1] crisis; and I worked with a brilliant lawyer, Charlie Allen. Everyone around the country came to Charlie with their S&L issues, whether they were trying to buy something from the government, keep it from the government, merge on the private side, recapitalise it on the private side. So it exposed me to a very transaction-oriented practice, working with distressed financial institutions.

In the early 1990s I moved to investment banking with Merrill Lynch in London, working in mergers and acquisitions, corporate finance, and distressed financial institutions, especially in Scandinavia. Later I moved to Deutsche Bank, where I managed the financial institutions group in debt capital markets globally. For about two years, I also managed the high yield business for Deutsche Bank in Europe.

In 2002 I came back to Washington DC and learned that the IMF was looking for people who were not macro-economists and not emerging markets focused. Horst Köhler[2] was the Managing Director at the time. I went there for almost six years, and helped establish the Capital Markets and Financial Stability Group at the IMF.

At the IMF I worked with central bankers, policy-makers and regulators in the G7 and G20, as well as the Basel organisations. The group I set up dealt with financial markets issues in the G7 and G20, so my clients were central banks, treasuries, finance ministries and regulators.

After that I was the chairman of AIMA,[3] mainly because they wanted someone who knew the policy-makers and regulators, and who could be more active in messaging in Washington DC, London, Brussels, Hong Kong and elsewhere.

In 2009 I decided it was a good time to go on my own, so I've been consulting and serving as a board director for hedge funds.

Frances: *Who were the people who influenced you during your early career?*

Todd: Charlie Allen at Hogan & Hartson for sure, and a variety of colleagues at Merrill Lynch and Deutsche Bank. It was especially rewarding to be able to advise my own bank on various significant financial transactions and issues, it was a very enjoyable experience. Among policy-makers I was fortunate to work with

Jaime Caruana,[4] a very thoughtful and hard-working central banker, and now the Managing Director of the BIS. I was also fortunate to meet, while at the IMF, Paul Tucker[5] from the Bank of England. Paul was, and is, a brilliant thinker in the area of financial stability and macro-prudential policy. While at the IMF I saw him often, and later I brought hedge funds or private equity guys to the Bank to exchange views and discuss market activities with him. He is a very good thinker, and I always enjoyed speaking with him, as well as reading his speeches and papers.

Frances: *What made him, in what way, a great thinker?*

Todd: He would regularly talk with market participants, he was a good listener, and importantly he would ask great questions. In some respects, it was a Bank of England style. His questions were often meant to send a message. A real example (which I can't directly attribute to Paul Tucker) is in the mid-1990s, as lending in commercial real estate area was becoming a concern in Europe. The Bank of England identified it as a potential bubble or risk, and they asked people: When you give me your next credit report, please break out your commercial real estate exposure in continental Europe. The fact that they asked the question caused my phone to light up as an investment banker: clients seeking credit derivatives, securitisation, other risk transfer tools. The Bank of England is concerned about commercial real estate because they are breaking it out in reports.

It affected people's behaviour, and that was a very good way to regulate. But that is not easy. It requires regulators like Paul, who understands markets.

Frances: *Tell us more about the consulting you do.*

Todd: A lot of regulatory consulting, a little bit of risk, a little bit of strategy. A US firm that wanted to expand overseas asked me to advise them on London and Hong Kong possible expansions. All financial markets, often with a strong regulatory angle.

Matthew: *Do you think, as the regulation in banking crowds in, the hedge funds will become more important?*

Todd: You mean, shadow banking?

Matthew: *Shadow banking, yes.*

Todd: That's a complex question. In an ideal world, yes. But the way the regulations are stacking up, no. Because they are squeezing all sides. Regulation is definitely squeezing banks and bank risk appetite, but much of it is also squeezing shadow banking. And in a very real sense, these two groups need each other and are very supportive of each other. Interestingly, as we begin to withdraw central banking liquidity (at least in the US), my friends in the public sector often say that the shadow banks will help fill that liquidity void. I say: You vastly overestimate the liquidity that the shadow banking system will bring to bear, and (even more so) the price of that liquidity.

Matthew: At the November 2014 G20 meeting, an agenda to apply numerical haircut floors[6] to non-centrally cleared securities financing transactions took a further step. The proposals seem to be seeking to change collateral test for all prime brokers to that of a through-the-cycle view as opposed to the shorter time horizons typically used to determine margin requirements in normal markets. If adopted, this requirement may bear down on the business model of prime brokers. One might conclude that global regulators are trying to discourage the leverage that we saw in 2007–08; or to bear down on speculation financed by prime brokers. Do you think something will replace the prime brokers? Will some sort of shadow banking or something else emerge?

Todd: There's no more innovative, entrepreneurial industry than the hedge fund, private equity space. But if you do that with prime broking today, it will squeeze out a lot of traditional trading (and liquidity) by hedge funds, especially smaller or start-up hedge funds. Even a year ago, and certainly in 2007 or before, a start-up hedge fund with a reasonable pedigree would have at least four or five prime brokers seeking business and offering financing. They didn't know if you were going to succeed or not, but they were willing to advise you, and lend you money, because they had balance sheet. Now you see it starting to tighten up, increasingly, and I think it has only begun to tighten up, and will tighten up much more.

Matthew: What do you think will be the broader implications?

Todd: If you are a hedge fund today and if you don't have a phenomenal pedigree from a successful hedge fund or big investment bank, the prime brokers are going to spend much less time with you. So the barriers to entry to this part of shadow banking – an important market liquidity source – are pretty high.

Regulation and investors' attitudes have changed. I think the regulations have become a bit extreme. When I was chairman of AIMA, we met with the SEC,[7] CFTC[8] and regulators and legislators from the US, Europe and Asia. AIMA supported registration of managers and periodic reporting of systemically relevant information. We would debate what that information was or should be, because it is a cost item to us as an industry. And we were really trying to "do the right thing", per the G20 Roadmap. However, I remember saying (I may get my numbers wrong now, because it's been a while since I made these arguments to regulators or politicians): If you focus on managers of $1 billion AUM[9] or more, you will cover about 20–25% of hedge funds, but you'll cover about 60% of the AUM in the industry. So you will get a very good picture of the industry, and focus on a limited and reasonable number of managers more relevant to you as a regulator, because you don't have the resources to cover hundreds or thousands of managers. You should focus your attention and efforts.

The FCA (the FSA at the time)[10] understood that argument, but I think they too were pulled along by IOSCO, ESMA,[11] the SEC, and the CFTC. So regulators today have a very broad reach across the industry, and in some cases seek position-level data. And I believe they sought too much data: they will miss the forest for the trees. So when a market stability event occurs, they will be called up in front of Congress, and Congressmen will say: You have the data, but you don't know what to look for or where the important information is because it's tucked away in the mounds of data you are gathering. So we asked them to figure out what they really wanted, work with the industry, and the industry will work with them. If you go to the industry and say: We don't want 100 data items, the industry will say: God bless you! But tell them the 30 data items that really matter, and the industry will help you figure out a way to get it done.

Matthew: *The global regulators may also be rethinking their emphasis on internal models for risk calculations. They did a review of internal models in December 2013, where they gave people the same positions and 30 institutions all came back with different answers with a very wide dispersion. And so there is some serious thinking about the benefits of* *standard models. They reduced it to simply requiring how much capital you need in a relatively standard manner, and to some extent that appeals to me, because of the amount of effort that the regulators put into proving that a regular internal model works: the tests, the interviews, the back testing. Risk departments can become a cross between a policeman and a compiler of data for the regulator.*

Todd: That's a serious cost consideration.

When I was at Merrill Lynch, in corporate finance, working with banks in Europe, a senior regulator in the Bank of England put me in contact with a central banker in Australia, active in Basel regulation and capital rules, and suggested I meet with him. When I did, I found that he was of the view – and you can hear central bankers, some treasury officials using the same language – that you are better served to focus on the liability side of banks (and, by extension, all financial institutions). And in doing so, seek to enhance market and balance sheet liquidity. Securitisation is one tool, but there are others. Banks fail because of liquidity crises, such as bank deposits and funding going away, a run on the bank. And it is often the illiquid nature of bank assets, exacerbating the issue. So, seek to enhance bank and market liquidity, and move relatively illiquid assets to balance sheets better able to hold them, with better matching liability structures, such as insurance companies, pensions, private equity and hedge funds. In a less direct manner, today regulators speak about "runs" on different markets of asset classes – all reflecting increased focus on liquidity management,

Society needs medium or long-dated assets, such as mortgages and four- or five-year corporate loans. But when bank liabilities are theoretically one day (even though in economic terms these liabilities have much longer maturities) there is no perfect match, and the liability structure can change depending on the external market environment. So various forms of "risk transfer" is how you get certain asset markets to be more liquid, and transfer some assets and risks to pension funds, insurance companies and the shadow banking world, which have longer dated and more predictable liability structures.

So for me, it is often more useful to focus on the liability structure of balance sheets. I am not really worried about hedge funds. I am not overly worried about insurance companies or pension funds (at least on this issue ... longer-term or solvency gaps are another issue). On the other hand, most money market funds look like a bank: they borrow short and lend longer. That's a bank. So with all the noise about shadow banking, the greatest focus, I believe, should be on money market funds.

When I arrived at the IMF and started participating in the IMF at various macro-prudential fora, I frequently sought to increase the policy of regulatory focus on liquidity conditions and differing balance sheet liability structures, rather than the continuing focus on capital against assets. Same point, different example, why make a pension fund mark its assets to market each quarter when its liability structure can tolerate a 15–20-year view? It has actuarially predicable liabilities. Do you want to turn big pension funds into investment banks? No, but we are often, through regulation and accounting policies, incentivising them to behave like banks. This raises another issue – market diversity. We should encourage market diversity; but this is less likely if we regulate all participants as if they are banks.

Matthew: *There is a lot more academic discussion about liabilities-side regulating and leaving the asset side to look after itself. But then every bank I've been at, the incentive, the compensation structure, is to write the assets.*

Todd: That is not easy to change, but it is changeable, and has been changing in the last 10–15 years. At a bank in Europe that I did some work for, a relatively new board member said: I figured out what has gone on with our balance sheet. The guys in commercial banking, particularly corporate lending, are compensated for the size of their balance sheet. We needed to get them to think about the risk-adjusted return on assets, and the capital required against those assets. No sooner had they got into a conversation at the board level, than the HR people said that you have to start by changing the compensation system. You change the compensation system, then you change the way people think and behave.

And that bank did a really great job, in my opinion. It took several years to change that mentality and to understand that bigger is not necessarily better. Greater profitability is better. A focus on return on assets and cost of capital. It matters more, and can be done.

Matthew: *And you get that "too big to fail" and "we'll get bailed out" mentality. That happened in Australia where all the bank deposits were guaranteed. It wasn't that they needed to be, the banks were in a strong position. But they lost confidence in each other's liquidity and trade dried up.*

Todd: Liquidity is important, the most important macro-prudential consideration in my opinion, but how to measure or regulate liquidity is complex. A policy official involved in drafting Basel II once said to me that if an asset had an AAA rating you could give it low or zero capital treatment based on a perceived high liquidity profile. I knew him well, and said: What were you thinking? Capital can be an easier prudential tool, and liquidity or liability structures much harder, so it has frequently been concluded that the best proxy for liquidity is AAA or high credit ratings. Of course, there is no such correlation. I have had similar conversations regarding primary market demand versus secondary market liquidity. The two things don't relate, so liquidity is something that I think is poorly understood. And it's too easy to say: Throw more capital at it.

Matthew: *Do you think big banks should be allowed to fail?*

Todd: This might surprise you, given my background in the private sector and belief in markets, by and large (I understand there are many flaws, but they are better than most of the alternatives), but I believe "too big to fail" is a misplaced goal. I think we will inevitably need to bail out the largest institutions operating at the heart of our payment (and now clearing) systems. Certainly executives should lose their jobs, equity holders should lose their money – or a lot of their money. But I care much more about liquidity shocks, so I would rather wipe out equity, keep institutions in place, or break up institutions (which is a conversation occurring) and protect the core, systemically important, units. But let's recognise that as soon as we say something is not a core unit then its funding cost will go up. We saw this in the insurance world, driven by S&P[12] 15 or more years ago. S&P sought to define core and non-core businesses within insurance companies. And immediately, if you were doing business with a non-core unit of a big insurance company, you acted differently vis-à-vis that counterparty, for good reasons. But such signals may not be bad: maybe they're a good or valid signal to give.

However in the banking world that is a fairly complicated conversation.

Matthew: *But while you can postulate that there are these too-big-to-fail institutions, I don't think anybody likes the way they got that status.*

Todd: Really? Why is big automatically a bad thing? Here is an example of some reasoning: In Europe, Merrill Lynch was an adviser to a particular government related to a domestic banking crisis. As part of that assignment we created a large institution comprised of many smaller, often distressed institutions. It became evident this institution really wasn't going to be a sustainable ongoing entity. Yet it had an attractive core deposit base and in part also served a necessary rural market, so we broke it up and sold it to the large banks in that country. However, at the same time, with an emerging EU and euro, banks felt pressure to grow with their core corporate client, in order to properly serve them. So the largest banks merged and eventually only two remained. And they, I think properly, began to view themselves as regional or pan-Europe institutions as needed to service their clients. I don't think they grow for the sake of growing. If the marginal return on equity is not positive, you just don't do it.

Matthew: *So do you think they're taking a broad brush to everything (i.e. capital standards) because of a problem in what basically started with loans to Californians that were packaged into CDOs? It was similar with the S&L crisis. Some excesses seem to push regulators to try to stop it happening anywhere else.*

Todd: That would likely mean extending capital standards to off balance sheet and shadow banking activities, and I do think the transparency today for regulators regarding off balance sheet activities is much better. I don't understand why it wasn't better before, because banks have had off balance sheet activity for many years. When I moved to London in 1989–90, few national regulators looked at consolidated and unconsolidated accounts for regulatory reporting; often simply looking at "bank financials".

Frances: How do you stop abusive banking or lending behaviour?

Todd: Well I go back to what I referred to earlier as the Bank of England style of regulation: you ask good questions. But that is harder than broad-brush rules, and is probably best as a complement to rules or principles. You meet with CROs, treasurers, you go down into the management structure and you ask good questions. And similar market dialogue must be had with non-banks as well. Regulators need such dialogue to understand the landscape.

　　While at the IMF, I would meet with CROs of investment banks. And one fellow constantly spoke of risk in terms of VaR. I recall asking him if he really believed so strongly in VaR. And he said: Well no, a lot of it is garbage. If you don't have proper liquidity, VaR can be quite misleading, and in the credit world a lot of assets or instruments have infrequent, inconsistent liquidity. So I asked why he was talking like that, and he said: Well, the SEC asks me to report in terms of VaR, so I assume all regulatory policy and folks focus on VaR. That's the power of the question, the power of the reporting model. If you ask me to report my risk framework a certain way, you influence how the regulated entity talks, thinks and possibly how they act or manage risk.

Frances: It's hard to communicate that to voters.

Todd: It is hard to communicate that nuance to politicians, and I can imagine to voters. They had an opportunity because of the crisis to do some things, some important, others as part of their political agenda, and they often don't understand the issues, and I understand that. Look at liquidity: they produced new liquidity rules, some even useful, and then they watered them down: for some banks almost anything will qualify for regulatory liquidity. So we may get to the point where people no longer care about liquidity rules, and they will go away with time.

Matthew: Do you think caveat emptor is used too much as a scapegoat or a way of using new product packaging; not worrying too much about whom you sell it to? Should you put more tests on the production cycle of the banks?

Todd: An example today may include the Cayman Islands and new guidance and considerations regarding hedge funds, private equity and mutual funds. Cayman has always been an institutional market, and some may say that means a buyer beware, caveat emptor market. The focus is on disclosure, and a belief that if we get proper disclosure standards, then sophisticated parties may negotiate transactions. And sometimes refine that to qualified parties, depending on what we define as qualified: net worth tests, experience tests, corporate tests, a variety of things.

When I first came out of law school and worked on a few private placements, I said to a senior associate: So the rule is, if I am wealthy enough, I am allowed to be stupid. And the guy said: Well yes.

Caveat emptor or buyer beware sounds politically incorrect, particularly in the post-crisis world. But the truth is, if you are in an institutional market, you should focus on getting disclosure right, and then allow sophisticated parties or institutions to transact.

A related policy debate was whether "disclosure" was better designed for the market place or for regulators. Continental Europeans have long advocated for more regulatory reporting, arguing that market-oriented disclosure simply fails to reduce systemic risk or market excesses.

I do not agree with this view. It may not be 100% wrong, but I would ask what they were going to do with all the information and data they sought. Because there will be another crisis or market disruption, and they will have all the data, but will not know what to do with it. How will a regulator, with all the data in the world, know better than the market and its millions of participants, when to lean against markets and bubbles? I sincerely believe that, ex-ante, it is a very hard task, if not impossible and naïve; so I prefer to develop disclosure for the collective minds and money of millions of market participants voting every day in the market.

Matthew: *Post the CDO crisis, there were schools closing down, fire departments closing down, the local municipalities, having bought these things. They had a budget, they tried to fund a little bit more and then they saw a good proportion of their financial assets default.*

Frances: *Did they understand what they had?*

Todd: A lot of the trustees or CIOs of smaller investment entities may not have been qualified to understand some of these complex credit securities, and many relied on consultants. Some have also questioned their expertise or due diligence. I don't know. But responsibility can't always be with the bank. Somebody is saying: Yes, I want to buy that asset, or a home that they can't afford, or a CLO that they don't fully understand.

In 2006 and 2007, policy-makers were asking: Who is buying these complex credit assets? Someone, I think with Citigroup in London, wrote a research report saying that a lot of these assets were being bought in Spain, Italy, Germany and the Benelux. Is there a common feature? And they described it as savings banks, *caixas* in Spain, cooperative banks in Germany and Italy, mutual insurance companies in Germany, mutual insurance companies and cooperative banks in the Benelux. What a lot of people may call dumb money. However, the other interesting thing is many in that group have equity shareholders, and some are often relatively ratings insensitive (except that they want to buy assets of a certain rating, and a few may be subject to certain capital regulations that depend on the rating of the asset). So given their structure, both lack of shareholder and fewer short-term pressures, why shouldn't they act and invest longer term, as buy-and-hold investors? The CLO may go to $0.40 in the short term, but in the longer term some of these assets were going to work out. However, the short-term volatility was tremendous and pushed many investors to sell, exacerbating the down-draft.

Matthew: *My other point was the scale. How could it have been tolerated? Part of the problem was that the loss given the default number made it cheaper for a major player to lose a little bit of money on the auction that cleared positons in defaulted paper and associated derivatives because they were making so much money on the overall strategy, which may have been priced using the likely overall, rather than position-level, loss given default.*

Todd: I think I know what you mean, but I may come at it slightly differently. Consider various shocks to the financial system, and how individual market participants (logically) think about risk and risk management around crises. Who is the one participant and the only asset that can address financial instability? It's the government, and the "asset" they provide is time. It is guarantees, back-stops, some kind of liquidity bridge. Regarding LTCM (which I don't rate as a systemic event), the government got everybody in a room and agreed everyone would hit the pause button. Indeed, some of the "smart" money even tried to buy LTCM risk of exposure on the cheap. We can see other examples in times of severe market stress and volatility. Likewise, when governments take over a failing institution, they usually end up making money (as opposed to bailing out car companies or union pensions).

Matthew: *At Credit Suisse, 2008 bonuses for the senior management group included participation in an illiquid parcel of leveraged loans and commercial mortgage-backed debt, which was smart. It was good alignment of interests with shareholders and regulators as it preserved capital.*

Todd: Yes, when the crisis in 2008–09 hit, many investors were trying to sell their hedge fund and/or private equity positions, but often couldn't get out of them. There was a secondary market. It wasn't terribly efficient or liquid, but it was there. There were some state pension funds trying to buy discounted private equity positions. I think they were very smart, playing the long game as allowed by their liability structures. Given their liability structure, why not? But not everybody was that smart or that nimble, or blessed with a similar liability profile.

Matthew: *The market cleared.*

Todd: So here is another related question asked: Japan relative to Anglo-Saxon countries, or Japan relative to the US (pre-2008). Which model or approach better deals with crises? Bankers and officials in Japan said they were tired of Western bankers telling them that they needed to flush the system, that capital will come back, and you will rebuild more quickly and move on. But culturally they questioned the wisdom or correctness of such a "free market" approach. "We don't want to see people or families hurt, or people out of work for long periods. We are prepared to go through five, ten (or more) years of an economic downturn, and come back slowly. We don't want the V bottoms that you guys have in London and New York." However, suddenly, everyone seemed to sound a bit Japanese after 2008 and 2009.

Matthew: *I was stunned by the revelations in 2011 of how the Olympus Group had managed losses that seemed to mount from asset bubble investments in the 1990s. The press at the time were likening the activity to an example of a Tobashi[13] scheme. You might recall around that time*

Japanese corporates issued bonds with attached warrants and used the proceeds to buy shares listed on the Nikkei to immunise their exposure to the issued warrants.

Todd: I think you are referring to the regulatory debate regarding disclosure and to whom. From the 1980s until the crisis, the British and Americans won that argument in the international arena, and it was effectively agreed in G7 and Basel circles that good disclosure to market participants enhanced market discipline, and that market discipline was the best defence against financial instability.

I remember a related issue in 2007, when the Germans had the presidency of the G7 and the G20, and I think they may have held the EU presidency then as well. So they were quite influential in setting the international policy agenda that year. Among financial market topics, they identified the growth of the hedge fund industry, and what it may mean for financial stability, a topic for the G7 finance ministers.

Normally a representative from the central bank, or the finance ministry would come to Washington and meet with IMF staff on such proposals and outline the desired work programme. However, this proposal got a lot more attention. Also, in the Spring of 2007, the US Treasury created the President's Working Group on Private Funds, and a group of UK hedge funds created the Hedge Funds Standards Board,[14] both I believe as a reaction to the German G7 initiative.

Public and private sector officials expected the Germans to propose significant regulation of hedge funds. But they threw everyone a bit of a curve ball, and, especially after the crisis, significantly influenced the policy debate. They stated that they were not sure what the right regulatory framework was for hedge funds and similar entities, for example: are they systemically relevant? If they are systemically relevant, what are the features that make them so? We do not have enough information, so they did not push for more regulation at the time.

The Germans also said that the British and Americans have long argued that market discipline is the best defence against financial instability, and that they may be right. But market discipline cannot work without better transparency, better disclosure, including, importantly, for regulators. And that was the beginning of a noticeable shift in the direction around more disclosure tailored for regulators, public officials, rather than the markets.

As the crisis played out, regulatory disclosure was materially ramped up, and greater direct regulation was politically acceptable, even required, across the G20. At the G20 meeting in Washington in November 2008, many officials referred to prior reliance on market discipline. And, of course, calls for regulation. So the Washington Action Plan was produced by the G20 in November 2008.

Matthew: *As a director of hedge funds, can you tell us what you think directors should do that is perhaps slightly out of the box? For example, should they challenge or test the material presented to them by the CRO? Are they asking if the risk is well managed or are there things they could be looking for?*

Todd: I ask good questions. Some are simple. For example, what is the market convention for pricing or measuring exposure for that asset class or that trading style? Is there a market convention? Is there a right way or wrong way that we should be adhering to? Why is the administrator not on board with one approach compared to another? And interestingly, market conventions can be hard to define for some asset classes, trading styles or transactions.

In this regard, a director is kind of like a good regulator, and the key is to understand the proper questions, and hopefully, in an intelligent manner, interact with the risk manager and the CEO and COO of the firm. They are going to know the fund's risk/return picture and portfolio details better than a director because they are living it. And, when required or requested, I try to help the manager reach an outcome we believe a reasonable investor, collectively representing all investors in the fund, would expect or desire of the fund they have invested in.

You have to ask: Does this seem reasonable to me? Is this the right way to think about an issue, or disclose a fund activity, or resolve an outstanding issue or question? And if it is not, how do we get to the right place? Again, exercising your judgement and fiduciary responsibilities to the fund investors collectively.

Frances: It comes down to common sense.

Todd: Very often, yes. And, based on prior experience, the ability to ask good, relevant questions.

Matthew: Do you think that pro-cyclicality, which is as a function of recent market volatility, warrants more attention? How could this risk be addressed by regulators?

Todd: Policy officials are all rightly worried about pro-cyclicality. However, I believe many of our regulations, tax rules and accounting policies for financial institutions are often pro-cyclical. Said differently, when the lightning bolt strikes and markets stress, through many of our regulatory policies and actions, we broadly incentivise many different market participants to react the same way. Pre-lightning bolt, everybody is creating similar risk management systems, risk reporting systems and risk strategies, so when the lightning bolt hits, everybody goes to the left side of the boat, and that boat is more likely to tip. That is how market volatility becomes financial instability.

Frances: Do you think that more transparency can help smooth volatility?

Todd: Transparency is a good thing, but too much transparency may actually hurt liquidity in some markets. People must have incentives to go out and do homework, and possibly gain an edge. But you also want enough transparency to bring a lot of people to the market. There's a balance needed. Our mothers had it right: "everything in moderation". We should strive for areas of improved transparency – to the market place; and I would also like to see regulators focus on what they really care about in the data and not overly burden the providers of such data (by which I mean regulated entities).

Frances: What innovations do you believe have been effective in managing risk?

Todd: No big individual breakthrough, but a lot of important smaller, idiosyncratic improvements, for example, CDS. But let me give some background. One thing I took away from the Greenspan era was that one important objective of central banks may be to reduce the volatility of GDP, within the framework of stable monetary variables.

For some, that is an interesting, or possibly radical, statement in itself. But how would you do it? First: central bank credibility, which takes a long time to build and is easy to lose. Second: once you have credibility, proper signalling: because the more I signal with credibility the more the market is going to react to my signal, which, it is hoped, may reduce financial market and economic volatility, since I am less likely to surprise you with interest rate or other policy decisions. From the Volker era, when the Fed "beat" inflation, to Greenspan, who came after him, you will find, I believe, that GDP is less volatile: the standard deviation of the business cycle was reduced. So Greenspan, by many measures, was hugely successful if you accept that one aim was to reduce the volatility of GDP, or economic output or aggregate economic wealth.

From a macro-economic and macro-prudential perspective, I believe CDS can perform a similar volatility (market, GDP, systemic risk) reducing function. CDS is all of us voting on certain credit quality over a certain period of time. Why is that not a credible signalling device by and for the markets about credit? Since banks and credit are typically at the focal point of financial stability and economic analysis, I believe it can be a tool both to signal credit conditions and dampen down volatility and crises.

Frances: *What developments would you like to see?*

Todd: As a policy-maker or a regulator, I would seek greater market diversity. Diversity of market participants is good, shadow banking is not bad, banks are not bad, insurance companies are not bad. Markets are most efficient, effective and, I believe, more stable when we observe markets with all of the balance sheet structures present and active. They bring different attributes and strengths, typically reflected by their liability structures and balance sheets. When lightning bolts hit, if we regulate everybody like a bank, they all go left on the boat. But if we regulate insurance companies, pension funds and others more based on balance sheet features, we allow their differences and strengths to persist. Similarly, if bank and money market funds are primarily creatures with short-term liabilities and longer-dated assets, regulate them in a more similar manner. If we can preserve such balance sheet differences and related differing market behaviours, when the lightning bolt hits everyone does not react in the same or a similar manner. That diversity of reaction and diversity of behaviour enhances liquidity in good times, and makes liquidity less likely to run for the exit (the same, crowded exit) in bad times. Today, I see many regulators seeking to treat all market participants like banks. That is not good policy.

Lastly, as concerns innovations, there are some fascinating things being done in the insurance world, defined in the broadest sense. Firms like AXA and Swiss Re, banks like Deutsche Bank, JP Morgan, Morgan Stanley and Goldman Sachs have developed, with differing market take-up, some very innovative risk management and risk sharing tools.

They've created tradable securities and indexes for the purpose of risk transfer, risk sharing and risk management. They have looked at environmental and demographic changes. At the IMF, we would encourage finance ministries and treasury departments to be the CRO of their country, and strive for greater financial flexibility, which means evaluating more closely the term structure, probability and severity of various real and contingent liabilities. Are they liabilities that you can handle through your own strength, your own management of cash flow or, through investments, including your education systems? Or are there certain liabilities that you cannot manage alone? So consider insurance. There are some really smart people working on financial market and real economy issues from the "insurance" world.

In the early and mid-1990s, JP Morgan was selling a product to banks that gave them the ability to sell certain liabilities or assets, or alternatively the right to issue certain capital securities if they experienced a capital deficiency event. Now we have COCOs,[15] which are being created through regulatory mandate, but JP Morgan was developing that market in the late 1980s and 1990s with banks and insurance companies. Today, institutional investors are starting to show greater interest in a variety of insurance risk transfer securities, related to demographics, agricultural prices, wind, rain, drought, tsunamis. New York City is reportedly considering the issuance of a catastrophe bond. These are interesting and potentially very positive ways to transfer a variety of risk to market participants better able to manage and hold such risks across the cycle. Diversity of markets, diversity of market participants.

There are people at the World Bank working with African nations to hedge certain agricultural risks. They work with insurance companies to structure traditional insurance-like products or, in some cases, very non-insurance products and sell them into the capital markets. They may be able to hedge meaningful portions of their GDP. This is important work, and I believe policy-makers fail to appreciate the potential or to support properly such efforts.

Frances: *Not the sort of insurance you write on an annual basis.*

Todd: No, but it can be attractive to many types of investors, since it is generally uncorrelated to financial markets.

Matthew: *Earthquake bonds?*

Todd: Yes, that is a version of it. For Ethiopian drought bonds, they priced 19 or 20 micro-climates in Ethiopia and created indices for each, and that is how they structured the bond.

Matthew: *Apparently they do it on F1 tracks. They forecast the temperature in various places around the track.*

Todd: All types of insurance are possible, even yak life insurance in Kazakhstan, for yak farmers.

Frances: *That's the origin of the CBOT[16] and the Sydney Futures Exchange not long after. They both started in agricultural commodities. Futures, rather than options.*

Todd: There is a consulting firm in Chicago that tried to develop an index for health care inflation. Wouldn't it be great if a small business or an individual could buy that index and hedge (at least in part) health care inflation, which has run at 15% or more a year. In the UK, when the housing market was rising rapidly in the 1990s and later, I think it was BNP that created an index so you could buy exposure to a home in London or some other relatively specific locale, for example, via the index, and your investment would keep pace with the average home inflation in that post code. An attractive hedge for some and a savings tool for those looking to buy a home ...

Frances: *There is a property derivatives market in the UK that does something similar.*

Todd: The UK has also sought to manage better longevity risk. A number of UK banks tried to develop a tradable index. Morgan Stanley was also considering how to match opposing exposures, such as pension funds and health care and pharmaceutical firms: companies that profit the longer we live and increase our consumption of their products, while the pension funds must pay out more with longer life spans. Why don't we execute a swap? For drug companies doing research on product X, sell a bond in the form of a longevity swap to pension funds, with the opposite exposure.

Frances: *Weather derivatives work exactly the same way: some people make money when it rains, others lose. There are lots of examples.*

Todd: Insurance, broadly defined, is a great way to transfer risk. I hope and expect to see more innovative insurance products like these. And ideally they will be used by individuals, corporate or institutional entities, and (very importantly) governments to manage and mitigate the economic effects of a wide variety of real, postulated and contingent liabilities.

Notes

1 The Savings and Loan crisis of the 1980s and 1990s was the failure of 1,043 out of the 3,234 savings and loan associations in the United States from 1986 to 1995.

2 A German politician of the Christian Democratic Union. He was President of Germany from 2004 to 2010. He was President of the European Bank for Reconstruction and Development from 1998 to 2000 and head of the International Monetary Fund (IMF) from 2000 to 2004.

3 Alternative Investment Management Association.

4 General Manager of the Bank for International Settlements (BIS) and Governor of the Bank of Spain from July 2000 to July 2006.

5 A retired British economist and central banker. He was formerly the Deputy Governor of the Bank of England, with responsibility for financial stability, and served on the Bank's Monetary Policy Committee from June 2002 until October 2013 and its interim and then full Financial Policy Committee from June 2011.

6 To increase minimum margins, or collateral, required.

7 US Securities and Exchange Commission.

8 US Commodities Futures Trading Commission.

9 Assets under Management.

10 UK Financial Conduct Authority, previously the Financial Services Authority.

11 European Securities and Markets Authority, a European Union financial regulatory institution and European Supervisory Authority.

12 Standard & Poor's, a credit rating agency.

13 A financial fraud where a client's losses are hidden by an investment firm by shifting them between the portfolios of other (genuine or fake) clients. Any real client with portfolio losses can therefore have their accounts flattered by this process.

14 A private sector standard-setting body for the hedge fund industry.

15 Contingent convertible bonds.

16 Chicago Board of Trade.

11 | Richard Meddings

London, 27 November 2014

Ring fencing banks and simplifying risk models are supposed to impede financial contagion, help compare banks and make the financial system more resilient to shocks. They could have the opposite effect.

Richard Meddings is Former Group Finance Director at Standard Chartered Bank and at Woolwich. He now serves on the boards of Legal & General and of HM Treasury.

He explains why he believes another big crisis is on the way.

Richard Meddings: Although a banker for over 30 years, I am a chartered accountant by training. I started at Price Waterhouse[1] then moved to Hill Samuel, a merchant bank and then BZW[2] and CSFB.[3] I spent overall 15 years in corporate finance and capital markets (so originally an investment banker). Then I became Group Finance Director at Woolwich, where I had been an

227

adviser. John Stewart[4] was the CEO at the time. I helped
de-mutualise and float it on the stock exchange. We sold to
Barclays around three years later, where I became Group
Financial Controller and then Chief Operating Officer of the
wealth management businesses. About three years later I joined
Standard Chartered as the main board director of risk, serving on
the board from 2002.

At Standard Chartered I took responsibility for Risk, Legal,
Compliance and Audit and from 2005 I also looked after all the
non-Asian countries, of which there were over 50 across Africa,
the Middle East, Latin America, Europe and North America.
From 2006 I became Group Finance Director, responsible for
Finance, Risk, Group Treasury, Group Strategy and Corporate
Development.

I left Standard Chartered in the summer of 2014 and, having
stepped down from the board of 3i PLC after six years as a
non-executive, now serve on the Boards of Legal & General and
also HM Treasury.

Frances: *Who are the people that influenced you early in your career?*

Richard: Two people have been significant influences on me. One is
Christopher Castleman,[5] who, having gone to Australia, founded
Hill Samuel Australia (which was of course the progenitor of
Macquarie Bank), with David Clarke. He came back to London
as the Chief Executive of Hill Samuel Group and I had the good
fortune, when I was in my mid-20s, to work as his executive
assistant. He was hugely formative for me. He taught me a couple
of things in particular. First of all about "the organisation of
decisions" and a discipline of follow-up, a real action-oriented
follow-up. But the main thing he taught me was simply that you
have to make a decision even if the decision is proactively to do
nothing. And not to be worried about making a decision that
might be wrong, because if it is, you simply have more
decisions to make. Castleman was legendary, a brilliant, brilliant
man, genuinely high integrity and he was a really good
banker.

The other influential person in my career was Mervyn
Davies,[6] who was the CEO of Standard Chartered. He is
absolutely superb at, has an amazing instinct for, judging

people – putting people in the right place and so freeing them up. He awoke Standard Chartered from a rather nervous position where it had been a banana skin bank. He gave it confidence and focus and he moved people around and took chances on young people. But equally you had to be very open to Mervyn. You had to exchange views with him. He was a very open manager, a bit cult like, but a very open manager who proactively sought to manage people and bring people forward.

Frances: *He sounds like a very good leader, which is important because finance is not about managing money, it's about people.*

Richard: Try to understand their motivations, why they are thinking about certain things because that affects the judgements and recommendations they make. Mervyn was very good at that. He also had a superb ability to network, which he still has. So from a risk perspective, he was always out there listening so he would pick up comments from the corporate world, and he would come back and say to me when I was his risk director: Maybe nothing in it, but I hear a bit of noise about x company and we would go and have a look. He wanted to stay alive and alert to signals even though most of them were bound to be false signals. Mervyn was also an excellent banker – inspirational and confidence-giving. So Mervyn Davies and Christopher Castleman.

The third person who has been really important to me is Peter Sands – I worked alongside him for 12 years on the Standard Chartered board. A great partner, a fast, numerate mind and a very clear strategic thinker. We worked closely together in the transformation of Standard Chartered and through a very successful period of growth.

Frances: *Have there been particular events that have been formative?*

Richard: I suppose everybody has said the financial crisis. But it was especially remarkable because of the role Standard Chartered played here in the UK in helping to design what the government adopted as the bail-in plans for all the banks. We created it here in Standard Chartered, understanding practically how a bank had to fund itself in crisis. The plan and, importantly, the urgency of the need for it and in scale, went to Darling[7] and then Brown[8] adopted it. We had written it through a Thursday afternoon and night. It was presented on the Friday; we remained over the weekend in touch with government as it was further developed with other inputs. It was the genesis of the scheme that emerged on the following Wednesday, where the banks were all offered more capital, huge injections of liquidity and also funding – importantly all in one scheme and in scale – and it then got replicated around the globe. I think the financial crisis, in all that it meant, has been a key event in my working life, importantly because its effects still continue today.

Matthew: It is almost like the regulators were stepping up the response.

Richard: Yes I think the regulators had to step up. The regulatory world is full of very able people, though I do worry there are not enough of them for the scale of the agenda they have in front of them, and I think that is a real challenge for the regulatory world. The fundamental challenge for the banks is that there is no single cogent design that anyone is working to. Anyone: academics, economists, regulators, politicians, are all coming at the issues and they are often in contradiction with each other. There is an overall theme, which is more capital, more liquidity and so on. But there are very, very inconsistent and often contradictory rules between jurisdictions – most recently you can see it in the various imposed ring-fences. Actually I think it's making the world much more fragmented and fragile. I'll give an illustration. Not all banks do this of course, but at Standard Chartered, if there were a local crisis in some part of the bank, we would support that area with funding and liquidity. We would in essence dampen a crisis down, not transmute it. It's now much, much more difficult to do that because of ring-fence forced fragmentation.

Matthew: Because of all the new legal arrangements for branches?

Richard: Subsidiarisation[9] is making the world more fragmented in many ways – and yet we persuade ourselves that it's stronger. I think it will be sorely tested. There is no single architecture of what we want to get to. They have the same thematic objective but you've very different structures. So you've got Vickers[10] ring-fencing in the UK, you have the US increasing, for banks over a certain scale, the amount of capital requirements and funding limitations that capture the liquidity and funding of a particular bank's assets within that jurisdiction. Capital is increasingly not fungible to where the next stress might come from.

Matthew: *It is a kind of de-globalisation.*

Richard: They're essentially creating innumerable small fractures within the banks, which may under stress crack and I think that will be the challenge.

Matthew: *They don't know if anything was really wrong with banking itself. It was really liquidity.*

Richard: It goes back to US real estate being fraudulently sold, packaged up and sold around to the rest of the world on a very structured basis. The US real estate market just exploded in scale and with very poor or fraudulent risk attributes and then was sold as investment, a very big risk being sold around the world. Then it was spotted for what it was and everyone lost confidence.

The Western markets and central bank authorities had allowed money to be too cheap for far too long. If you were a banker in 2005 or 2006, were you going to stop lending? You could and should be making sure you were managing credit well but you were not going to say: I won't lend any more money. It would have been very difficult to do this plus, importantly, the belief at the time was that risk had been "distributed" – remember the "new paradigm"?

Frances: *How could you explain that to your shareholders?*

Richard: I don't think you can. You have to be thoughtful and change your profile but the machine is going to keep going, albeit you were distributing more and more of the originated risk. So I think you had a big bubble coming because economies grew and grew and became hugely over-leveraged. Society and politicians liked being able to afford the lifestyle but essentially largely borrowed against over-optimistic views of future growth fed by very cheap money – a virtuous circle of conceit. What's now happening is that society's leverage is being reduced, albeit government borrowing is growing, causing real economic activity to slow, and causing huge pain to many, many people. But it isn't necessarily that the lending in itself was wrong, it was that economies had grown too big on far more credit than we are now comfortable with. You had money too cheap for too long. US real estate was being mis-sold and you had some complex developments in bank products, which made risk harder to see. Remember all that language that you were distributing risk around the markets?

But when the crisis broke, the regulators were uncomfortable that they couldn't understand or see where the risk had gone. I think that's perfectly understandable. So they said to the banks: Take your risk, all the SIVs[11] and equivalents, back on balance sheet. They didn't want to live with the possibility of lots of grenades going off, dispersed throughout the system, even though they might have been quite small.

So we brought it back into the banks' capital structures. This means that if leverage is 25 times then for every pound of bad debt you lost you took 24 back of good lending.

So by centralising it back in the banks it caused very, very real stress in the banking system. I am not sure we'd have been better or worse off – perhaps we'd have been worse off if we hadn't done that, so it was probably the right thing to do. The alternative would have been to have left the sold risk to explode wherever people had bought it. That would have been quite interesting, but that's what would have happened. That was what the "new paradigm" was believed to be, that risk had been distributed and therefore spread, but it never operated.

In summary, society was very highly leveraged in a cheap money world, where risk was being distributed aggressively. And as soon as the crisis came, people reversed it and took the risk back centrally.

Matthew: *Is it because some of the things like standby lines were mis-priced for the stressed liquidity that eventuated?*

Richard: They weren't usable.

Matthew: *Nobody really factored them into their liquidity because the standby line was a way of getting securitised mortgages off the balance sheet.*

Richard: So if you touched it you would signal distress and that was a great problem.

Matthew: *I don't know whether there couldn't have been other institutions who might have taken on those assets, I suppose they're still trying to find them. Those sub-prime mortgages were still good: they were still going to pay off.*

Richard: Yes, and they did do, they have done, in fact. I don't think it was a solvency crisis. It clearly created a solvency crisis but I don't think it was a solvency crisis in itself. It was liquidity. Because people got very, very nervous and they couldn't see who had what, and so they just withdrew from each other. And then at the retail level, markets started to run. But it was liquidity effectively that caused the real distress, asset values plunged and the lack of liquidity forced the sale of assets into collapsed markets. This caused the losses and hence the solvency crisis.

Frances: *The moves to try to make these instruments more transparent by bringing them onto exchanges, is that going to be effective, is that going to work?*

Richard: I think it has real merit as an idea. It is really trying to remove opacity and complexity from the industry and from the instruments themselves, and I think that is a necessary good. Often it was in that complexity itself where some of the super profits were being made. There was too much rent being taken out of the market in those types of transactions.

One of the reasons that one goes to central clearing I think is that it makes the products less complex and more vanilla. There are of course certain types of bespoke risk that you can't cover with those, but you can still write those products, it's just that you can't centrally clear them. The advantage generally of central clearance is that you can still have a reasonable vega[12] return because you put zero or minimal capital up against a centrally cleared product.[13] And that's part of the incentive: although you earn less income, return is probably much better. The challenge, I think, and where regulation is right and where Mark Carney[14] was focusing recently, is that you had better have very substantial backing behind those central clearers because they are nodal points in the system, and are going to be vital in terms of scale and volume of transactions. They need to be very well backed. They also need to be very well stress-tested for things like operational risk and systems efficacy. And because of such concentration one needs to be very thoughtful. Overall, however, I think it's a very good idea to take the opacity and complexity out of those products.

Matthew: What questions can directors ask of risk managers? What standard should they set for their risk people? What discussions should they have about risk, perhaps without the executive present?

Richard: That is interesting: why did you say: Without the executive there? And by executive do you mean the individual head of risk? Because that suggests a sort of culture where you think heads of risk are not senior or where one is concerned that head of risk may be too oppressive or not transparent or not open, or that he or she has not employed people who have enough integrity to speak their mind.

I think the culture should be open because people often don't agree on everything. These things are rarely black and white, it is always a spectrum of grey. If you have got a culture where you have to have people talking without the head there, I think it suggests the culture is not a very good one. The main thing about culture is that risk is owned by the whole group. I think you are in real difficulty if risk is seen as a unit, which says yes or no like a gateway. Risk must be owned by the person at the front line who is actually engaged with the customer, engaged with the transactions. The risk function can be part of it. You can't have risk separately owned just by the risk function, while the businesses regard it as an add-on process with the exhortation of risk to sign off. Incentives have to make risk owned at the very front end of the business. Often this got lost I think.

Frances: What do you think defines a good risk culture?

Richard: The front line owns it. Healthy, transparent, senior level debate. Risk should be owned in the front line and also discussed at board level and senior management level. Clarity of model explanation, so you cannot easily have a complex model presented with a generalist executive team. You can, but it needs to be translated clearly enough that they can understand it. I think the use test is really important. The business has to use the model of the day and I think regulators are moving away from that – which is unfortunate. Now the amount of regulatory imposition of multiple adjustments to models means they are increasingly not used or are less reflective of the risk. And finally how you incentivise is really important.

Matthew: *Do you think the front office are trained sufficiently in risk techniques and process?*

Richard: One thing that risk managers, heads of risk and CEOs should do or the board should do is to ask how well trained their people are for the business they are in. A key foundation is to make sure people are very well trained for their job – this is true for bankers – both commercial and central – and for regulators. An important control is that one delegates functions to people who are capable or experienced in managing them. Over-reliance on generalists can be very dangerous.

Matthew: *Many of the tools that people used to make decisions, in trading rooms for instance, became embedded, so that nobody knew the assumptions that are germane to the models.*

Richard: That leads to another theme which I care hugely about. I do think we are getting it wrong now with this proactive avoidance of model complexity that says: Make it simple, get back to Basel I, for example. But actually, that's still a model. It is just an utterly crap model. It may mean that you can see the apparent ratio, but actually what you do know is that the asset measure is not risk sensitised at all, which means that in fact it could be a much, much riskier profile than your numbers are showing. To run away from model complexity because there has been a financial crisis doesn't make sense.

I think a better approach is to try really hard to make the models better, even if they do remain complex. I wouldn't be dumbing them down to enable more seductive, easier comparisons – so that everyone can say that this bank looks like this bank looks like this bank. It only looks that way because the underlying risk profile has been hidden in very simplified risk weighting.

Matthew: *The Basel Committee did a survey in December 2013 and found dispersion between banks' asset risk weightings.*

Richard: Why is that, do you think? I'll give you an illustration. Consider two identical loans, each of $100, from two different banks. They have identical product terms, they are both unsecured with three-year tenor, same interest rates, same payment instalment profile. Why might one bank give the product a lower risk weight than the other bank does?

Matthew: I would struggle, on a loss given default model or risk metrics model, to see the difference.

Richard: One reason might be that the banks have different risk appetites and different portfolios of loans. For example, one might be a cavalier bank that doesn't really care about a $100 loss, so it doesn't carry the cost of risk officers and risk programmes to assess loans of this amount. It might be happy to write off losses on 100% of loans of this amount. Of course this means that it has much lower costs of risk infrastructure and lower P&L costs of debt pursuit but higher credit costs. By contrast, the other bank might be much more conservative and prefer to pursue every dollar. The cavalier bank simply chooses to have a lighter risk team, a lighter collections team, no automated diallers, all the rest of it. The conservative bank has a much higher P&L cost of its risk infrastructure but it will suffer much lower credit loss.

There are perfectly good reasons why banks have different appetites for risk, which make the risk weights attributed to apparently identical loans different. That is wholly appropriate. Given the banks' different risk appetites, structures or strategies, you would not want the same loan to be given the same risk weight. That very straightforward, simple point has been misunderstood.

Frances: There is also a portfolio effect, which takes into account what the rest of the loan book looks like.[15] This is basic portfolio management.

Richard: In fact forcing them to weight the same, as if the product is designed the same, ignores the fact that the risk appetites, the risk structures, the risk cultures and risk investments of those two banks are different. If I were a regulator, from a structure of market perspective, I don't want homogenisation: I do want $100 loans to have a differential impact if they start distressing. I don't want herding pressure coming through the market or the economy.

Frances: Basic diversification.

Richard: It's a diversification of loss rate and treatment. But I think we are going in the wrong direction by seeking simplification because it allows people to think that they are analysing banks on a comparable basis, when in fact they are doing the opposite: they are effectively masking differences in those banks. And the same applies to trying to avoid complexity in models. You want your models to be empirical to your structure of risk, to your collections, your method of sales or distributions, to what it is modelling. You want it to be used, i.e. the use test, to price that risk. In that sense Basel II was going in the right direction, and instead of junking it and going back to over-simplified structures that mask levels of risk, we should just keep working really hard at improving those models.

The perspective in a global market product set is differently I think because the ability to model and draw the three-dimensional risk shapes of particular structures is much, much more difficult.

Matthew: *One view is that complexity can creep into structured investment products without people knowing about it. I'm thinking of modelling co-dependence or correlation.*

Richard: They are very hard pictures for management, general management, to pick up and understand.

Frances: *Where complexity is blamed, often the real issue is that it is not the complexity itself, it is that not enough people understand it.*

Richard: At senior level.

Frances: *Yes, it could be a bright young thing sitting in corner who might not have the communication skills, or who doesn't see the overall picture.*

Richard: I think the bright young thing might be doing something very straightforward. But it's the old problems, it's the hiding of the position, it's having the nine zeros account or whatever it is that masks an issue until the loss gets bigger and bigger.

That doesn't invalidate the point about whether your senior management really understands what happens to a product's shape under stress: it can be deeply mathematical, formulaic, hard to get to grips with. So I would be watchful of those sorts of products. I think that one of the lessons from this conversation is, while I think it is important to distinguish that rather easy $100 personal loan example from a financial markets product – and it is generally very easy for managers to understand the $100 loan product and what it might do – and to model outcomes and stress them. But there are probably not enough managers at senior levels who understand how the financial market product or an array of such products might behave under stress. There is not enough knowledge in that space. Many boards are light on people who can engage deeply enough with the head of markets or head of market risk on how that portfolio is moving or can move under stress.

Frances: We're hearing how important it is for boards to have the experience and skills to pose the right questions.

Richard: Or understand whether you have been given the answer to the question you asked. Sometimes – it shouldn't be the case, but it is – some non-executive directors may not be willing to look foolish. You need to persuade people that it is okay to ask for an explanation of, say, butterfly swaps[16] and the risk pattern of those.

Matthew: It seems that the regulators and their masters are trying to re-order the world based on one or two errant types of activities that caused a lot of pain, for good reasons I suppose. It's related to the issue of distribution of risk that you mentioned earlier and how they're pulling back on that.

Richard: Would you agree with that as a thesis or not? I often wonder. We came under quite a lot of pressure from the Bank of England to bring back our SIVs. We had a small SIV but we refused. I think we were the only bank that refused to do that because we saw honest reasons not to. People said our reputation would suffer, but we said: We will take that risk. What we did was we shrank the SIV and shrank it and shrank it. We kept offering people the chance to take their slice away, so for example if they had 3% they could take 3% of every asset in the piece and if they took their asset slice and funded it themselves, it would have performed very well. It enabled them to avoid the fire-sale price of a liquidity event. But the fact was that the assets continued to pay their interest, they were very good value assets but the liquidity crisis was forcing people to sell them out into a distressed market. We had some difficult phone calls with some clients but in the end all of them recognised that that was the basis on which they had bought. I think we handled that SIV, Whistlejacket,[17] really well.

Matthew: Yes, but when credit derivatives first started, there was talk about a new source of credit appetite, but many people buying them may have been making inappropriate decisions. And the regulators may have reflected post-crisis that buyer beware is difficult to modify (legally). So that might have been another reason why they were bringing it back on board.

Richard: I do think that one of the things that led to the depth of the crisis was not so much the complexity of the products but the complexity of the system that developed to distribute them. A lot of people who never had any connection to the underlying assets could trade at several stages removed in the instrument, or some combination of instruments. And this contributed to a massive ballooning of financial instruments. It goes back to Lord Turner's[18] phrase in his 2009 interview[19] about socially useless activities. And many of them were socially useless, but not all, because you do need to buy risk protection. As these markets built and built they produced an ever greater scale of instruments packaged and being traded in high volume for small margins, which meant you ended up with a very sizeable product volume. And it wouldn't take much to make you nervous in that environment would it? And a great deal of this activity was traded between financial institutions for its own sake – well away from the original transaction that originated the first deal. To an extent – and this is important – it's a necessary deepening of market liquidity to have some of this activity, but it became far more extensive than necessary and traded on a non- or low-cost basis, establishing apparent profitability but at ever greater scale.

If you ask me what happens when we look back five or 10 years from now, I'm quite bearish. The circumstances leading to the financial crisis were cheap money and the pursuit of yield. And what have we got today? Even greater equivalent issues. QE and central bank liquidity may continue to blow the bubble for some time yet – but there will be a reckoning and it is getting bigger all the time.

The second aspect of financially useless activity is the opportunity to take rent out of the system. It comes from the combination of that search for yield, very smart people and of very capable technology. It helps build market activity that lacks a central valuation brake. And what's happening with the markets today?

Michael Lewis's book *Flash Boys*,[20] it's a polemic but a very good book about dark pools[21] and the speed of trading, and the scale of the speed of trading. I'm still struck by the October 2014 volatility of US treasuries.[22] I believe it is a combination of the breadth and depth and pace of market activity now, which is fearsomely bigger and more powerful than it was 10 or 15 years ago, combined with the fact that the regulation of liquidity for banks makes the banks look like they are more liquid than they are. That's because in reality the majority of liquidity can't be used because the banks have to maintain their regulatory minima. So you have an apparently large liquidity pool, when in fact you have got only a small inch below the surface level that's available for those banks to use to dampen volatility. So liquidity is apparent but not real in significant depth and this is while the markets are themselves getting faster and bigger all the time. I think that is a really difficult combination that regulators and central banks have to deal with. It suggests that with people ever more aggressive in the hunt for yield, asset bubbles are appearing all over the place. I think we are going to see another very big correction. Bleak! I know. Do you agree with that?

Frances: *It seems that what they did in 2008 was necessary though: the immediate reaction had to be to pump liquidity into the system.*

Richard: I am not criticising at all what they have done, it was necessary but it didn't put the fire out completely. It is going to be a long fix, this.

Matthew: *It has gone on for a very long time, and there is a lot of collateral damage, for example pension earning rates that are going to be nowhere near adequate.*

Richard: I think, too, the single currency of Europe is a moral question as much as an economic question. With 40 or 50% unemployment rates amongst the young generations in southern Europe, casting them out for the sake of a single currency experiment is morally wrong. I don't disagree with a single currency as long as the politicians are prepared to fix the underlying foundations that will enable the single currency to operate. But where is the evidence for that?

Matthew: *The purgatory of savings is that you can stay in cash at very low margins to avoid the bubbles. But if that goes on for 10 years, you are going to be going to 3% yield on equities in nine or so years.*

Richard: I don't disagree with you at all, I think it is a very difficult question, it is the devil's own task to get out of. But I think we're too comfortable in our assumption that it has been mended. Rather, I think, the conditions are setting us up for another very real crisis somewhere. For example, if you think about where most people have investments, how their portfolios are positioned, very few people take the highest risk category and very few people take the lowest risk category. Most people sit somewhere in the middle categories: moderate or cautious. To get a cautious portfolio you need a high weighting of bonds. What do we think one of the bubbles is? Bonds. So if you have a sudden reset of bond prices and bond valuations, you are going to find perfectly bright, intelligent people who believe they made sensible, cautious investment decisions suddenly finding their asset portfolios have dropped somewhere about 20 or 30%. Then what happens?

Matthew: *And then there is, say, a school system in America that needs a certain interest rate return to finance operating expenses. These are unintended consequences of low interest rates, which are not just to do with investor preferences or liquidity traps. They're to do with funding gaps.*

Richard: They are fundamental to assumptions on future funding. I agree. You could probably tolerate it for one or two or five years, but it has been going on for nine, so suddenly you are facing much greater deficits. It is an increasing problem for pension funds.

Frances: *What do you think is the industry view of compartmentalisation of risk functions into investment, counterparty, operations, legal and compliance, reputational risks and so on?*

Richard: It is blindingly obvious that we should maintain a continuing stress-testing environment of both external stress tests (as the regulators ask) and internal management ones. And if something goes wrong anywhere in a small part of the group, you take that issue and stress it across the whole group. And reflect on it honestly. Hold the mirror up and ask: What do we look like? Learn from problems.

I understand why risk gets compartmentalised: it's a necessary management or structural convenience. But there is a danger of missing risk as it emerges because risk transmogrifies: it appears as one thing and becomes something else or turns up somewhere else. Risk doesn't fit and stay in only one compartment. It is often

in multiple compartments, or it moves. So I think it is an
organisational or structural challenge how to organise risk
functions. But when you pause and reflect on that, the key is that
we require there to be a behavioural reflection across the whole
business.

*Matthew: You could have a group of experienced risk managers who can
stroll across risk silos in a non-threatening way, drill down on things that
strike them as over-zealous risk taking or unusual build-ups of risk. To
challenge and bridge the silos.*

Richard: And ask: If that assumption is wrong, are we still
comfortable?

*Matthew: Many organisations may find it difficult to take that approach
because they are trying to manage regulatory demands. One of the benefits
of the standardised regulatory approach is that compliance is simpler. It
makes the regulatory burden of proof of your internal model simpler.*

Richard: I thought none of those internal models were allowed to
operate without regulatory approval and sign-off. In Basel II, there
was a use test. You had to use that model to run your business, for
pricing risk and in how you managed and modelled risk weight
for capital attribution. That is a very good discipline to make sure
it is working correctly. If you wanted to make changes to model
assumptions you were also required to get regulatory approval.

Matthew: Can models properly capture the human response to crises?

Richard: I think this is a very good question that really made me
think about crisis management. I don't think it does and I think
that is a question. You can model hypotheses, but how well do
you put in how humans respond? How do you model their
behavioural reaction and response? I do not think people model
that well enough. By human response, I do not mean the
customer reaction, for example, I lose my credit card before my
house. More, it is how the executive, risk managers and front line
of a bank react – and also how the regulators react.

*Matthew: Some people have type A or type B personalities if you will. Let's
say type A seek to help the firm survive and type B say: If we go down,
everybody will go down so let's not worry.*

Richard: I think that it is not just the banks' own executives' likely
reaction, but also the regulatory and central bank reactions. I
think it could be modelled, for instance: I have this stress

happening, I am not going to be left on my own to deal with it. Essentially run proper "war games" of stress situations. It is just as important that the regulators do this as also should the banks.

Frances: *How can regulators satisfy popular demand for visible and simple controls, such as leverage limits and at the same time manage the natural response of organisations to circumvent regulation through various forms of regulatory arbitrage.*

Richard: There is generally a very low level of popular financial literacy, which is why we have hopefully responsible management and very good regulators. So asking for visible and simple controls may not be what you should be asking for even though people might understand it. Leverage limits are a very real example. I think it should only be a back-up control: it should never be a lead constraint.

But I also don't think organisations seek to circumvent regulation. We actually want to be in a banking system where the other banks are strongly regulated. I do not want to exist in a world where there are cowboys out there, who are allowed to be cowboys, because that endangers me. A number of investment banks or other intermediaries in the immediate aftermath of the crisis offered us capital regulation arbitrage products and we said: We won't do it. I think the penalty should be quite significant for senior managers who try to circumvent regulation, if they are found to be doing so.

I think complexity of regulation is absolutely a source of risk. We now face such a confused mosaic with different interpretations about what counts for core equity and what doesn't count for core equity in different jurisdictions. It is that point I made earlier about fractures in the system, the lack of any single, coherent design; the ring-fencing debate is a very good example, the actual methods of ring-fencing, one method competing with the other.

Matthew: *So why do you think that is happening in the IOSCO[23] sub-framework where they are trying to make it collegiate?*

Richard: The people who gather round the table are under very real pressures. They are subject to the shape of their own domestic industries and their own domestic economies and their ability to provide those particular activities. So commonality can't easily be achieved absent a better shared understanding in the political response and given the economic circumstances of each jurisdiction. And here the regulators are also necessarily politicised. I don't blame them because the financial crisis was such a major feature of political debate, so politicians listen to their electorates and then pursue banks via the regulators and I think as each major economy is coming from a different place, this also places pressures on what they feel they can do, so harmonised rules are difficult to agree on.

Frances: *How do you see the balance between rules-based risk management and principles-and-judgement-based risk management – with a dose of caveat emptor – that reflects the intention of the regulations?*

Richard: Principle and judgement-based regulation is generally better than rules-based. But it requires a level of investment in skills and transparency, firms and regulators, one with the other, to make that work.

I do think that caveat emptor, translated as personal responsibility, is important but has been largely lost: if anything goes wrong it must the institution's fault: they must have mis-sold in some way. The onus has certainly shifted. It has not disappeared but shifted. It is more by public and political demand; I think that is a natural consequence of a pretty deep crisis.

PPI[24] is a good example. This is very difficult space because the media and politicians and public opinion only portray one view. And let me be clear, banks absolutely should compensate customers where they have mis-sold. But what did the regulators think the scale of PPI was? I think £2 billion. What is it today? £23.5 billion and rising. Do you know how many times a week people in the UK get calls or texts from people saying: Make a claim, make a claim. The claims industry is now huge. You can check with Barclays and Lloyds, I think they would tell you around 50% of the claims they get are from people who have never had a relationship with them. So there is a different point, a societal responsibility point, which is that the pendulum has swung too far. I would be absolutely hammering the banks for mis-selling and insist that they compensate, but I would equally say: Society functions better if personal integrity is strong. I don't want a society where you just claim and claim, even when you know you haven't been mis–sold anything. What does that mean for popular behaviour and expectations?

Matthew: *How effective do most practitioners think ongoing stress tests can be?*

Richard: I think ongoing stress tests are really insightful, but you have to continuously search for correlations[25] and hidden correlations.

Matthew: *Do you believe that the pro-cyclicality inherent in margin calls, which are levied as a function of recent market volatility – and therefore are prone to underestimating in the calm that often precedes a crisis – warrants more attention?*

Richard: It's a potentially significant problem. Much of regulation is pro-cyclical. As economies slow down default probabilities move up and so risk weight moves up and capital needs move up and so banks come under more stress. They can't always access capital so they then deleverage so the economies slow down more. I think it is set up in a way where that pro-cyclicality is a challenge.

Frances: *What can you do about it?*

Richard: Recognising it more overtly and explaining it better in thinking about the evolution of regulations would help. What regulators have tried to do about it is to use counter-cyclical capital buffers although in reality we have yet to see them operate. Yet you'd assume they would be operating now. Moreover, it will be interesting to see how regulators or markets allow these capital buffers to operate within an actual stress. But in forming those buffers we've now got a world where the world-wide capital structures have become, on a regulatory basis, more complex. For example, the idea that every bank has 8% or 7% or whatever capital is no longer true. So, for example, HSBC might require a regulatory minimum of 11% and Standard Chartered might be $9\frac{1}{2}$%. Why would that be? It would be because Standard Chartered hasn't the same level of G–SIB[26] as has HSBC. Standard Chartered also has a lower pillar 2A[27] buffer requirement. Yet the market still says: Yes, but 11% is 11% is 11%. That complicates communication of the bank's relative capital strength compared to the regulatory asset requirement. The capital structures involving several different regulatory buffers – each different for different banks – is not yet accepted by the market, which in the end is the lightning rod judge of a bank's capital strength.

Frances: *It depends on where in the cycle you are.*

Richard: And then there is that – hence the counter-cyclical buffer concept.

Matthew: *The G20 were debating a change to the margin collateral rules to make them more across the cycle rather than span one year of history. They were also looking at minimum collateral measures for the prime brokers. One outcome was that the prime broker business model would become less attractive. A corollary may have been that leverage will sort of drop out of the system. People were expecting some steps towards not allowing prime brokers as much freedom with the statistical foundations of their risk models. For example, by using 90 days rather than 120 days in their statistical models so that their collateral goes down x and they win more business. So I wonder whether there are some things that you can do to slow down that behaviour.*

Richard: I suppose it is understood with the thinking about expected loss provisioning in the banks. It comes back to the point that there is no single architecture. As a bank it is a bit like shooting the ocean. Everybody has a view, academics, economists, politicians, regulators, different regulators and different academics and different judges are all suggesting different things. You can engage and say: Yes, that makes sense, or: Sorry, that does make sense but some of that just doesn't make sense. So you shoot into the wave and it comes again, it comes again. Where is the single design?

Matthew: *Glass-Steagall[28] was a harmonised approach: a bank is a bank.*

Richard: It took nine years from the final demise of Glass-Steagall for the investment banking industry to bring the banking industry to its knees. Of course it's stupid to say that the investment banks are bad. They're not at all, they are just different businesses. Investment banks are not banks, they are market intermediaries. The investment banks brought Wall Street and the markets and the power of those markets, particularly as I said earlier, with massively growing technological capabilities, speed of trading and scale of trading, into the banking system.

 With my finance hat on, I take a very unpopular view, which is I don't agree with a growing use of a fair value[29] or exit value of banks' assets. For example, if I lend you money for five years and you are servicing it, why would I move the value of the loan to you up and down with some market proxy? It should be accruals-based accounting. If you start to look unable to pay or I thought you were not going to pay, then I would provide.[30] Imagine what happens to the capital structures, the ratios of banks if exit price applied more broadly to all these assets? It's the same with deposits.

Matthew: About five years ago some American banks revalued their liabilities mark-to-market, which gave them a credit in their income statement of some enormous number.

Richard: Because their debt was trading at a low price. It's at that point where you get these massive accounting profits because your own debt apparently falls in value and you take it as a credit to your P&L.

Matthew: If your falling debt is a harbinger for the rest of the economy, then the assets are increasingly likely to be provided for. And this brings us to the point about shadow banking. It's similar to the diversification effect that Greenspan thought he was getting with credit derivatives.

To what extent do you think that the diversity of services and organisations shadow banking produces will, as some observers believe, be a possible solution to the "too big to fail" problem, and associated moral hazard?

Richard: I think you should allow risk transfer to shadow banks but you have then to stand by it. If you allow risk to be distributed more broadly into shadow banks or into investment institutions, wherever it is, it should stay there: they buy it, they keep it.

Matthew: If they fall foul, they fall foul.

Richard: And that would make their risk assessment of it better and tighter I think. And the caveat emptor principle is right. You might want to have clear caveat emptor for sophisticated investors, however defined, so that they have to have an explicit licensed capability to buy particular types of assets.

I think shadow banking does change the financial landscape and risk distribution too: it is a significant change in the way credit markets operate. But I also think that what's often misunderstood is just how central to a modern economy the banking system is. I mean, the other words for leverage are what? Credit capacity.

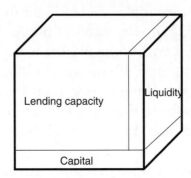

Figure 11.1   Asset Capacity of Banks

To illustrate: this is a very simplistic representation of a bank, shown here as a cube (see Figure 11.1). A bank has capital, which it lends over and over again. We have ignored fixed assets because they are never going to be material to this. A certain amount of the bank's assets has to be held in liquid form – as liquidity, in case people decide they want to come and ask for their assets back. What's left – the larger box – is asset capacity, commercial asset lending capacity.

What's happened in regulation? What's happened to capital? It's doubled. What's happened to liquidity? At least doubled. Of necessity what's happened to credit capacity? It's now much reduced as the available commercial asset capacity is squeezed as capital and liquidity ratios perforce rise. And now look at NSFR.[31] A bank isn't selling daily consumables, it sells tenor. Banks borrow short to lend long so that society can do the opposite.

So all this commercial asset capacity is lending capacity. That big face used to extend right to the back of the box, so there was a lot of capacity in there. But as the maturities of the assets fall with NSFR, the depth of the box comes in (see Figure 11.2). And the face is no longer the big face, it's the smaller face and it only goes back halfway or so. There's a massive three-dimensional squeeze on credit capacity.

It's also only apparent liquidity, not real liquidity, if assessed in terms of its availability into the market because you have to keep so much of it as your "regulatory eligible minimum". As the regulatory minimum threshold – in both capital and liquidity – rises,

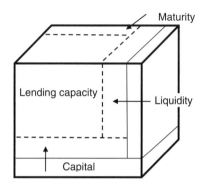

Figure 11.2 The Squeeze on Credit Capacity

then the collapse point for the banks emerges sooner. Capital may be higher, but the first 7–8% of it can't be used.

This smaller amount of commercial asset capacity has also now got to service double the capital. So no wonder returns are much lower – and they probably ought to be much lower still. You are going to see an increase in pricing coming through to the customer for this credit.

It is a very good, easy portrayal of what's happening in the banks. I think something like £1.5 trillion is the amount of customer lending provided by the top six banks in the UK. GDP in the UK is £1.3 or £1.4 trillion, national debt £1.7 trillion. Banks are clearly the main engine and as you squeeze them, so your economy squeezes.

It's not that capital or liquidity shouldn't be higher – these have been eminently sensible regulatory changes – but we cannot make these changes blind to the economic consequences. Understanding the impact on the economy is important.

Frances: *I think it is a very clear way of portraying what you have been saying.*

Richard: Yes. It is a very good illustration and then you can also draw it using risk weights vs assets and you will see the other thing that is happening here is that, for the same $100 nominal asset, the risk weight attribution is moving up. And therefore if you have higher capital cost, it is another squeeze that is coming in addition to the nominal asset example.

Frances: *The risk weighting is moving the capital demand up.*

Richard: Absolutely.

Frances: To be effective, what position should risk management hold in the organisation?

Richard: I do not think the risk director absolutely needs to sit on the board, but it depends on the board structures. Clearly they need to be very senior in the organisation and report directly to the CEO. It absolutely has to be one of the top roles in the bank.

Matthew: In the experience you have of how authorities and market participants tried to cope with events such as the GFC or LTCM, can you describe enduring principles you adhere to in running your practice?

Richard: Enduring principles are the obvious ones. A lot of the old language is still the same. No surprises. Continuous stress tests. Look for concentrations and avoid them. They are not always obvious but you have to continue to search for hidden correlations and understand them. Balance sheet strength. You have to keep a balance sheet of undoubted strength. Capital. Liquidity and funding. So you can ride through periods of distress and people know you can ride through them.

   Another practice that has stood the test of time, and it may sound prosaic, but credit committee approvals are better than round robin signatures. Because you never quite know the force of someone's thinking behind a signature. Debate and open exchange of views are really important, not just for culture, but actually for the right decisions. It may be more bureaucratic to have committees engaging on an issue but I think they are very, very important.

Frances: It's where you say: Has anybody thought of this? And assumptions can be challenged.

Richard: There was a very good book by Roger Lowenstein on LTCM,[32] *When Genius Failed.*[33]

Matthew: Because LTCM started the determination to save the banks. They didn't just save LTCM, they saved the banks from the counterparty risk. That was the "too big to fail".

Richard: And that was the model risk issue. It wasn't that it was a complex model, they just assumed that those particular assets would always be liquid. Failure to understand illiquidity tends to be the biggest risk that people need to worry about. "How long can you sustain any illiquidity stress?" would be a good question.

Frances: *Paraphrasing one of Keynes' remarks: The markets can stay irrational longer than I can stay liquid.*

Richard: The converse of that is how to beat a casino. Superficially, as long as you can cover your loss and bet again, fine, but you need immensely deep pockets for that. As a strategy it is utterly, utterly flawed.

Frances: *Liquidity risk is also the hardest risk to model in my experience. I often see in investment management that liquidity risk is ignored, just because it is hard to model or estimate. To put it undiplomatically: You cannot see it therefore it cannot see you.*

Matthew: *If we were in this room in 10 years' time, looking back, what do you think we will be surprised by?*

Richard: I think what will absolutely surprise us is, and even though we can already see its dynamic, still the pace of technological change. If you think of the last 10 years and go forward to the next 10 years, look at big data, the use of proxy data. Both for the insights it gives us, such as the ability to manage risk but also for the creation of risk, I think it is continually going to surprise us.

Matthew: *Somebody reflected on the LIBOR[34] scandal that that behaviour was probably always there even 20 or 30 years ago, but it was just down in the pub, whereas now, with technology, chat rooms and so on, it is more observable.*

Richard: I also think there is a big difference between what happened with LIBOR and FX.[35] FX I think was utterly shameful. On LIBOR there was a period where I believe the authorities knew perfectly well that people were not submitting properly, and they did not require them to, because what are you going to say: I'm the biggest bank in the UK and I cannot borrow, no one will lend to me, at any of these rates? The authorities undoubtedly knew, and may even have winked at what was going on. The challenge is whether it is ever appropriate to do that and when is it not. Clearly there was also some gaming being attempted in the banks themselves, which was shameful, that some traders were trying to make money for themselves by gaming the system. That is unacceptable and wrong.

In 2009, there was a hell of a crisis going on and I think everybody was trying to make sure the system stayed up. And I don't think that there is anything wrong with trying to make the

system stay up. You can argue that RPI and CPI[36] are both
"guided" in the sense of what they choose to measure in the
basket. I think in the UK most people's cost of living is going up
far faster than the official measures of inflation. What's in the
basket of goods that gets measured? Now, is that a sleight of hand
or not? I don't think so. But the cost of living is, much of the
time, much higher than the official inflation number says it is.
Does it matter? Well it does if you consider the many contracts
that are x% plus CPI or x% plus RPI. Are we going to go after
the people who set CPI and RPI? No, of course not, and partly I
think because they don't use it in trading to take advantage from
their positions. But it can be challenged as a real measure of
society's inflation and indeed we've seen recent adjustments as
these measures get better scrutinised.

One reason I think why democracies and politics are
struggling so much is that people absolutely don't believe what
the politicians are telling them about their standards of living
when they see what is actually happening in their lives and in
their wallets and purses.

If you keep inflation measures artificially low, real cost goes up
and people's living standards are not increasing consistently with
the political narrative.

Frances: *There's a danger that the complexity of regulation is sort of
snowballing and at some point it will collapse under its own weight.*

Richard: I do think this politicisation and continuous growth in
regulation at some stage has got to be rebalanced. Not because I
hold a torch for banks – except without them the modern
economies don't work. I think a lot of new regulation is very
difficult to deal with and it is burning up huge amounts of
resource. The danger I see is that, increasingly, institutions are
managing to the regulations and not to the actual risk. Particularly
with more rules-based regulation rather than regulation based on
principles or judgement. Institutions are managing to what the
regulations say they ought to rather than the actual risk they
should be thinking about. That's what the sheer quantum of new,
detailed regulation will cause and that's what simplified models
will do. They will incentivise banks to lend more unsecured,

high-risk because they will get a better return and this activity will
be masked.

The vast majority of bankers try and do a good job, but that's a
minority view at the moment. I also agree that it is an overpaid
industry, which naturally invites attack. But maybe that is more
the investment banking-type activity that does that. There is
definitely a sense of entitlement across the financial service
industry more broadly. So there are lots of issues within banking
and financial services. But fundamentally a modern economy
doesn't work without a modern banking system and a modern
banking system is leverage and leverage is credit capacity.

That also means maturity transformation: that banks essentially
borrow short and lend long so that society can do the opposite. I
love that phrase: it's what banks do. Stand on a hill in the UK and
look at all the roofs of all the houses, and think that the vast
majority of those are bought with borrowed money: long-term
loans that may get paid off over many, many years. That
broad-based home ownership wouldn't be happening if it
weren't for the major banking system that transforms maturity
risk.

Matthew: *I don't disagree with you, but I think there is the banker's
simplification: this is what a bank is. I think what's lost, what the
regulators are coping with, is that that's not all they do. This is more
common in America, but they claim that they need huge balance sheets so
they can provide services to huge corporate customers; and all these rules
and regulations will dampen that, which will dampen our globalisation
and our trade. I think there is a link between regulation and trade
theory. I think there is a bit of throwing out the baby with the bath
water.*

Richard: There is a danger of that. What's happening is what we
should have expected to happen, given the depth of the crisis,
given my point about money being too cheap for too long. US
real estate, fraudulent real estate that was sold to everyone. The
banks were the translators of that and they still are the translators
of that. People borrow from banks, not government and now
government wants to cut as the economies de-leverage. The
banks de-leverage, face up to customers and withdraw the loans.

So it's a wholly natural reaction that the pendulum will swing like – indeed it's over-swinging – here at the moment. But there must at some stage be some rebalancing back the other way to allow proper functioning. A better question is to ask the Bank of England or the Chancellor: What's the amount of credit or leverage you want in the economy, and how do you want it disposed?

Matthew: *If I were running a big bank, I would be disposed to getting rid of some of the high-risk banking activities.*

Richard: I absolutely agree with you, particularly when you look at the structures. So, for example, the return in financial markets businesses looks high for some products. But if you factor in the real cost of capital plus market and operational risk, a lot of that activity should disappear because much of the return was made when capital requirements were much lower. And capital requirements now, rightly, have to go up if you don't centrally clear. On the other hand, if you centrally clear, then your complexity comes down, and profit margins with it. So whichever way you go, that business is going to shrink. You therefore need to take out significant costs, lots of people or take their remuneration levels down, and that's a very difficult thing to do.

And for the banks and ring-fencing, I think you can still offer very good derivative products to your wholesale customers, centrally cleared, without this complexity. That should provide the vast majority of the risk product range they want and have minimal capital, zero capital to put up. You wouldn't make anywhere like the income but your return will be good. The problem is that you do not have the income to cover the cost of your very heavily-paid mouths. It forces you to rationalise the financial markets and investment bank activities out of the banks. I think that will happen anyway because very clever people and systems will go to the shadow banks and the regulator will need to watch that. But if I'm a corporate, I don't need to write some really complex product but I can still risk-protect myself on interest rates and commodity prices and currency risk over sufficiently long forward periods – without the levels of complexity in product design we have seen created in financial markets over the last 20 years or so.

Matthew: *It's a hedge fund product, so the hedge funds can play with the other shadow banks. I think that happens.*

Much of that business was led by the traders. I have come from a market risk background and I looked into copulas and so forth. But nobody could really understand them, the risk people were almost racing to keep up with the front office guy and the front office guy had never had a mortgage in his life.

I sat down with the CFO of an investment organisation and he offered to show me these mortgages they were securitising and he gets out an Excel spreadsheet and he says: There they are. I said: But some of them don't have the tracing number of the mortgage. And he said: It's coming, its coming. An attitude seemed to me one of "As long as we get the product done!"

Richard: This was exactly what happened. If you read that book on Washington Mutual.[37] It's a really good book about how culture goes wrong and then you see its impact and that they had this massive machine writing these mortgage products and packaging them up for the investment banks, who were demanding more and more to distribute. And you think: The USA is 25% of global GDP and this asset category – real estate – is vast and was abused.

The crisis will come again. In a different way, but it will come again. I'm nervous of a world where we are chasing yield and money is really cheap. It stayed cheap for the right reasons to start with, but nine years now and the experiment looks likely to continue. How will it be settled? And your point about schools – or pension funds – is true: you've got a growing long-run funding issue. How can they generate enough income to meet their longer-term obligations in a low rate environment? Their obligations, particularly in the West, are dictated by very demanding current societal expectations, which are not easily reduced. That's a real long-term challenge for our political economies, which is increasingly the challenge to society's expectations of wealth creation and of the contribution from the financial services industry.

Notes

1 Now part of Price Waterhouse Coopers (PWC).
2 Barclays de Zoete Wedd was the investment banking arm of Barclays Bank PLC.
3 Credit Suisse First Boston.
4 Chairman of Legal & General Group since March 2010, a member of the Court of the Bank of England, a non-executive director of the Financial Reporting Council and Chairman of Guide Dogs for the Blind. Previous roles include a director of the Telstra Corporation, a member of the Australian Federal Attorney General's Business Government Advisory Group on National Security, a member of the Australian Prime Minister's Task Group on Emissions Trading, Chief Executive of Woolwich (1996–2000), deputy CEO of Barclays (2000–2003) and Chief Executive of National Australia Bank (2004–2008) (legalandgeneral.com).
5 Chief Executive of Hill Samuel, and subsequently as a director of Standard Chartered and a senior adviser to UBS Investment Bank, Castleman was widely admired in the financial world for his straightforwardness, his ability to motivate those who worked with him, and his formidable intellect and stamina (telegraph.co.uk).
6 A former banker and a UK government minister until May 2010. His role as Minister of State for Trade, Investment and Small Business involved oversight of UK Trade and Investment – the United Kingdom's export support and inward investment agency – and he had dual accountability to the Department for Business, Innovation and Skills and the Foreign and Commonwealth Office. Davies was Chairman of Standard Chartered PLC between November 2006 and January 2009, and Chief Executive between 2001 and 2006. He was appointed a director in 1997.
7 A British Labour Party politician who has been a Member of Parliament (MP) since 1987, and Chancellor of the Exchequer in the Labour Government from 2007 to 2010.
8 A British Labour Party politician who was the Prime Minister of the United Kingdom and Leader of the Labour Party from 2007 until 2010.
9 Operating the foreign banking activities of global banks as separate subsidiaries of the parent bank rather than as branches.
10 The Independent Commission on Banking was a United Kingdom government inquiry looking at structural and related non-structural reforms to the UK banking sector to promote financial stability and

competition in the wake of the financial crisis of 2007–08. Chaired by John Vickers, it was established in June 2010 and produced its final report and recommendations in September 2011.

11 Structured Investment Vehicles. See also Appendix B.

12 The sensitivity of a derivative position to the volatility of the underlying asset.

13 In contrast to a bank or investment bank counterparty, for example, which demands more capital as collateral.

14 Governor of the Bank of England and Chairman of the G20's Financial Stability Board. He was previously the Governor of the Bank of Canada.

15 For example, because the rest of its loan portfolio is uncorrelated with that loan, or the loan is a relatively small component of the overall portfolio.

16 A limited risk, non-directional strategy that is designed to have a large probability of earning a limited profit when the future volatility of the underlying asset is expected to be lower than the implied volatility.

17 The name of a Standard Chartered SIV.

18 A British businessman, academic, a member of the UK's Financial Policy Committee, and was Chairman of the Financial Services Authority until its abolition in March 2013.

19 How to tame global finance, *Prospect Magazine* interview with Adair Turner, 27 August 2009 (prospectmagazine.co.uk).

20 Lewis, M., *Flash Boys: A Wall Street Revolt* (New York: W.W. Norton & Company, 2014).

21 Decentralised, electronic trading platforms in securities such as listed equities, which are normally traded on a centralised exchange. Unlike conventional exchanges, dark pools do not publish the queue of bids and offers for the securities traded on them until after the transaction is completed.

22 On 15 October 2014, yields of the benchmark 10-year Treasury note fell to as low as 1.87%, the lowest yield since May 2013, then swung sharply up to close the day at 2.09% (market realist.com).

23 International Organisation of Securities Commissions.

24 Payment Protection Insurance, also known as credit insurance, credit protection insurance or loan repayment insurance, is an insurance product (especially in the UK) that enables consumers to insure repayment of loans if the borrower is unable to service the debt.

25 Correlated or conditional stress tests take into account the relationships or correlations, including lagged correlations, between the shock factor

and other elements in the portfolio or ensemble of holdings and the factors that affect them.

26 Global Systemically Important Banks, banks so identified by the Financial Stability Board (FSB).
27 Capital buffer under the Basel III accord.
28 The US Banking Act of 1933.
29 Mark-to-market.
30 Make provision for a doubtful loan.
31 Net Stable Funding Requirement.
32 Long Term Capital Management.
33 Lowenstein, R., *When Genius Failed: The Rise and Fall of Long-Term Capital Management* (New York: Random House, 2000).
34 London Inter Bank Offered Rate.
35 Foreign Exchange.
36 Retail Price Index and Consumer Price Index, two official measures of inflation.
37 Grind, K., *The Lost Bank: The Story of Washington Mutual – The Biggest Bank Failure in American History* (New York: Simon & Schuster, 2012).

12 | Adrian
Blundell-Wignall

Paris, 28 April 2015

At the heart of the crisis was under-pricing of risk that was made possible by the emergence of the universal bank business model following the repeal of Glass–Steagall.

Adrian Blundell-Wignall is the Acting Director of the Directorate for Financial and Enterprise Affairs (DAF) and Special Advisor to the Secretary General for Financial Markets at the OECD and a former official of the Reserve Bank of Australia.

He contends that how some new regulations facilitate both concentration and under-pricing of risk, so could have the effect of aggravating the next crisis.

Adrian Blundell-Wignall: I went to a government school, in a relatively poor area, and didn't have any of the silver spoons things that some people get in life. In my third year at high school I wrote an economics essay called, "What Is the Market Mechanism?" This won me my first ever A+ for an essay and

259

encouragement from my teacher, so I concluded that I must be good at economics. It is amazing what influence a good teacher can have on your life. Even at this late stage in my career I still have this enthusiasm of my youth when it comes to looking at what's happening in the world and why. After school I did an undergraduate degree and a PhD in Economics at Cambridge. My first proper job was as a junior economist in the Economics Department at the OECD.

After six years in the OECD I went back to Australia as Assistant Secretary at the Economic Planning Advisory Council. I quickly learned that the Canberra wasn't really for me (too political) so I joined the Reserve Bank of Australia (RBA), where some years before I had spent some time doing work as a student on my PhDs. The professionalism and independence of the RBA was a breath of fresh air. At the Reserve Bank I worked through various jobs and ultimately became head of the Research Department. From there I joined Bankers Trust Funds Management (BT) where I became an Executive Vice President and ran the futures markets overlay business, working with Olev Rahn in asset allocation.[1] Olev had quite an influence on my thinking in many ways. For example, he used to say: "Don't let your position become your view", which struck me as a good piece of advice. He was always willing to abandon something that he thought was wrong, and I think that requires disciplined research to carry out well. When Olev retired I was appointed Head of Asset Allocation in BT.

When Bankers Trust was taken over and was about to be sold to Westpac, I had the opportunity to take out my equity and (with a colleague) to go to Citigroup, where I worked for a few years as head of equity strategy. Then, following a major tragedy in my life where a nuclear bomb went off in our family,[2] I sought a lifestyle change and I came back to the OECD in Paris again after all those years, where I had some very good friends of long standing. That was before the financial crisis in February 2007, and it turned out to be quite a good move in helping me survive and because my background was perfect for giving insights into what could happen in the markets. Having worked in the markets running derivatives portfolios it gives you a very good idea of how the plumbing of the financial system works. Structured products based on derivatives and counterparty relationships were to be the epicentre of the crisis, particularly via a shortage of capital and a severe liquidity crisis.

In March '07 I gave some speeches saying there was going to be a really big problem with structured products, at a time when few people were taking the issue seriously. Most senior policy-makers thought the next crisis was going to come from hedge funds and private equity, as opposed to the regulated banking sector. The outcome is now history, but my markets background helped my career at the OECD greatly, and the Secretary General of the OECD appointed me as his special adviser on financial markets. I am now running the Directorate on Financial and Enterprise Affairs in the OECD.

Matthew: *Your recent paper on bank business models and the Basel system seemed to me to be spot on the money. But a slightly deeper question is whether there is a cultural problem with the regulators themselves, with their quest for risk measurement.*

Adrian: When talking about the culture of the regulators themselves it helps to take as global a view as possible. You can think of the world as having four blocs, each with its own way of thinking about and running its economy. One of them is the emerging markets, who run their economies and banking systems with a strong emphasis on cross-border controls, financial repression and a heavy involvement of state-owned enterprises (SOEs). Within the advanced countries there is the Eurozone, which has some very special characteristics: open banking systems and markets but cross-cutting issues relating to the common currency without fiscal union. Then there is the Anglo-Saxon economies, which tend to have more open and competitive markets. Finally there are some more advanced economies that are relatively open but have a corporate governance culture that is quite closed to the market for corporate control. Regulations are therefore thought about according to very different philosophies in each region. This is unfortunate, as the most basic regulatory principle should be that all financial instruments need to be regulated in the same way in every jurisdiction, and if you can't get that you will always have regulatory arbitrage. The goal of the Financial Stability

Board (FSB) is regulatory coordination, but it doesn't cover all countries and it is dealing with cultural approaches that differ greatly. It is very difficult to achieve this most basic regulatory requirement.

Frances: *A priori, we're aiming for a world view, but because the crisis mostly affected American and European markets, principally the Anglo-Saxons, that is where a lot of the attention has naturally been focused. Having said that, those economies of course don't operate in isolation, so we are very interested also in the emerging market perspective.*

Adrian: Well, I think of the crisis as a rolling bubble, a bubble that was rolling from one crisis to another long before 2008. Emerging markets have been the centre of the storm before – as in the late 1990s. China had already recapitalised its banking system in the 1990s. Emerging economies use financial repression as a development strategy: cross-border capital controls, interest rate ceilings, ownership restrictions, state-owned banks playing a large role, and many other controls to force a huge amount of savings to finance an investment programme intermediated through SOE banks. This often creates inefficiencies where state priorities and subsidies result in investments that are not necessarily those that would be financed in a competitive system, and so it can result in bad loans and more importantly a misallocation of resources. In that environment recapitalisations become necessary once non-performing loans get to a critical level and can't be hidden any more.

At different stages of development financial repression can be very useful, but as the financial system develops, there is a need to deregulate and open economies up to gravitate to a level playing field. Unfortunately some countries can cling to their "developing" status for too long and using techniques claimed to be essential for financial stability, but which also serve to target exchange rates for a net-export-led growth strategy. This is a great source of tension in the global economy today.

Frances: *But you draw a distinction between continental Europe and the Anglo-Saxon blocs.*

Adrian: To understand how regulation in the continental European bloc differs from the Anglo-Saxon (America-dominated) bloc, it helps to understand how banks' business models developed. In my view, the differences and similarities between the two blocs are somewhat aligned with the debates about universal versus segregated banking, as in the "Glass-Steagall world".

Under Glass-Steagall, which separated investment banking and insurance from insured deposit banking, we got on very well indeed.[3] Investment banking was done by a separate group of institutions. Under that system following financial deregulation in the 1970s and early 1980s, and despite a significant recession in 1991, the Asia crisis and the failure of a large hedge fund, there was an equity bull market and prosperity until things began to change from about 2001. There were no major banking crises prior to the regulatory changes that started with the repeal of Glass-Steagall and culminated in Basel II and SEC rule changes in 2004. Pressures began to build through the 2000s and these finally erupted in the crisis of 2008.

Certain large banks pressured regulators to remove Glass-Steagall and to change other rules that would allow US banks to compete with Europe on a consolidated enterprise basis. Combined with financial innovations involving derivatives, these changes led to increasing system-wide interdependencies. At the same time the relaxation of capital requirements with Basel II permitted a great acceleration of leverage. Those who favour the universal banking model in Europe point out that this model has served Europe well for hundreds of years. I don't know how many times since I have been working on these issues that people have said to me: "but Adrian you know we have had universal banks in Europe forever, and all Citigroup and others wanted to do was just to become universal banks like the ones in Europe, so what was wrong with that?"

There are big problems with that line of thinking. Markets were largely "incomplete" for most of the 20th century, especially as regards banking products like mortgages, consumer loans, etc., which were based on private information and were not a part of public capital markets. Then along came securitisation, tranches, credit default swap guarantees (which rating agencies took seriously) and much more. Derivatives played a big role in structuring products, and interdependence between capital markets and banking rose via counterparty credit risk, maturity mismatch and the like. Markets became complete: you could go long or short virtually anything and banking products were very much a part of it. Just when the US should have stuck to Glass-Steagall and the Europeans should have introduced it, it all went in exactly the opposite direction.

The US banks moved to the European universal banking model, where deposit banking and investment banking were mixed. The rest as they say is history.

Matthew: *What was the ultimate cause of the crisis in your view?*

Adrian: If you had to say in a couple of words what the cause of the crisis was, it would be this: "the under-pricing of risk." Why was risk being under-priced? Part of the reason for this was the mixing of insured depositors – mums and dads – with investment banking activities. No government could let the insured deposit entity fail. This is just the policy-maker side of the "too big to fail" problem; private participant incentives also play a role. I remember an incident at BT when we were trying to set up a new counterparty facility with a well-known bank entity and our back office came back and said: "they are offering us as counter-party a subsidiary in the Cayman Islands with very little capital." We wanted the big complex bank entity as the counterparty. Why? Because you know you will always get your money back, whereas if you are dealing with a subsidiary that has little capital in the Cayman Islands, you know that you won't get your money back if something big goes wrong. Everybody wants to deal with somebody that can't fail. So when you put all this together the system ends up cross-subsidising risk.

Risks need to be priced in the businesses where the risks are taken. If you don't, you end up mixing implicit guarantees with private incentives and the result is something like what we saw in the crisis: too much leverage, too much counterparty credit risk, too much maturity transformation mismatch, and so on.

A deposit bank can remain technically insolvent for quite a long time if it can hide its non-performing loans and trade its way slowly out of it. Insolvency isn't what takes the bank down quickly. It is liquidity, or more correctly the lack of it, which does that. Liquidity is the short route to having to close your doors. If you hold positions that require collateral top-ups or margin payments then you have to make them. And if you can't make them, then a legal process starts to stop the clock and to go into close-out netting.

The failure and subsequent rescue of AIG was an important moment in the crisis that illustrates well the under-pricing of risk. AIG was essentially writing low spread CDS contracts, which banks bought to help them avoid guaranteeing assets, and vastly reduce the capital required under the Basel rules. Nobody expected the defaults and liabilities that the writers of CDS were exposed to. The risks were under-priced.

In the rescue, once close-out netting began, the pay-outs that the US Treasury made were enormous. The cheques for most of the large banks that run the world derivatives markets were often as high as 30–40% of the banks' capital. They were all exposed to each other. I once heard the CFO of one of them say that they were "fine" because they bought a CDS contract on AIG. But of course they could only do that with another large bank, and that bank must have been in the same position as they were. Were they really protected? This is the problem with interdependence. Saving AIG was important. In my own view that was the single most important policy action that probably avoided a global financial meltdown.

While markets are calm, nobody needs capital in a bank. In the Goldilocks days, nobody needs to worry about anything in the derivatives markets, because the repo[4] market was always there and you could always borrow what was needed. It is when people say: "we won't lend to you because we are worried, we don't know what your position is; we don't know the risk we face", and then the whole system freezes up.

Matthew: *And that's when you need quantitative easing (QE)?*

Adrian: Quantitative easing came along because the margin call on the global banking system was so big. The amount of collateral that changed hands, just prior to when the crisis hit in 2008, around the time Lehman started to fail, was roughly speaking $1 trillion worth of collateral. Then, when the crisis hit, volatility forced that up to about $4 trillion; so there was a $3 trillion margin call on the global banking system. At the time, the capital of the global banking institutions involved in derivatives was about $1.75 trillion, so they received a margin call collectively that was bigger than the combined capital base of the GSIBs[5] that run the world derivatives markets. And of course the inter-bank and broker–dealer repo markets stopped: nobody would lend to pay out the margins that were due. So the central bank came in and they had to do it.

    The crisis was not about sub-prime mortgages as such; it was more about the liquidity crisis caused by margin call given the huge pyramid of leverage and counterparty positions that had built up. Of course as banks have gotten stronger by 2015, so the continuance of QE is not about saving the banks today. QE has metamorphosed into quite a different policy agenda about transmission mechanisms for monetary policy at the zero bound for interest rates.

Frances: *Moving some over-the-counter derivatives on to exchanges and insisting on clearing for all OTC derivatives was intended to address some of those issues.*

Adrian: Yes, but it is worth remembering that risk cannot just be wished away, as some commentators seem to think it can – that if you put everything through a central clearing platform then suddenly that has got rid of all the risk. All it would do is to shift the risk to the clearer, which becomes the "mega node" of all the interconnections in the market. In a sense one would have reconstructed a potentially larger too big to fail institution. Imagine that a central clearing party was about to go under, with everybody exposed to it. That couldn't possibly be allowed to happen, and everybody knows that they would have to be supported in a crisis. Straight away you get the same problem again: the under-pricing of risk.

Matthew: *And progress has been fraught.*

Adrian: Since the crisis the banks have been very, very effective in fighting against the regulatory changes. Most recently, during congressional proceedings to pass the budget at the start of this year I understand that a US senator sponsored a bill added on to the budget bill that amended the Swaps Push-Out Rule that had been a key part of the Dodd-Frank Act. There were already a lot of exceptions in the Dodd-Frank Act for the Swaps Push-Out rule, including interest rate swaps and currency derivatives. Its aim was to put all dangerous swaps like CDS and commodity-based swaps onto swaps execution facilities that were to be excluded from public support in a crisis. The press pointed out that a very large US bank basically wrote that legislation and it was adopted word for word. So the big banks are very effective at protecting their profitable businesses and stopping sensible policy action that threatens it.

Frances: *Some people believe that shadow banking can be part of the solution, but is it just shifting the problem somewhere else?*

Adrian: Well, yes, in part that is true, financial markets always adapt in response to new rules. But to be clear shadow banking refers to the process of intermediation involving lots of business segments. It is about broker-dealers (often part of a banking group) and the way they interact with non-bank financial institutions. If you are going to have rules about gearing, if you are going to have rules about quality of collateral, capital buffers and new liquidity requirements, rules about funding stability then both banks and non-banks will be affected. For example, pension funds and insurance companies are part of this process and must adapt as a consequence of new collateral and margin rules. Pension funds and insurance companies are cash poor (invested in bonds and equities), while money market funds, sovereign wealth funds and petroleum funds are cash rich.

Pension funds and insurance companies need the cash to invest in alternative products, and the repo markets serve this purpose well. They feel the need to do this as they face insolvency given the very low level of interest rates that may be around for a very long time. Pension funds and insurance companies risk insolvency because the relatively high-yielding bonds that they bought in past decades are maturing and dropping out of their portfolios, and they face replacing them with extremely low (possibly negative) interest rate bonds. This development reduces asset values at retirement in defined benefit schemes and raises the price of annuities. Pension funds will find it hard to meet their promises because liabilities also rise as interest rates fall. So pension funds and insurance companies are trying to find ways to "dodge the bullet". And that means they feel forced to move into alternative products. These include private equity and real estate, which are highly illiquid, but also a new class of alternatives such as absolute return funds, total return funds, risk parity funds and a variety of hedged products designed to provide better yields with reduced downside risk. Such products help to avoid selling risk assets imposed by regulatory rules in periods of volatility. But these products also require collateral and margin call management. So broker–dealers intermediate the re-use of securities between cash-rich and cash-poor funds in shadow banking. The cash–rich funds need to borrow riskier securities so that they do not sit on zero returns. The broker–dealers intermediate the re-use of securities and they attempt to maintain matched books to avoid any balance sheet risk for themselves. But of course in periods of extreme volatility unwanted balance sheet inventories will occur once again, as for banks in the crisis. Just as we move to regulate banks in a better way we can now observe leverage, re-investment, maturity mismatch and re-hypothecation risk building up in this shadow banking intermediation process.

I worry that the growing business of shadow banking is not doing any country's people a favour, because it's compensating for the distortion of zero interest rates. The pension funds have made all these promises, which everyone's assuming will be kept. Bank and broker-dealer executives are not the ones who need to worry, because they have worked in the finance industry and accumulated a good "pot of gold". But the majority of people are not in this position, and they really depend on these promises being kept. The misallocation of resources always has real effects. And what we are seeing at the moment with zero interest rates and the preference of shareholders for buybacks is that the real investment and the productivity growth needed to make bonds and equities worth something in 50 years' time isn't happening.

Matthew: The regulators are attempting to introduce what they call through-the-cycle buffers and minimum margins, but of course that's been pushed back against, and I wonder why that is. Is it competition amongst the futures exchanges? Is it the way the futures exchanges can set their margining to draw on much shorter time periods, taking a lot more information from recent trading movements? Put another way, is the capital applied to broker-dealers and prime brokers and futures too low? Should we be allowing those agents to self-appraise their capital requirements?

Adrian: There are two issues here: the use of models to appraise bank capital needs and dealing with the problem of pro-cyclicality. The former issue goes back to before the crisis and the Basel II decision to allow banks to self-appraise their capital using their own risk models to determine risk-weighted assets and this has been carried over into Basel III. We at the OECD were the first to point that out at an RBA conference in 2008 and subsequently at multiple official meetings. The OECD received a lot of official flak for pushing this argument. But finally, about 18 months ago, the BCBS[6] did their own exercise where they sent out an identical portfolio to all the major banks and asked them how much capital they would need to support it. And guess what! They were all different with about a 300% difference between the lowest and the highest capital needed. Of course banks shouldn't be allowed to assess their capital needs, because the moral hazard is just enormous. As Sheila Bair[7] once said, it's like having a football match where all the players have a different rule book.

You know at BT we were pioneers in developing Value-at-Risk models. But as soon as you say: Well, that is great, you have done all this great work, so now why don't you use those risk frameworks to tell us how much capital you need to hold? As soon as you do that, you pollute the process. All CEOs want to manage their risk and look at it every day. But as soon as banks use the models to tell regulators what capital they will need to hold, the incentive to cheat gets mixed in. This results in games being played with the modelling and risk management process because it is a process that banks can influence and that directly affects a bank's return on equity.

The latter pro-cyclicality issue can be illustrated by the use of regulatory haircuts[8] with respect to collateral for credit. So when the markets go up, you have automatically room for more leverage as the value of the securities offered rises in value. But then of course when the markets go down, you find you are in exactly the opposite position, which is what tends to happen in a crisis. Suddenly you have to find more collateral to manage the haircut.

Frances: *This raises the argument that investors ultimately pay, as banks' increased costs are passed on to them.*

Adrian: So many times I have had bankers say to me: "you realise that this and that regulation is going to greatly increase the costs of doing derivatives businesses, and this is terrible." And I look at them and feel like giving the Homer Simpson response: "D'oh!" That is the whole point. If risk has been under-priced, then you want it precisely to be more expensive. The risks need to be priced correctly where the risks are being taken. If you are going to be writing CDS for banks so they can avoid capital rules, you had better be charging them a price that reflects what those risks really are. If you're not then you have a huge financial stability problem in the making.

There are very good reasons for having derivatives. In the "Main Street" world, derivatives are essential for numerous reasons. For example, the airlines need to hedge their fuelling costs, pension funds hedge volatility, shipbuilders are going to sell their ships in five years' time, so they need to be able to hedge the currency, so they can know what returns they are looking at when they're investing today. These are all good reasons for using derivatives. But why banks think morally that they need to do structured products to avoid taxes for clients or use the CDS markets and swaps to arbitrage regulations and other less-than-socially-useful activities is altogether another issue.

One statistic I like to quote is the share of the earnings of the financial sector in the S&P 500. In 1980 the share of the earnings of the financial sector, banks and insurance in the S&P 500 was something like 10%. By the time you got to the crisis it was over 30%. Now this is the sector that is supposed to be oiling the wheels of capitalism between real savers and real investors, who create jobs and economic growth all of which underpins the real value in bonds and equities. Should banks be taking one third of the earnings of the entire listed sector themselves? The US earnings share is now already back to what it was before the crisis, and Europe is following suit.

Frances: *Sounds like rent seeking.*

Adrian: It is rent seeking. GSIBs and their broker-dealers are essentially oligopolies. And the regulators have all sorts of rules and regulations that actually facilitate that. They are making the banks safer in some senses, but in others they are creating more concentration. For example, take some of the more detailed rules about derivatives, and capital rules.

The Basel system, because it is a system that has to be analytically tractable for regulators, is based on the principle of portfolio invariance, which is a linear additivity principle where the riskiness of an asset is idiosyncratic. So under that framework pillar 1 portfolio-wide concentration risk is not penalised (this is left up to supervisors in the pillar 2 aspect of Basel).

Netting rules for derivatives are another aspect of this problem. Cross-product netting is allowed for the CVA[9] charge for derivatives under the Basel system. The charge is based on netting pools with a bank's counterparty and the charge is then additive across netting pools. If you have a netting pool between two huge banks, you have a huge amount of scope for cross-product netting. But vis-à-vis smaller banks there is less scope for cross-product netting. So in this case regulation encourages concentration in the derivatives business.

Matthew: *What do the people at the BIS (Basel) say when you point that out to them? If you attempt to criticise their system, they get very defensive, they can't see anything other than their methodology.*

Adrian: I don't think they get defensive and claim they have a perfect system. I think what happens with regulators is a sort of fatigue plus all of the long processes. Even with good arguments it is like trying to change the direction of a big slow oil tanker. Their ability to change quickly and adapt is constrained.

With portfolio invariance the Basel system is like a medusa: everything can just be added on to it. If something moves and causes a problem in such-and-such a market, then there is a new Basel rule for it that can be added on.

The other mathematical principle on which the Basel system rests is the assumption of only one single global risk factor for the world banking system: essentially because the rules are supposed to fit all banks. That risk factor can only be the global macro cycle. The mathematics of the entire Basel system depends on the idea that, if there is a single risk factor affecting all banks, the global risk cycle, and for that risk the capital should be adequate. But if you have idiosyncratic risk, for example sub-prime securitisation in America, the Basel system has nothing to say about that. And of course they are the sort of issues we have all the time: something happens somewhere, some specific thing, and then, because all the banks are interconnected, suddenly it isn't the global macro cycle risk at all. It is an AIG–like specific problem that everyone is connected to.

Matthew: *So what about mark-to-market? Some people say that causes a problem due to the volatility of markets. You are in solvency one day and not the next.*

Adrian: Mark-to-market is an accounting concept. As a broad proposition, I would say that insurance companies, for example, in normal circumstances genuinely want to hold liabilities to their full maturity. To meet long-term liabilities they want to hold assets to term. So they like to buy say a 30-year bond and hold it for 30 years. I don't know why an insurance company or a pension fund doing that should be called insolvent and told they have got to de-risk in their first year of a 30-year bond because its price went down by 20%, when they intend to hold it for 30 years. What applies to banks under Basel III shouldn't apply to pension funds and insurance companies under Solvency II.

Mark-to-market is what should apply to bank assets that are in the "trading book", or which are "available for sale" and all trading in the repo and derivatives markets, so supervisors can follow what is happening to inventory on bank and broker–dealer balance sheets. Pension funds and insurance companies shouldn't necessarily have to be treated in the same way. Yet there is a caveat to this in the zero–interest–rate world: which is causing the institutional investors to take on new alternative (riskier) products.

Institutional investors moving into high risk securities to beat the low yields is a big issue that policy-makers are focusing on. Another is the worrying use of techniques reminiscent of bank behaviour prior to the crisis. There was a great article in the *NY Times* on 11 April 2015, by Mary Williams Walsh, about the business models of insurance companies. It is very interesting how you can find ways to give insurance reserves back to shareholders via the creative use of subsidiaries called "captives", owned by the parent, and entities without businesses issuing notes to insure the parent. It's an article definitely worth a read.

Matthew: *We are wondering if the system is too complex. If the managements don't understand it, how do you, as an independent observer, step back and point these things out?*

Adrian: Companies, both Main Street and Wall Street, don't perceive corporate governance as a problem; indeed quite the contrary. The board appointment process is problematic – independent directors are often not independent at all and are connected to the bank management in some way. Nor are directors required to meet tough standards of knowledge about accounting, the plumbing of the business and risk management. Running a safe transparent business will sometimes get in the way of making money for shareholders in the short term and of course management remuneration, the timing of buy-backs (executives hold options) and much more. The world deserves responsible business conduct at all levels, but we are currently very far from that at present. The mentality of bank management today is "it's time to stop bashing the banks". The claim is that regulators and policy analysts don't understand the complex business and their actions are holding up economic growth. Arguments are even being made that banks should be allowed to regulate themselves. Imagine.

One of the advantages that I have had in my job in the OECD has been that I worked as a fund manager for a long time but now work on the policy side. They don't like to engage with people who have been insiders, but rather focus on politicians who are more easily impressed with arguments about complexity and the need to let banks get on with it.

When I was a panellist at an interesting conference in Stanford a few years ago, one of the questions I got from the floor was: "So Adrian, how do you handle the following problem: there is a guy at the Fed who is earning $100,000 a year and is supervising a guy in the financial markets who is getting $10 million a year? How does he or she do that?" That is a regulatory capture problem, because if that Fed guy tries to push hard against bank interests he will be blacklisted. He won't be able to do what people like to do, which is "to go for the gold" after their years in the regulatory

institution. He will want to have his turn to make the $10 million
a year too. So people don't do it. Regulatory capture takes on
different forms all over the world, related to the very
different financial systems and business cultures in
operation.

Frances: *Apart from future job prospects, what other factors affect "capture"
in the relationships of organisations with regulators?*

Adrian: The moral hazard issue goes right through the system. The
big problem is that the system has become so complex that even
talented regulators have trouble dealing with it. If the central bank
has 300 people working on regulation for all banks, one single
large bank can bring huge resources of qualified and more
highly-paid people working on all of the issues that concern them.
When a regulator comes to see them the bank can whip up a
snow storm. The rocket scientists are wheeled out and supervisors
don't know the right questions to ask and places to look in the
granular details where problems reside. At the political level the
CEO can say: If you do this regulatory change you will hurt our
business and the economy terribly. You don't know all the
complexity and competition we are dealing with. Be very careful!
It is like the TV series *Yes Minister*. The politician pulls back. That
kind of thing goes on all the time. In Europe there is a feeling of
the need to support national champions against the evil of unfair
competition from America where banks are (claimed to be) less
regulated. The amount of money that gets thrown at lobbying in
some part of the world with professional lobbyists and donations
to political campaigns can be another form. The point is there are
lots of reasons for capture and it is quite pervasive.

At this point in time, the banks take the view that the crisis is
ancient history. It is time to move on. And this is getting a
sympathetic ear in business and politics, if not with the ordinary
person that bore the costs of the crisis.

Frances: *Do you think all of this has affected trust in the financial system?*

Adrian: I think so. I don't know if you read *Flash Boys: A Wall Street
Revolt* by Michael Lewis.[10] It is one of the most useful books to
read, because it gives you a very good insight into what goes on in
markets. The topic in the book is about algorithmic
high-frequency trading and the problems that this is causing for

the market. When the UK did a big inquiry into high-frequency trading in Britain a few years ago, I was on the academic board of the inquiry. Of course this was before Michael Lewis's book. Through speed alone and the complicity of broker–dealer banks in providing proximity to electronic stock exchanges that receive commissions, trading became a source of taking value out of bid-ask spreads by false expressions of interest, cancelled trades, and jumping queues when trades that would happen anyway are taken over and value in the spread extracted for the high-frequency trader. What is very clear is that trust in the financial system and in the equity markets in particular has really plummeted.

Another book really worth reading is Liaquat Ahamed's *Lords of Finance*,[11] which is about central bank policy in the Gold Standard days. For me what is happening in Europe today is very much related to the subject matter of *Lords of Finance*.

When you have a single currency you have your own special brand of problems.

Frances: *Unifying the currency in America wasn't altogether that straightforward either. Certainly, it was a much smaller economy when it was established, but still wasn't a given. And currency unions have been tried in Europe before. This is not the first.*

Adrian: There was a lot of misinformation about the euro from the outset; that somehow being in a currency union would cause economic convergence. There was a currency union between the United Kingdom and Ireland between 1820 and 1920. For 100 years Ireland used the pound sterling as its currency; and that was when Britain was the America of the day. During that period, the British population doubled and British GDP rose 600%. In that same 100 years, the Irish population fell by 40% and Irish GDP barely grew. A currency union doesn't bring about convergence. It is more likely to bring about divergence, if the fundamentals of a currency union are not in place. When countries are subject to asymmetric real shocks like the industrialisation of Great Britain in the case of Ireland or the current industrialisation in China and other emerging markets, then either you have a fiscal union, so rich areas can compensate poor areas, or you have the exchange rate as a shock absorber. Unfortunately, taxpayers in the richer countries of Europe are not willing to see those taxes used to support the unemployment insurance of the poorer countries, as happens automatically in America or Britain. England has a workable currency union with Wales and Scotland because the fiscal union allows transfer to poorer regions. Europe is doing sensible things such as the banking union and plans for a capital markets union. But it is difficult to regulate all that into being if you do not have the same bankruptcy laws, tax laws, corporate laws, labour market laws, bribery and corruption enforcement, market trading regulations and the like.

Frances: *Iceland?*

Adrian: Iceland got out of it by reneging on deposit insurance. They didn't have any choice.

Frances: *With the algorithmic trading, do you think the transaction tax being proposed will help, or will it be introducing more problems?*

Adrian: Transactions taxes can't target algorithmic trading without hitting everything else – there are other solutions for that issue better targeted on stock exchange mechanics. In general I think transaction taxes on securities that trade on liquid exchanges is a weak idea; it just reduces liquidity and causes problems. However, where you have markets that are by their nature illiquid, such as the OTC derivatives market, I don't see any reason why you shouldn't impose a tax on the notional values. For one thing, it would encourage them to move securities onto exchanges. OTC securities aren't liquid instruments anyway and so a tax would have no negative effects on liquidity. It would be a useful source of building up an insurance fund so that taxpayers do not have to foot the bill in future crises.

Disclaimer: The opinions expressed and arguments employed herein are solely those of the author and do not necessarily reflect the official views of the OECD or of its member countries.

Notes

1   Olev Rahn, BEc, ASIA served as a Director of Constellation Capital Management Limited since 2003, and a founding Director of Bentley International Limited, then known as BT Global Asset Management

Limited and is a Member of Advisory Board at Business Spectator Pty Ltd (Bloomberg.com).

2   My daughter died and as a consequence I set up the Anika Foundation, information about which can be found at www.anikafoundation.com.

3   Insured deposit banking, refers to taking deposits that are explicitly or implicitly guaranteed, retaining a capital buffer and on the asset side lending to small and medium-size businesses and to households.

4   Repurchase agreement, whereby a bond is sold with a contract to repurchase it at a given date and price in the future. In effect, short-term borrowing.

5   Global Sytemically Important Banks.

6   Basel Committee on Banking Supervision.

7   President of Washington College from 1 August 2015, previously Chairperson of the US Federal Deposit Insurance Corporation (FDIC) from 2006 to 2011.

8   In finance, a haircut is the difference between the market value of an asset used as loan collateral and the amount of the loan. The amount of the haircut reflects the lender's perceived risk of loss from the asset falling in value or being sold in a fire sale. The lender will, however, still hold a lien for the entire value of the asset. In the event the collateral is sold to repay the loan, the lender will have a higher chance of being made whole. Expressed as a percentage of the collateral's market value, the haircut is the complement of the Loan-to-value ratio: together they equal 100% of the value.

9   Capital Value Adjustment is defined by the Basel Committee as the difference between the value of a derivative assuming the counterparty is default risk-free and the value of a derivative reflecting the default risk of the counterparty.

10   Lewis, M., *Flash Boys – A Wall Street Revolt* (New York: Norton, 2014).

11   Ahamed, L., *Lords of Finance: The Bankers who Broke the World* (New York: Penguin, 2009).

13 | Innovations

How many disasters have we had where Value at Risk was completely irrelevant?

John Breit

The global financial crisis furnished both the necessity and a means for a cluster of innovation in financial risk management. The necessity is that a lot of risk management failed during the financial crisis and we need to understand why and what needs to be done to make it work in future. The means is the rich source of data, which, together with increasingly powerful data analysis capabilities, has added scope to our thinking about risk and how it should be measured and managed.

This chapter reviews six new insights resulting from recent research and one that derives from earlier work that now benefits from modern computational power. They address six themes arising in our interviews, including:

- How to analyse risk appetite and risk tolerance for individual investors
- How to quantify risk appetite for an economy

- Why models seemed to fail
- How to quantify illiquidity
- Signals of market instability and
- Analysis of connectivity and contagion in the financial system.

How to analyse risk appetite and risk tolerance

> At present firms don't understand risk tolerance, sufficiently. The sort of structure we need is one where there is top-down allocation according to clear decision processes and maximum transparency.
>
> Carol Alexander

Supervisors are encouraging financial organisations to think about their risk appetite in a more analytic and structured way than they have done in the past.

Until now, the risk appetite of an organisation was treated at best as a matter of estimating how much risk was needed and could be tolerated in order to achieve given investment or business outcomes. New areas of research show that risk appetite and risk tolerance are in fact much more complex than would justify this relatively simple approach.

Kinked utility functions – idiosyncratic intolerance of loss

Work on kinked utility functions shows that individual investors' risk appetites and tolerances of losses respond in often complex ways to changes in the investors' circumstances and expectations.

Most investment selection processes assume that investors' appetites for risk can be described by a smooth, relatively simple function of the amount of wealth they have. But in practice most investors face thresholds whereby, if their portfolio depreciates by a certain amount, they may be in violation of some covenant, which in turn can cause a sharp increase in their risk aversion or otherwise cause abrupt changes in their appetite for risk. These are called kinked utility functions.

Adler and Kritzman[1] shows how full-scale optimisation[2] can help solve kinked utility functions and define portfolios that are suitable for investors with discrete thresholds in their risk appetites and tolerances. Full-scale optimisation looks not just at the moments[3] of the return distribution, but at every single observation within a given data sample, thereby taking into account every single feature of the data given any set of return distributions. This type of research is becoming ever more feasible with modern computing power: algorithms are now available that test half a million portfolios in a few seconds to identify the one that maximises this more realistic utility function.

First passage probabilities – risk during the investment path

Research based on first passage probabilities[4] demonstrates that the risk profile at the start and at the end of the investment period is only a small part of the overall risk story: often most of the risk comes from what happens in the meantime.

Investment organisations typically express investment risk as some outcome, or range of possible outcomes, at the end of a defined investment horizon, such as a year or 10 years, often ignoring what could happen in the interim. For example, a risk analysis might say that there is a 5% chance that, at the end of the 10-year period, a portfolio will have lost 10% or more. Yet there may be a 50% or 60% chance that somewhere along the way the portfolio will be down by that amount. And what happens within the 10-year period is important, especially if, during that time, an investor has reason to transact part of the portfolio and crystallise losses, for example because he needs to redeem some of it or because some threshold is breached.

Analysing investment paths can uncover sources of risk that are quite different from, and masked by, those given in the end of period profile. In fact, portfolios can be exposed to much more risk within the horizon than they are at the end. This happens because there are many possible paths within the horizon, some of which might breach a particular threshold and then recover.

How to quantify risk appetite for an economy

Fluctuations in risk appetites have a material effect on financial markets and the real economy: sudden declines in risk appetite are often cited as a contributor to contagion that leads to serial failures of financial organisations and spreads financial crises from one economy to another. Regulators and supervisors therefore have an interest in quantifying and tracking aggregate risk appetite over time. Yet most methods of estimating risk appetite are only partial solutions, measuring only either changes in aggregate risk appetite – without calibrating its level – or the level of risk appetite at a single investor type rather than capturing the whole distribution.

Work carried out by Prasanna Gai and Nicholas Vause at the Bank of England following the Asian crisis of 1997 sought to understand the reason for contagion from one emerging economy to the next that could not be explained by pure economic variables. It was attributed to a flight to the safety of developed markets associated with a general decline in risk appetite.

In their 2006 paper,[5] they describe the nature of risk appetite as a function of two factors: risk aversion, which they argue is relatively stable for individual investors; and perceived uncertainty in economic and market conditions, which of course fluctuates. Both factors can be estimated from readily available market data.

An approximation of collective risk aversion in the overall economy is given in discount rates, which in effect quantify the price that compensates for the uncertainty of delayed consumption. Extra information about changing investor risk preferences over time is given in sovereign yield curves.

Economic uncertainty is estimated as the ratio of the distribution of certainty equivalent outcomes to the distribution of subjective probabilities of expected payoffs. The certainty equivalent distribution is quantified using options of various strike prices on the VIX index, while the distribution of subjective probabilities of expected payoffs is derived using a GARCH model. By capturing, in each case, the whole distribution of perceived economic uncertainty, including higher moments that characterise asymmetric and fat-tailed distributions, they are able to derive a measure of perceived economic uncertainty for the overall economy.

Together, measures of risk aversion and estimates of economic uncertainty can give measures of collective risk appetite that can be tracked through time using easily observed information from frequently traded instruments.

The authors also show how this result can be used to estimate the risk premium embedded in asset prices. Just as risk appetite is a product of risk aversion and the economic and market environment, the risk premium can be estimated as a function of risk appetite and the riskiness of an asset or class of assets.

Why models seem to fail

I like to say that risk modelling is a great place to start but a terrible place to finish.

Sir Michael Hintze

It has been widely recognised for some time that some of the criticism aimed at risk models was more to do with how the models were calibrated and used, rather than the modelling itself.

A common failing was inappropriate sampling from past market data.

Recent research shows that ill-timed observations can capture risk that is irrelevant to the investment strategy or that masks risk that is critical to it. Giving thought to how often risk is measured and when observations are taken are two relatively simple adjustments to existing analyses that can materially improve the accuracy and practical usefulness of risk estimates.

Risk as a function of measurement frequency[6]

How often data are sampled determines how volatile assets and portfolios appear to be, how correlated pairs of assets and portfolios appear to be with each other, and therefore how useful the risk estimates are that are based on them.

It is common practice to estimate volatilities and correlations frequently, from, say, monthly – or even daily – returns and then use them
to analyse the risk of portfolios with much longer investment horizons
of, say, three, five or 10 years. This implicitly assumes, first, that correlations do not vary according to the return interval used to calculate
them, second, that returns are normally distributed and exhibit neither
autocorrelation nor serial correlation and, third, that volatility scales
at the square root of time.[7] But in practice all three assumptions are
flawed because of the tendency of markets to trend and to reverse. This
is why daily price fluctuations often net out over longer periods, such
as weeks or months.

A good example of this is the return of emerging market equities
and the US stock market measured monthly for the 20-year period
starting in about the mid-1990s, which were both about 9.5% annualised, with a correlation of about 70%. Intuitively, this would suggest
that the returns for the two assets followed similar paths. Yet there was
one three-year period where the return to US stocks exceeded that of
emerging market stocks cumulatively by 60% and another three-year
period where the returns to emerging market stocks exceeded that of
US stocks cumulatively by 130%. This happens because, although the
correlation of their monthly returns is 70%, the correlation of their
annual returns is only 40%, and the correlation of their three-year
returns is 0%.

The main implication for risk estimation is that how frequently data
are observed should be consistent with the investment objectives of the
portfolios concerned. For example, relatively infrequent observations
are relevant to long-term investors, while frequent, such as daily, observations are necessary for investors, such as banks, investment banks and
some hedge funds, who adjust their holdings frequently.

The reference day effect – risk as a function of measurement timing

The reference day effect is the distortion of risk estimates that results
when data are sampled only at the end of each period. Correcting for
this distortion can materially improve risk forecasts for medium and
long-term investors.

It is common practice to measure investment risk using data samples based on end of week or end of month prices. Daniella Acker and Nigel Duck[8] asked what would be the effect of using prices on, say, a mid-month trading day instead of the closing price on the last trading day of the month. The resulting risk estimates turned out to be significantly different, as they report in their 2006 paper.[9] This happens because end of period trading often differs from mid period activity as many derivatives positions are closed out at the same time, and as some market participants rebalance their portfolios ready for end of period reporting and valuation – often reversing the transactions at the start of the following period.

For this reason, some argue that, in order to avoid this distortion, risk should be estimated from observations taken from any point other than the end of the period. Supporting this view, risk estimation techniques that correct for the reference day effect have been shown to give more valid risk forecasts than those that do not make the correction.

How to quantify illiquidity

Many people observe that financial crises often begin with a crisis of liquidity, which, if poorly managed, can become a solvency crisis. According to Richard Meddings, "A failure to understand illiquidity … tends to be the biggest risk that people need to worry about." But measuring liquidity is surprisingly difficult to do, and the shortcomings of the currently accepted method are widely recognised. As Todd Groome has mentioned, "Liquidity is important but how to measure liquidity is really complex." Yet it is important to measure it meaningfully because, as Todd explains, "If you don't have proper liquidity, VaR can be quite misleading, and in the credit world a lot of assets or instruments have infrequent, inconsistent liquidity."

Holding illiquid investment instruments bears a cost: buying and selling them can be slow and the price realised can be worse than the price at which they had been valued. To compensate for this cost, investors demand that illiquid instruments deliver either higher return for a given level of risk, or lower risk for a given level of return, collectively known as the liquidity premium.

The accepted methodology for estimating liquidity for an investment portfolio is to analyse recent trading activity in each instrument held in order to gauge how easily it could be liquidated in the event that it were necessary to do so. From this, a liquidity score, say, on a scale of one to five, can be assigned to each instrument. This method has two flaws. The first is that trading activity tends to be sampled from stable market conditions, whereas illiquidity is of most concern when positions must be closed in a hurry, which is most likely when markets are stressed or turbulent. The second flaw is that recent trading activity may be atypical if it is distorted by one or two large transactions, or because some trading activity in the instrument takes place off market.

Because of these flaws, the cost of liquidity for any position cannot be known in advance, and is difficult to estimate with any confidence, which means that liquidity cannot be expressed in terms of either return or risk. What is needed is a way to quantify the liquidity premium in order to map liquidity onto return and risk so that it can be objectively taken into account in a portfolio.

Kinlaw and Kritzman[10] propose an innovative and robust method of estimating the liquidity premium that both compensates investors for the cost of holding illiquid investments in their portfolios and overcomes the shortcomings of existing best practice.

Their solution is to integrate liquidity into the portfolio selection process by treating illiquidity as a shadow asset or a shadow liability, whereby the expected return or cost reflects the portfolio level return-risk premium that the investor demands for holding part of his portfolio in illiquid instruments. Where the investor holds illiquid instruments out of choice, for example in order to earn a liquidity premium, illiquidity would be represented as a shadow asset. If, on the other hand, the illiquid positions are held out of necessity rather than choice, illiquidity would be modelled as a shadow liability.

Signals of market instability

Bubbles are functions of unchangeable human nature. The obvious question is how to manage them.[11] The other obvious question is how to know when market bubbles are about to burst.

Risk modelling methodologies adapted to measure risk in stable market conditions often fall short when markets are stressed. They have been criticised for underestimating both the likelihood of an extreme event and the scale of the extreme event when it happens.

The likelihood of an extreme event is underestimated because most risk modelling techniques use data sampled from recent periods, which are mostly stable. Data samples thus rarely include a shock. Add to this the fact that many crises are preceded by a period of abnormal calm, and the underestimation can be greater still. The most intuitive solution, which is to include longer return histories in the sample data, introduces other, often less tractable problems, such as structural changes in the composition of markets (think of how the wave of privatisations in the early 1990s and the dotcom boom of the late 1990s changed the shape of investment opportunities) and stock survivorship bias,[12] which render much data irrelevant and bias risk forecasts.

Risk models understate the severity of shocks because they assume that correlations between assets and risk factors are more or less stable, and that the returns in consecutive periods are unrelated to each other. They also often assume that markets are always liquid. These assumptions are violated in extreme or turbulent market conditions, as normal trading patterns are disrupted.

- Correlations between assets change, sometimes dramatically: "diversification fails just when you need it", as investors sell both cheap and fairly priced assets to meet redemptions and other short-term demands.
- Sequential returns can become correlated: extreme markets can trend sharply down, as margin lending and dynamic hedging provisions are triggered. They can also reverse sharply as long-term investors perceive they have overshot their fair price and step in to take advantage of bargains on offer.
- Liquidity dries up unpredictably.

The logical, and usual, response is to conduct comprehensive risk analyses with profiles for both stable and stressed, or turbulent, market conditions. This then raises the question of how much importance to give each profile for the purpose of risk positioning and hedging strategies. What is needed is some way of predicting the likelihood of imminent market turbulence or instability, or at least to recognise it in its very early stages.

Plenty of research has aimed at devising reliable signal mechanisms that take into account not just the sequence of recent returns, but also changes in return volatilities and correlations between asset prices and risk factors, two of which are reviewed here.

Financial rogue waves

Insights made possible using satellite technology show that rogue waves, which cause maritime tragedy from time to time, are not entirely random.[13] Steve Ohana saw parallels with crises in financial markets and asked if similar mechanisms could be at work.

His work draws on Systems Theory, which says that, in nature and elsewhere, processes can be either self-correcting or self-perpetuating. An example of a self-correcting process is spontaneous bush fires, which clear away old growth, make way for new plants to flourish and reduce the likelihood of a very big fire. Similarly, excess profit in a market segment attracts competitors whose effect is to push prices down until the sector's profit approximately compensates its financing costs. These self-correcting processes are also known as negative feedback systems. But some feedback systems are positive, including rogue waves, where a small imbalance causes a wave to grow bigger than those about it. As it does so, it sucks in water from neighbouring waves, becoming bigger still, until it collapses under its own weight.

This research shows that financial rogue waves, while not necessarily preventable, can be observed and possibly modelled from observable concentrations of risk factor exposures to signal a build-up in market imbalances. Analysis of the evolution of risk concentrations and factor exposures can be used to give early signals of market stress.

Mahalanobis Distance as a signal of market instability

Managers typically rely on measures of the skew and kurtosis of return distributions to estimate how stable or otherwise asset returns are. But these measures are limited by the fact that they can indicate market instability only when it has already happened.

Work carried out by Prasanta Chandra Mahalanobis[14] in the early 20th century, which sought to determine whether or not two separate groups of human skulls were from the same race as each other, derived the Mahalanobis Distance as a measure of statistical separation that takes into account both dispersion and correlations within the two groups of skulls.

Kritzman and Yanzhen[15] show how this can be applied to financial markets, to give a measure of how unusual recent asset returns are compared to returns to the same assets over a longer period that is known to be stable. From this it can indicate how atypical the recent period is for those assets. Returns from one period can be thought of as unusual relative to returns from another if:

1. There is an extreme price move that is very different from what the average volatility for a particular asset implies;
2. There is decoupling of two assets that are normally highly correlated; or
3. There is convergence of assets that typically are uncorrelated.

The Mahalanobis Distance distils information about both the unusual returns of individual assets for any given period and unusual interactions between asset returns to give a single indicator of whether market imbalances may be building up that might herald market turbulence.

Analysis of connectivity and contagion

Systemic risk due to contagion in the financial system is a primary concern for regulators and supervisors. Todd Groome makes the point that "[t]he ability of a financial system to weather a severe shock depends, among other things, on how closely connected the institutions that make it up are, as well as how vulnerable or robust the most connected institutions are".

The financial system comprises a network of banks, insurers, investment banks, pension funds and hedge funds, with the central bank trying to map all the connections between them. The puzzle with financial system complexity and connectedness is that neither the connections nor the nodes that make the connections are known with certainty.

It is as if, in visualising, say, the London Underground,[16] all the lines are known, but not the significance of all the stations. For example, it is not known that Wimbledon South, which is on only one line, is not as important as Oxford Circus, which is the junction of several lines. Similarly, the map of what is thought of as the financial system is incomplete, and in fact is much bigger than it seems. The system is also evolving continuously.

When Lehmans failed in 2008 it was widely assumed to be peripheral (Wimbledon South, in the Underground analogy) because central bankers underestimated the systemic importance of hedge fund prime brokers. But because Lehmans was one of the five major global prime brokers, it was in fact a huge artery, more resembling Oxford Circus.

Following the crisis the G20 gave the Financial Stability Board the task of identifying and measuring the most systemically important global financial institutions. The intuitively appealing approach to this is to use fundamental analysis of individual financial institutions to identify the balance sheet connections, exposures, contracts and so on between them. This is difficult, and possibly unrealistic to do in practice because things like private transactions and securitisation obscure many connections. This was made worse by the scale and complexity of open contracts, for example Lehman is thought to have had over a million derivatives on its books when it failed.

Because modelling the connectedness of financial organisations using this kind of analysis is both time consuming and prone to misestimation, it can be carried out only infrequently. But regulators and supervisors really need a quick and cost-efficient way of carrying out frequent analyses of how closely integrated the financial system is and which organisations are most central to it, so they can understand how connectedness varies over time and spot potential flashpoints before they become a problem. Recent research[17] finds that this can be achieved using the absorption ratio, which is a quick and cost-efficient measure of connectivity in the financial system and of the organisations that make it up.

The absorption ratio draws on the fact that connectedness can be inferred statistically from the behaviour of security prices. To do this, principal components analysis (PCA) is used to identify all the factors that explain the variability of returns to individual financial sector securities. From this, the absorption ratio gives the fraction of return variability that is captured by, say, the ten most important factors identified in the PCA. A high absorption ratio suggests that the system is very connected, which means that shocks travel very quickly and very broadly. A low absorption ratio indicates that these few factors explain only a small fraction of variability of returns, which means that risk is distributed broadly throughout the system. When it is diffused that way, markets are much more resilient to shocks.

The absorption ratio can also be extended to identify how systemically important a particular entity is. Three conditions are given for systemic importance:

1. Vulnerability to failure, because if the entity is not going to fail it presents little risk;
2. Connections to other entities in the system, because even if it is going to fail, if it's not connected, it is not systemically important;
3. Connections to other entities that are themselves risky, because if it is connected only to safe companies and institutions, then again it presents little risk to the system.

Not only does this method allow connectedness to be estimated quickly, cheaply and frequently, the measure it gives is more robust than those given by earlier methods. In the past, average correlation was used as a measure of how diffused or compact markets were. But average correlations do not distinguish between systemically important assets and systemically unimportant assets. For example, an increase in the correlation between low-volatility assets is unimportant; but an increase in correlation between high-volatility assets is much more important. Because the absorption ratio is based on the covariance matrix, it takes into account volatility as well as correlation, which means it recognises precisely the relative importance of all the assets.

It is thus a much more reliable signal than the average correlation; in fact, the absorption ratio and the average correlation often move in opposite directions.

Notes

1 Adler, T. and Kritzman, M., Mean-variance versus Full-scale Optimisation: In and Out of Sample. *Journal of Asset Management* (2007) 7(5): 302–311.

2 A term introduced by Paul Samuelson, also known as direct numerical maximisation of utility.

3 For example, average, standard deviation, skew and kurtosis.

4 Kritzman, M., Risk Disparity, *MIT Sloan School Working Paper* 5001-13, 2013.

5 Gai, P. and Vause, N., Bank of England Measuring Investors' Risk Appetite, *International Journal of Central Banking* (2006) 2(1): 167–188.

6 Kinlaw, W.B., Kritzman, M. and Turkington, D., The Divergence of High- and Low-Frequency Estimation: Causes and Consequences, *Journal of Portfolio Management* (2014) Fortieth Year Special Anniversary Issue.

7 For example, estimates of monthly return volatility are annualised by multiplying by the square root of 12.

8 Acker, D. and Duck, N., Reference-day Risk and the Use of Monthly Returns Data: A Warning Note. University of Bristol, Department of Economics, Discussion Paper No 04/557. April 2006.

9 Ibid.

10 Kinlaw, W.B., Kritzman, M. and Turkington, D., Liquidity and Portfolio Choice – A Unified Approach, *MIT Sloan School Working Paper* 4959-12, 2012.

11 Alan Greenspan, in an interview with *Market Watch*, 27 July 2014, www.marketwatch.com.

12 Data relating to failed or otherwise discontinued assets are excluded from the sample.

13 Ohana, S., Financial Rogue Waves, Presentation to CFA UK, November 2010.

14 1893–1972 An Indian scientist and applied statistician who also conducted pioneering studies in anthropometry, founded the Indian Statistical Institute and contributed to the design of large-scale sample surveys.

15 Kritzman, M. and Yanzhen, L., Skulls, Financial Turbulence and Risk Management, *Financial Analysts' Journal* (2010) 66(5): 30–41.
16 For this analogy, thanks to Gerald Ashley of St Mawgan & Co.
17 Kritzman, M., Yanzhen, L., Page, S. and Rigobon, R., Principal Components as a Measure of Systemic Risk, *Journal of Portfolio Management* (2011) 37(4): 112.

14

Interpretation

Directors of financial enterprises and readers in other important stewardship roles will draw their own conclusions from these conversations. The key seems to be to use information from risk analyses only as a starting point, according a healthy dose of scepticism to the reported numbers, which often emanate from inflexible machinery, a diminished view of through the cycle exposure and an expectation of normal liquidity in all market environments.

Simple questions add to understanding: What short cuts are being taking to get all the work done? Is the risk department itself undergoing personnel changes – planned or unplanned? Does the revenue budget in the trading room encourage excessive risk taking by, for example, embedding expectations carried over from windfall events of the previous year? Special attention should be given to new and rapidly growing activities, which are often predicated on untested assumptions about asset price behaviour. All suggested that directors need to spend more time challenging management perceptions of risk and that the model of the specialist risk director may see those directors called to longer engagements with each firm they steward and an increase in compensation to reflect the necessary demands on their time.

What struck us as we talked with all the interviewees was a common belief that for all the good work undertaken by regulators during and since the financial crisis there was an expectation that such a dislocation would occur again. Why do all hold this expectation while still managing risk much as before? Even now each interviewee can pinpoint activities that raise their antennae to excessive risk. These activities are not being reformed quickly enough or are subject to resistance by dominant participants.

Opportunity wasted?

The financial crisis provided an opportunity to bring up to date supervision and regulation in the global financial system, to streamline, coordinate and reinforce the pre-crisis confection of ad-hoc rules and guidelines. The opportunity was to clean up rules that no longer served their original purpose, remove contradictions and inconsistencies in legacy regulations and plug loopholes that allow controls to be circumvented. Importantly, gaps could be filled that had appeared in the course of continuous evolution of a complex financial system as it responded to the needs of global commerce and cross-border investment, fuelled by new technology in communications and information processing.

Failure of regulation

The crisis of 2007–08 showed up a broken system misunderstood by bankers and regulators alike. Despite thoughtful regulation, the financial system had developed a scale and complexity that belied unrealistic assumptions about the power of globalisation. In particular, the capacity of home governments to support their legal entities was overestimated. Settlement of cross-border margins and collateral calls was nowhere near as fluid as had been supposed, as the netting of exposures between derivative houses – designed to reduce counterparty exposures – were disrupted when key operators in the network collapsed, in turn exposing the lack of capacity of the payments system to cope with the impairment of principal agents, such as the global banks.

The comparison is, in some ways, not entirely fair,[1] but were the standards of regulation that govern the financial system applied to, say, aviation or food processing, few people would be as relaxed as they are about flying, and more people would find ways to grow and prepare their own food.

Politicians have taken steps to correct perceived failures that made the crisis worse, and plenty of well-conceived new regulation has been effected. In addition to the public recapitalisation of financial institutions and ongoing pump priming via quantitative easing programmes, reforms continue to be sought amongst the international community to strengthen the system. The quest for a better, more stable system has seen a seemingly permanent expansion in what gets measured, what gets stress tested and how much capital is required in the supervised system to support its activities. But most would agree that managing a crisis of this scale quickly goes beyond the skilled deliberations of a single entity, and although their first instinct is to prevent catastrophes, regulators arguably are at their best solving problems rather than preventing them.[2]

Many contend that the crisis could not have been foreseen. This is contestable. For example, the Financial Crisis Inquiry Commission, reporting in 2010,[3] found that the crisis was completely avoidable. While on nowhere near the same scale, similar problems with CDOs had occurred in 2001, when technology companies were particularly implicated.

Some say that the public retribution sheeted home to bankers in the aftermath is somewhat unfair. But the crisis shone a spotlight on behaviour and governance in financial organisations, revealing a culture that seemed at best to turn a blind eye to some dubious practices. There seemed to be operating a wilful negligence in addressing issues that should have been obvious – too often motivated by the quest to extract as much rent as possible, with little regard for the broader consequences. Sir Michael Hintze makes the point: "… people who were very happy to keep dancing as long as the music was playing. They may have known about it but didn't give a monkey's."

This culture was exemplified by the sale, to relatively unsophisticated investors, of complex and opaque structured products, which often turned out to be much more risky than they had been represented to be. Financial organisations were accused of enriching themselves at the expense of investors by deliberately mis-selling overly complex and risky financial products.

On closer inspection, what appears to be about traders' incentives and governance within banks can be decomposed into three issues: the design of the products, their origination and the behaviour of traders who sold them.

Organisations designed products to meet investor demand for yield in a low interest rate environment. Investors, such as maturing pension funds, sought income to pay retirees' pensions, while other organisations, including schools and hospitals, sought yield to fund shortfalls in budgets that had embedded unrealistic investment return assumptions. With prevailing interest rates at historic lows, this demand could be met only by investing in high risk assets, including sub-prime mortgages.

But organisations like pension funds, schools and hospitals are often constrained to invest only in relatively safe assets. Structured products promised lower overall risk by bundling together large numbers of high risk, relatively uncorrelated individual assets. The problem was that the individual assets turned out not to be uncorrelated.

In originating the products, the problem of understated correlations between assets was aggravated by how individual assets were selected, which was primarily for their yield, often without due consideration of their risk characteristics. The products' complexity and lack of transparency meant that the assets' quality was not properly scrutinised, so those that were sold were often much riskier than had been supposed, as Sir Michael Hintze observes: "… they held things that they thought were AAA-rated, but they were effectively CCC. In fact they were D: they were default."

Many traders who sold the products took the opportunity to exploit their complexity and opacity to earn excessively high fees. In the interests of maximising revenue, many organisations seemed to wink at behaviour that was clearly unacceptable. At the same time, investors often were less diligent in questioning the risk characteristics of their investments than one might have expected. Sir Michael Hintze draws our attention to "mis-buying" by investors.

The example of structured products illustrates the inherent contradiction of demand for high yield in a low yield environment, and demonstrates problems brought about by a combination of market pressure, the motivation for organisations to satisfy investor demand, model mis-calibration and misuse, questionable trading and sales practices and inadequate governance. All of which contributed to often spectacular risk management failure, and amplifies the responsibility of financial organisations to monitor and scrutinise what their employees are up to.

Pressure is inevitably felt by politicians and regulators, who need to be seen to be taking all reasonable steps to prevent or avoid another crisis. This plays to the agendas of politicians, who find it easy to sound apocalyptic warnings about the consequences of whatever is their *bête noire*, and propose either more intensive or more extensive regulation – or indeed watering down of existing or proposed rules. Todd Groome talks about the intrusion of political agendas and Sir Michael Hintze recalls that "… Michel Barnier in effect said in a public forum that it was a political matter, a political issue". The result is sometimes regulations that have popular or political appeal but can be ineffectual or even counterproductive in practice.

The result is plenty of new regulation, much of it constructive and well conceived, but much of it less well thought-through, leaving plenty of scope for paradoxical outcomes and unintended consequences. They are now driving the financial markets agenda.

What has been done so far and how useful is it?

The urgency of risk management and governance is central to why regulators are insisting that risk management be pushed up the agenda, starting with the elevation of the risk management function within financial organisations. The European Systemic Risk Board recommended in February 2009: "Senior risk officers should hold a very high rank in the company hierarchy …",[4] while the IIF reported in December 2009: "Risk functions now have greater influence on firm operations and business decisions."[5]

Raising the risk manager's profile begs the following questions: What exactly is the risk manager's job, what skills and personal qualities are needed, and what conditions favour effective risk management?

We learn that, among other things, the risk manager needs not only an exceptional mix of skills and experience to counter-balance the power of profit-generating risk takers, but also the personal qualities to do so. Hollywood would doubtless cast Humphrey Bogart in the role. But why would Mr Bogart not opt to become a hedge fund manager instead?

Yet talented people do take the job and they nearly all agree that the best way to do it is to engage with risk takers in order genuinely to understand what they are doing and why. Sophisticated models and detailed risk reports are essential tools, but by themselves are no substitute for constructive and regular dialogue between risk manager and risk taker. Only when the risk manager understands enough about the fundamentals of the investments themselves to be able to apply the right reasonableness checks, are models useful. Without that understanding, complex models can be another source of risk.

Managers and traders, who use models for day-to-day risk taking activities, often do not really understand all the assumptions that are embedded in them, can easily calibrate them inappropriately and subject them to too few reasonableness checks. This means that the risk profiles they generate are sometimes misinterpreted, and data or computational errors can go unnoticed. A related problem is that few people, especially at senior levels in the organisation, understand valuation and risk models well enough to make informed governance decisions, as Richard Meddings notes: "… there are probably not enough managers at senior levels who understand how the financial market product or an array of such products might behave under stress."

Model complexity compounds the problem of lack of transparency in things like structured products, which makes managing systemic risk virtually impossible. Initiatives, such as to remove some opacity by encouraging derivatives to be registered on exchanges, are important steps to help regulators and supervisors keep tabs on concentrations of risk exposures, so go a long way to making complex systems more tractable. They also benefit investors directly by allowing them to build bespoke risk hedges using relatively simple and transparent instruments.

Watering down

But some useful reforms have been watered down by political bargaining to the point of emasculation and, in some cases, will actually add to the fragility of the financial system and worsen the next financial crisis when it happens.

Amendments to the swaps push-out rule under Dodd-Frank, for example, have the potential materially to relax limitations on the swap activities that can be undertaken by swap dealer banks within their federally assisted banking entity, thereby potentially increasing taxpayers' liabilities in the event of failure of the organisation.

The burden of rules

New regulation tends to impose ever more fixed rules on organisations. This has superficial appeal but less appealing side-effects. Rules are often more intuitive than "light touch", principles-based regulation, and so are easier to communicate to voters. But, as Hugo Bänziger puts it: "… whether we really need a regulatory rulebook with more than 10,000 pages (Dodd-Frank), I wonder." Regulations comprising hundreds or thousands of rules can be counterproductive, and in the extreme, can lead to Enron-type collapses, where the letter but not the intent of the rules is respected. According to John Breit: "These days, in the official (risk management) function you spend your life running a post office." This is hard to square with the Humphrey Bogart image of the pragmatic, savvy risk manager who keeps digging until he knows what is really going on. Many would agree with Richard Meddings that "[i]ncreasingly, institutions are managing to the regulations and not to the actual risk". Unintended consequences that defeat the primary purpose of regulation can become a feature of the financial and economic landscape.

Paradoxical and counterproductive

The increasing cost of complying with numerous complex and often contradictory rules punishes small and medium firms and adds to barriers to entry for new firms – arguably those that are potentially the most innovative and likely to challenge established norms. Not only does this do nothing constructive to manage risk, it also hurts investors by reducing competition between financial organisations, thus increasing costs and reducing investor choice. Sir Michael Hintze makes the point: "It is far from clear to me that the system is safer for all the regulation. It has created a barrier to entry for smaller start-ups. That may be good for some incumbents but not for business formation."

Some intuitively appealing, and arguably necessary, new regulation can have the effect of impeding economic activity. Most bankers would contend that forcing banks to hold more capital and liquid assets necessarily reduces their ability to lend. And ring-fencing the foreign country operations of global banks can lead to mis-allocation of resources. As *The Economist* contended in November 2013: "Balkanising (big wholesale investment banks) would hinder capital from moving to where it could be put to the most efficient – and lucrative – use. It would also distort competition by forcing international banks to hold far more capital in aggregate than their domestic counterparts."[6]

Worse, some new regulations are likely to render the financial system more fragile, not less. For example, the Basel guidelines for banks' regulatory capital requirements can have the paradoxical effect of rewarding risk concentrations. This is because the Basel protocol falls into the trap of thinking of risks as additive, ignoring the fact that similar risk exposures compound when held in the same portfolio. Together with the tiered nature of capital required, this encourages concentrations of risk – the opposite of risk diversification.

Also hard to understand is why the rules governing how derivatives positions can be netted for reporting purposes effectively allow understating of organisations' exposures to derivatives through the permitted use of netting pools, with the scale of the distortion increasing with the size of the netting pool.

As the burden and complexity of regulations increases progressively, it can reach the point where it actually impedes practical governance of financial organisations. Richard Meddings in particular draws attention to the confusion arising from different interpretations of core equity for bank regulatory capital purposes.

Could go either way

New to the regulatory agenda – and untested – is risk culture, which is generally understood to be about risk awareness throughout the organisation. But if a primary motivation for risk-taking behaviour is the inherent contradiction of demand for high yield products in a low yield economic environment, it could be argued that risk culture really extends beyond financial organisations, to regulators, investors and policy-makers. Managing the risk culture of financial organisations would, in this sense, be addressing only one of many of its facets.

It also begs other questions, such as: To what extent can risk culture, even within a financial organisation, be mandated? Should regulators be leading the charge? How much responsibility should shareholders and customers apply to encourage organisations to pay more attention to their risk culture? And if it is left to the regulators, does risk culture become, for financial organisations, just another regulatory burden?

Despite these concerted efforts, plenty of issues remain unresolved, and resolving them will inevitably take time. Richard Meddings warns: "… it didn't put the fire out completely. It is going to be a long fix, this."

It will also demand more coordination and planning. A worrying aspect of the reform agenda to date is its piecemeal and somewhat ad-hoc nature. Richard Meddings laments the lack of a coherent "design" to coordinate the regulatory agenda. In view of the watering down, lack of proper analysis of unintended consequences and sheer scale and complexity, it is now time to take stock of what is likely to work and what realistically can be achieved.

Time to reflect on theoretical underpinnings

A quick tour of established theories of regulation helps to understand why the current response to the financial crisis seems to be missing its point.

In 1974, Posner[7] observed that the costs of designing and agreeing regulation of a system, and then of enforcing it, increases with the complexity of the system. He also noted that even the loftiest intent of regulators can be thwarted if the task facing them is intractable.

Allen and Carletti[8] build on this in 2010, saying that, for regulation to be most effective, it must begin with a sound theoretical framework, together with a clear understanding of what it seeks to achieve, and what the potential costs of agreeing the regulation, implementing it and complying with it will be. It also needs considerable consultation with representatives of affected groups in order to understand likely and possible unintended consequences.

Efforts to present a properly thought-through regulatory design to sustain economic efficiency and fairness have been impeded by the combined effects of politicians' conflicting demands, such as short political horizons, the motivation to advance pet projects and the need to communicate simplified "solutions" to their voters. Politicians are also susceptible to the efforts of well-financed lobbyists, while regulators, for their part, often seek to avoid blame and encourage box-ticking. John Breit is frank about this: "The cynic in me thinks that ever since Barings, the regulators have realised they can't really stop financial institutions from losing tons of money, but they can stop themselves for being blamed for it."

More fundamentally, the regulatory methodologies now applied to Western financial systems are additive, in that each perceived failure leads to more intensive supervision. Yet capital controls intended to shore up resilience to adverse macro-economic events do not discourage concentrations of risk within bank balance sheets. Pro-cyclicality, introduced into the system by allowing all assets in a class to be marked to a simple closing price reference point irrespective of the size of position held or the investment objectives they are intended to meet, seems a convenience that does not reflect the reality of investment managers governed by specific investment mandates. Notwithstanding the good work undertaken by the various financial stability initiatives, concentration issues built up in netting regimes or within the payment system seem piecemeal and mis-aligned with competition theory. International brinkmanship underpins competition between futures exchanges, who seem to resist any change to margining systems that use trailing market data rather than through the cycle indicators.

Tower of Babel

People (including the authors) have their own "versions" of the crisis, usually according to their particular interests, including ineffective or failed regulation, mis-aligned incentives – of bankers, regulators and politicians; undue complexity – of models or regulation; failure of governance; overriding of risk warnings in pursuit of profits;

over-powerful financial services industry lobbying and the necessity to earn positive returns in a low interest rate environment.

The tendency to concentrate on one or two aspects of the crisis and generalise to the overall means that all are working to cross-purposes, and may be losing sight of the main question.

The problem of fragmented objectives is exacerbated by the unavoidable differences between regimes due to differences in local economic circumstances. In 2013, White pointed out that this impedes international coordination of regulations, such as between Basel and the EBA. "[In] the United States and the European Union, the relevant authorities have made firm commitments to rapid implementation of Basel III. That said, worrisome differences in the specifics of the suggested rules in different regions have been identified."[9]

Posner wrote that the potential effectiveness of regulation declines and cost of devising and enforcing increases with the complexity of the underlying system.[10] Regulation therefore needs to be as simple as possible (but as complex as necessary to achieve its stated objectives).

Regulations also date. Devising and implementing new regulations to meet changes in the financial landscape are obviously important. But at least as important, in the interests of keeping regulations as simple as possible and the burden of compliance light, is to get rid of obsolete rules before they begin materially to distort financial and economic activity.

These outcomes imply that what is needed is to simplify the underlying system while still meeting the needs of global commerce – a complex, adaptive system that will always seek to maximise profits and find legal ways to circumvent regulations. How realistic is this?

One simplifying measure would be to break banks up into separate retail/business bank activities and risky investment banking activities. Banking activities would thus be transparent, somewhat mechanistic and easy to manage and supervise, like managing the risk in a post office – with similarly constrained risk and subject to clear controls. In this scenario, investment bank activities would be easier to quarantine if they were in separate organisations and would not benefit from public guarantees. But would they still be allowed to fail?

Regulations could be simplified too, by targeting, not the assets, but the liability structure of each organisation. The reasoning is that organisations call for help when they are unable to meet their liabilities, not necessarily when the value of their investments falls. The liability structure of utility banks is materially different from trading organisations, such as investment banks, for example. Apart from being simpler, liabilities-based regulations would probably be less intrusive and more effective.

That is not to say that, under a liabilities-focused regime, the risk management of assets is dispensed with. Much in the same way as the corporate bond market operates today, one can imagine that bonds raised to support investment banking operations would need to comply with covenants on the risk profile of the assets that the borrowing (in conjunction with equity) supports. Directors would need management's reassurance that assets, whether trading assets or sophisticated loan assets, met certain through-the-cycle criteria. For a simple business and consumer finance firm, impairment calculations not very different from contemporary methodologies would seem satisfactory. In fact they are demonstrated in the form of residential mortgage-backed instruments.

When imagining the disaggregation that may ensue – either to banks facing off against specialist bond markets, or investment activity being transferred to specialist funds – one must reflect on the effect on the payments system. It would seem to follow that as riskier activities move to specialist organisations, there may be a need for specialist payment clearing houses, since the operators of payments based on consumer and business finance flows may be unable, or have insufficient capital, to support the clearing of "sophisticated" payments.

Limits to regulation

Is it time to step back and admit that the complexity of the modern financial system is such that no system of regulation is, or even can be, up to the task?

As we spoke to our panel of practitioners we found that an enduring aspect of their management styles is to run their business as if it were their own (which it is in some cases). As owners they are respectful of the efforts of regulators, but highly focused on simple indicators and common sense in dealing with their risk profile

Follow the debate about these and other open questions on www.riskculture.today.

Notes

1 It can be argued, for example, that modern financial systems are considerably more complex than aviation systems or food processing.

2 The counter-argument is of course that it is impossible to know how many crises have actually been prevented.

3 US Financial Crisis Inquiry Commission, Press Release Official Transcript. Washington, DC, 27 January 2010.

4 High-Level Group on Financial Supervision in the EU, Report, Brussels, 25 February 2009.

5 Reform in the Financial Services Industry, IIF Steering Committee on Implementation, December 2009.

6 *The Economist*, Balkanisation of Banking – Putting Humpty Together Again, 23 November 2013.

7 Posner, R.A., Theories of Economic Regulation, NBER Working Paper No 41, 1974.

8 Allen, F. and Carletti, E., New Theories to Underpin Financial Reform, Institute for New Economic Thinking, Cambridge, 8–11 April 2010.

9 White, W.R., The Prudential Regulation of Financial Institutions: Why Regulatory Responses to the Crisis Might Not Prove Sufficient. University of Calgary, SPP Research Papers, Vol 6, 33, October 2013, p 13.

10 Posner, R.A., op.cit.

A | Risk Silos

Financial organisations must manage at least five main types of risk: investment risk, liquidity risk, counterparty risk, operations risk and legal and compliance risk. A failure in any of the five can be the source of a sixth, which is reputational risk.

Investment risk

This is the risk of loss or shortfall associated with fluctuations in investment values.

Sources of investment risk

Organisations decompose investment risk according to how they select and manage their portfolios. For example, banks and investment banks distinguish between market risk (exposure to interest rate fluctuations), currency risk and credit risk (exposure to defaults or downgrades by borrowers or issuers of corporate bonds).

Investment managers think of investment risk as associated with either allocation to asset classes such as equities, bonds and property, or selection of individual securities within asset classes.

Measures of investment risk

Different sources of risk demand correspondingly different risk measures. For example, Value-at-Risk (VaR) and Conditional Value-at-Risk (CVaR), also known as Extreme Tail Loss (ETL), are designed to quantify short-term vulnerability to extreme events. Long-term investors are more interested in measures of sustained risk, such as portfolio volatility, tracking error and the portfolio's sensitivities, or betas, to factors such as the markets in which it invests.

Investment risk is measured either by parametric or analytic methods, such as variance-covariance or copula analysis, by simulation of possible future scenarios or by stress tests.

Liquidity risk

This is the risk that the assets held in portfolios take longer to liquidate than expected, or that the price realised for them is worse than the price at which they are valued, and therefore assumed to be tradable.

Organisations usually estimate the liquidity of their investments – and implicitly their liquidity risk, by comparing the nominal size of each holding with recent trading activity for each instrument in their portfolios. Yet liquidity estimated in this way may not always be a good representation of how liquid a position or a portfolio really is, because it is nearly always sampled from stable markets, while liquidity is of most concern in stressed markets.

Liquidity risk can also refer to the risk that assets held in liquid instruments by banks, investment banks and some hedge funds are insufficient to meet short-term liabilities,[1] such as demands for withdrawals, or to meet margin calls on derivatives positions.

Counterparty risk

This is the risk that a counterparty will fail to honour an agreement or obligation. In practice, most counterparty risk stems from over-the-counter derivatives contracts, such as interest rate and credit default swaps. Failure to meet counterparty obligations can happen when market fluctuations lead to an accumulation of unrealised profits and losses in the intervals between swap settlement dates. In this sense it is a type of credit risk, although most organisations account for and manage it separately. Importantly, counterparty risk can and does correlate with other sources of risk. For example, an organisation may have a swap agreement with an intermediary (and therefore be exposed to counterparty risk to that entity) and, at the same time, hold in its portfolio bonds issued by the same intermediary, which is accounted for as a credit exposure to it.

Operations risk

Operations, sometimes also called "back office", comprises functions that support risk-taking activities, including settlement of transactions, valuation of positions, reconciliation and accounting. It also provides data that support risk-taking decisions, such as up-to-date portfolio composition and positioning, market prices, data input to risk models and return and profitability calculations, as well as information technology (IT) support. In many organisations, operations also plays an important part in enforcing compliance with internal controls and regulation, for example by providing automatic pre-trade compliance monitoring.

By necessity operations functions follow in the wake of the activities of risk takers, as they respond to market developments, such as the emergence of new instruments and as they undertake one-off, bespoke transactions. Any malfunctioning in operations can be a material impediment to an organisation's ability to engage in profit generating activity, for example if valuations are inaccurate, settlements delayed or data unreliable.

Legal and compliance risk

This is the risk of breach of a regulation, mandate or contract. Compliance risk management is sometimes confounded with investment risk management, but the two are distinct in at least one important sense, which is that while compliance is usually binary – either a breach has occurred or it hasn't – risk management necessarily entails some degree of judgement. Compliance management is often automated using purpose-built software, for example to check that any proposed transaction does not cause a breach of a mandate or covenant. By contrast, while risk measurement can be automated, it is rarely effective without some human input.

Note

1   Investment managers are more likely to call this "liquids" or "cash".

B

The Mechanics of Selected Financial Products

This appendix describes the workings of selected investment products, and related market mechanisms and modelling techniques, including:

- Exchange-traded v over-the-counter transactions
- Swaps
- Securitisation and collateralisation
- Asset-Backed Securities (ABS)
- Structured Investment Vehicles (SIV)
- Collateralised Debt Obligations (CDO) and Collateralised Loan Obligations (CLO)
- Options and option implied volatility
- Volatility and variance swaps
- Option replication
- Gaussian Copulas
- "Do it yourself" structured products.

Exchange-traded v over-the-counter transactions

Derivatives are transacted either on recognised exchanges, such as CME, Euronext or EUREX, or over-the-counter, where they are agreed privately between parties to the transaction or via an intermediary, such as an investment bank.

The benefits of exchange trading include central clearing, standardisation of contract terms, liquidity, low transaction costs and transparency. The main advantage of over-the-counter transacting is that it accommodates customised derivatives products.

Central clearing is where the exchange is party to each transaction, in effect serving simultaneously as seller to the buyer and buyer from the seller. Should the buyer or seller of an exchange-traded derivative fail to honour his contract, the exchange bears the costs of recovering any losses and stands ready to honour all open contracts. It contains and manages the counterparty risk it bears by collecting margins on open positions at frequent intervals, usually daily.

Exchange-traded contracts are standardised by expiry date, mode of settlement or delivery at expiry, and by contract size (usually expressed as some local currency multiple of a market index or price, for example the value of an S&P 500 future is $500 × the nominal level of the index).

The centralised market helps ensure liquidity, which allows transactions to be implemented and reversed quickly and cheaply at any time, at the prevailing market rate, with minimal transaction costs.

Centralised markets usually also provide transparency of prices and traded volumes, whereby information about prices and open positions is publicly available, facilitating mark-to-market valuation of existing positions and estimation of available liquidity.

The advantage of over-the-counter markets is that they can be very flexible, accommodating any bespoke transaction that is agreed between buyer and seller. This allows things like precise hedging and non-standard delivery and settlement dates.

The disadvantages of over-the-counter transactions are lack of transparency, illiquidity, high transaction costs and increased counterparty risk. Prices and the size of transactions are negotiated between buyer and seller, so are generally not observable to outsiders to the transaction, which can be a concern to regulators and supervisors responsible for overseeing system-wide risk. Once established, the position is typically priced by modelling it from some reference indicator, such as a publicly quoted interest rate, exchange rate or credit spread. This means that the value derived can be subject to modelling error. Reversing the transaction can be expensive or impossible, usually depending on the issuer's willingness to accept the reversal – which he may not be prepared to do if it has been hedged with other hard-to-reverse, over-the-counter transactions. While the position is open, each party bears counterparty risk against the other.

Many derivatives markets, including interest rate, currency and credit default swaps, began as over-the-counter markets in order to meet demand for bespoke hedging products, but these instruments are increasingly being traded on exchanges.

Swaps

A swap is an agreement between two parties to swap revenue streams for some pair of assets without transacting the assets themselves. An example of a simple, single currency interest rate swap is where Party A, who holds, say, a fixed coupon bond, seeks to exchange that income stream for a variable income stream of, say, a note held by Party B. Party B is happy to pay the variable stream and receive the fixed stream, so the two enter a swap for a fixed time interval, such as one or two years. At fixed intervals throughout the term of the swap agreement, the two parties settle the net of accrued receipts to the bond and the note.

In the past, swaps were transacted only over-the-counter, where the two parties dealt directly with each other or via an intermediary such as an investment bank. This meant that, during the intervals between settlement dates, Parties A and B were exposed to counterparty risk against each other. As more swaps are registered on exchanges, counterparty risk is increasingly borne by the exchange, or clearer, and intermittent settlement is replaced by frequent, usually daily, margins called by the exchange.

Securitisation and collateralisation

These terms describe the pooling of a future income stream for sale as an investment product such as a Structured Investment Vehicle (SIV) or Asset Backed Security (ABS) for sale to investors. The assets that generate the income stream form the collateral of the product and can comprise any pool of assets, or a single asset, such as the future royalties of a celebrity or the revenue stream from a film. More usually, the assets that are securitised are large numbers of assets, each with small individual income streams, such as repayments on mortgages, credit card debt or student loans.

Investors in securitised products receive a regular income stream in the same way that bond holders do. To enhance marketability, most securitised products are accorded a quality rating by an independent rating agency.

Investors benefit from the diversification effect of the pool of assets, whereby the risk of the pooled vehicle is less than the average risk of the assets in it, and each asset represents only a small percentage of the overall pool of underlying assets. The magnitude of the diversification effect depends on how closely correlated the income streams are with each other: the lower the correlation, the more powerful the diversification effect.

The diversification effect can be unstable. Correlations between assets and revenue streams can change with market conditions, for example, income streams emanating from things like consumer loans and mortgages are affected by common factors such as conditions in the real economy, so that loans that might be relatively uncorrelated in normal economic circumstances become highly correlated in a downturn as many people lose their jobs and find themselves unable to repay their debts.

Asset-Backed Securities (ABS)

These are investment products whose income payments are derived from, and collateralised by, a specified pool of underlying assets. The pool of assets is typically a collection of small and illiquid assets that cannot easily be sold individually.

Structured Investment Vehicle (SIV)

This is a self-funded entity that holds specified revenue generating assets, such as the loans originated by a bank, for sale to investors via an ABS or a Collateralised Debt Obligation (CDO). SIVs are typically originated by banks, but have their own management teams to pool the securitised assets, manage risk and distribute income to investors.

Being separate entities from the banks that originated them can afford SIVs some benefits. For example, until about 2008 the assets held in SIVs did not form part of the bank's balance sheet. Being in this way self-contained and typically with less gearing than the originating bank, SIVs usually attract higher credit ratings, and can offer more transparency to investors, than can traditional bank investments – raising the price investors are willing to pay to participate in them.

Collateralised Debt Obligations (CDO) and Collateralised Loan Obligations (CLO)

These terms describe a type of ABS that is tranched and often bundled with guarantees of performance or of income. In the event of defaults, the lower, subordinate tranches bear the initial impact, with subsequent losses, if they occur, "cascading up" so that senior tranches are the last to suffer. Tranches might be, in order of risk: Senior AAA (sometimes known as "super senior"); Junior AAA; AA; A; BBB; Residual. CDOs thereby appeal to investors with different risk appetites.

"Do it yourself" structured products

As more swap and options transactions move toward exchange trading, the possibilities for investors to create their own structured products with bespoke risk profiles expand. Some flexibility is lost, but this is usually offset by the benefits of central clearing in terms of reduction in exposure to counterparty risk, improved liquidity and transparency, as well as much lower transaction costs.

Options and option implied volatility

Options are the right, but not the obligation, to transact a given instrument at an agreed price up to some specified time in the future. The price of an option depends on the ratio of the current price of the given underlying instrument to the exercise price of the option, the time remaining until expiry, the interest rate and the volatility of the underlying instrument.

Because the first three parameters are known in advance, it is possible to infer the volatility of the underlying instrument from a known option price. The volatility thus inferred is called the option implied volatility.

Option implied volatilities are often used as inputs to valuation and risk models, and are the basis of volatility and variance instruments.

Volatility and variance swaps

These are derivatives contracts that are settled against the option implied volatility of an underlying instrument. Because market volatility and variance[1] tend to be relatively uncorrelated with the direction of the price of the underlying instrument,[2] they can be a valuable source of diversification for portfolio investors.

The VIX is the best-known example of an exchange-traded volatility swap. It is derived from a weighted blend of prices of selected options on the S&P 500 index and is settled against observed option implied volatility. It translates approximately to the expected movement in the S&P 500 index over an annualised 30-day horizon.

Option replication

As well as being traded on exchange or over-the-counter, options can also be replicated using a combination of the underlying instrument and a risk-free asset, such as cash. The proportion of the portfolio invested in the underlying instrument is determined by the option's delta, a value between zero and one for a call option.[3] As the price of the underlying instrument increases, so does the delta. This means that a portfolio that replicates a bought option is always buying into a rising market and selling into a falling market – with a lag. When many participants replicate options on similar instruments, the collective effect of buying and selling can contribute to market-level pro-cyclicality effects.

Constant Proportions Portfolio Insurance (CPPI) is a type of modified option replication strategy that also entails buying into rising markets and selling into falling ones, and so can also contribute to system-wide pro-cyclicality.

Gaussian Copulas

Copulas are a technique for modelling the dependence between random variables in a probability distribution, such as the distribution of returns of an asset or a pool of assets. Many copula families are available, with parameters that control the strength of dependence.

Copulas were adapted for financial markets to estimate the probability distribution of losses on pools of loans or bonds. In investment risk management, copulas are used to perform stress tests and robustness checks to measure vulnerability to market events that can result in unusual losses.

Early copula families, including the Gaussian Copula, are able to accommodate large numbers of assets or risk factors only by assuming symmetry in the underlying distribution of asset returns.[4] This limits their ability to estimate the probability of extreme events (often referred to as the tail of the return distribution) and, importantly, the instability of correlations between assets that usually accompany stressed markets, as pro-cyclical effects cause disruption to normal trading activity. The result is often underestimation of both the likelihood of an extreme loss and its magnitude in the event that it occurs.

Notes

1 The square of volatility.
2 Typically equity indices.
3 An option to buy the underlying instrument. The delta for a put option, which is the option to sell the underlying instrument, ranges from -1 to 0.
4 Whereby gains and losses are equally likely.

C

Basel I, II and III – Risk Weightings

The 1988 Basel I Accord set minimum capital requirements for global banks, taking account of assets' risk weighting, with a focus on credit risk. Five asset categories were defined with risk weights of between 0% and 100%, according to assessed risk.

Basel II added market and operations risk to the credit risk of Basel I and defined three pillars:

- The first pillar, Minimum Capital Requirements, deals with maintenance of regulatory capital calculated for three major quantifiable components of risk that a bank faces: credit risk, operational risk and market risk.
- The second pillar provides a framework for dealing with systemic risk, pension risk, concentration risk, strategic risk, reputational risk, liquidity risk and legal risk.
- The third pillar develops a set of disclosure requirements to allow market participants to gauge for themselves the capital adequacy of an institution.

Basel III raised the capital requirements and simplified and strength-ened the capital base by requiring eligible regulatory capital to be of higher quality and genuinely loss-absorbing. It also introduced leverage as a back-stop.[1]

Note

1 Basel Committee on Banking Supervision, The Regulatory Framework: Balancing Risk Sensitivity, Simplicity and Comparability, Discussion Paper, July 2013.

Glossary of Terms

2 and 20	A typical hedge fund management fee structure, comprising a base fee of 2% p.a. on the capital invested plus 20% of returns above an agreed threshold return.
Absorption ratio	A measure of implied systemic risk. It equals the fraction of the total variance of a set of asset returns explained or "absorbed" by a fixed number of eigenvectors. The absorption ratio captures the extent to which markets are unified or tightly coupled.
ABX	Asset-Backed Security Index. A credit default swap contract that pools lists of exposures to mortgage-backed securities.
ABX index	A financial benchmark that measures the overall value of mortgages made to borrowers with sub-prime or weak credit.
Accrual	An accounting entry to recognise an impending transaction settlement.
Accruals-based accounting	An accounting method that values an asset by recognising economic events regardless of when cash transactions occur. Revenues are matched to expenses (the matching principle) at the time in which the transaction occurs rather than when payment is made (or received), allowing current cash inflows/outflows to be combined with future expected cash inflows/outflows.

ADR	American Depository Receipt – an instrument listed on a US exchange, backed by shares in a non–US exchange. See also SDR.
AIFMD	Alternative Investment Fund Management Directive. An EU initiative to regulate hedge funds and other alternative investment funds.
AIMR	Association for Investment Management Research.
ALM	Asset-Liability Management.
AML	Anti-Money Laundering.
Arbitrage	The purchase and simultaneous sale of two economically identical instruments or assets to yield a risk-free profit.
Arbitrage pricing theory	Stock valuation theory equating the value of an asset with the sum of market valuations of its subsidiaries.
Asset liability management	The practice of matching or optimising the investment portfolio according to the projected liabilities of a fund.
Asset swap	Transaction whereby two investors exchange the variation in value of nominated assets.
At-the-money	Asset price equals exercise price. An option with zero intrinsic value.
AUM	Assets Under Management.
Automated trading	A practice whereby computers are programmed to give instructions to trade on the basis of defined prices or price spreads between securities and derivatives contracts, with specified timing and quantity, but without routine human intervention.
Barrier option	An exotic derivative, typically an option on the underlying asset whose price reaching the pre-set barrier level either springs the option into existence or extinguishes an already existing option. Barrier options are always cheaper than a similar option without barrier. Thus, barrier options were created to provide the insurance value of an option without charging as much premium.

Basis risk	The risk that a derivative position will not exactly offset the physical asset that it is intended to hedge.
Basket or block trade	The aggregation of a number of individual purchases or sales to a single transaction.
BCBS	Basel Committee on Banking Supervision.
Bid–ask spread	The concurrent difference in the buy and sell price of a security or contract.
BIS	Bank for International Settlements. The central bankers' central bank.
Black box	A quantitative asset allocation or stock selection model, which does not permit the user to check intermediate calculations or carry out reasonableness checks.
Black pools	Decentralised, electronic trading platforms in securities such as listed equities, which are normally traded on a centralised exchange. Unlike conventional exchanges, black pools do not publish the queue of bids and offers for the securities traded on them until after the transaction is completed.
Black–Scholes	Fischer Black and Myron Scholes were the authors of the widely used eponymous technique of pricing options on assets and portfolios.
Bond volatility	The change in settlement value of a bond corresponding to a change in the interest rate of 0.01%.
Business risk	The risk that a business loses money or fails to make a profit.
Butterfly swaps	A limited risk, non-directional strategy that is designed to have a large probability of earning a limited profit when the future volatility of the underlying asset is expected to be lower than the implied volatility.
Call option	The right, but not the obligation, to buy an asset or futures contract at an agreed price at an agreed time. See also Put option.
Capital Asset Pricing Model (CAPM)	A framework for valuing equities and modelling equity risk, based on a single market factor.

Capital guarantee	An assurance by an investment manager that the return to the portfolio will not be below zero in nominal terms in a given period.
CAPM	Capital Asset Pricing Model.
Cash	Short-term low yield liquid instruments, usually issued by a government or a bank. See also Liquid assets.
Cash settled contract	A derivative contract that ends with a cash payment of the difference between the traded price and the final price of the contract.
Caveat emptor	Buyer beware.
CDS	Credit Default Swap – over-the-counter derivatives instrument linked to the default on a debt instrument.
CDO	Collateralised Debt Obligation – a type of structured asset-backed security (ABS). CDOs, originally developed for the corporate debt markets, evolved to encompass the mortgage and mortgage-backed security (MBS) markets.
CEO	Chief Executive Officer.
CFO	Chief Financial Officer.
CFTC	US Commodity Futures Trading Commission.
Chief Financial Officer (CFO)	The Head Accountant.
CIO	Chief Investment Officer.
Clearer	A bank or other financial institution, or a consortium that stands between parties trading assets or other instruments on an exchange. By taking part in exchange transactions, the clearer ensures performance of transactions taking place on the exchange. Also known as a clearing house.
Clearing house	A firm that guarantees performance of transactions by participating in each. Also known as clearer.
CLO	Collateralised Loan Obligation – an investment instrument constructed by bundling many small loans into securitised instruments for re-sale on the secondary market.

COCO	Contingent convertible bond.
Collateral	An asset held or pledged to support performance of the terms of a transaction.
Commodities Trading Funds (CTF)	Funds that exploit mispricing and trends in commodities, usually transacting in commodity futures contracts.
Commodity-linked notes and deposits	A type of exchange traded note that invests in commodities and commodity derivatives.
Conditional Value–at–Risk (CVaR)	A measure of extreme loss that describes the shape of the loss distribution in the tail, to the left of VaR, thus indicating how long the tail could be, rather than simply a point outcome. See also ETL, Expected Shortfall (ES).
Constant Proportion Debt Obligations (CPDO)	A structured product that is designed to deliver long-term exposure to corporate bond returns in a highly rated debt security.
Contribution holiday	A period during which members pay lower contributions than normal, or even none at all.
Convertible bonds	Instruments combining a bond and a call option on an equity. See also Converting bonds, Hybrids.
Convertible hedge	An investment strategy combining convertible instruments and derivatives or other instruments, designed to eliminate unwanted risk.
Converting bonds	Instruments combining a bond, a call option and a put option on an equity. Sometimes combines a bond and a forward agreement. See also Convertible notes, Hybrids.
Convexity	The change in duration of a bond or portfolio of bonds for a small change in the interest rate.
COO	Chief Operating Officer, responsible for non-trading activities in an investment management firm.
Copula	A multivariate probability distribution for which the marginal probability distribution of each

	variable is uniform. Copulas are used to describe the dependence between random variables.
Corporate governance	Exercising shareholder rights, such as casting votes at general meetings and voicing opinions on management policies of companies in which the fund has a significant holding.
Correlation	The degree to which the returns to assets or portfolios resemble each other. Correlations range from −1 (perfectly offsetting returns) through zero (no relationship at all) to +1 (perfectly similar returns). See also Covariance.
Cost of carry	Ancillary costs associated with holding an investment, including interest cost, insurance, income foregone.
Counter-cyclical stocks	Stocks that outperform other stocks in a period of economic slowdown or recession. Usually include basic foods, tobacco and discount retailers.
Counterparty risk	The risk that a person or entity participating in a transaction will be unable to perform his, her or its obligations under the terms of the transaction.
Coupon	Regular payments to holders of bonds.
Covariance	The degree to which the returns to assets or portfolios resemble each other. Covariances can be negative (offsetting returns), zero (no relationship at all) or positive (similar returns). See also Correlation.
CPI	Consumer Price Index.
CPPI	Constant Proportions Portfolio Insurance. An alternative technique to Black–Scholes for constructing portfolio protection programmes.
CQS	Convertibles Quantitative Strategies.
CRC	Capital Requirements Calculation.
Credit risk	The risk that a borrower will not be able to honour the terms of a loan or that the loan will be downgraded.
Credit spread	The difference in yield between interest rate securities with different risks of default.
Credit-linked notes and deposits	A type of exchange traded note that invests in commodities and commodity derivatives.

CRO	Chief Risk Officer.
Crowded trade	Where a large number of market participants concurrently seek to carry out the same or a similar transaction.
CSFB	Credit Suisse First Boston.
CSFP	Credit Suisse Financial Products.
CTA	Commodities Traders' Association.
CVA	Capital Value Adjustment is defined by the Basel Committee as the difference between the value of a derivative assuming the counterparty is default risk-free and the value of a derivative reflecting the default risk of the counterparty.
Dark liquidity	Decentralised, electronic trading platforms in securities such as listed equities, which are normally traded on a centralised exchange. Unlike conventional exchanges, black pools do not publish the queue of bids and offers for the securities traded on them until after the transaction is completed.
Dark pools	See Dark liquidity.
Data-mining	The practice of using historical data to test and validate investment models.
Delta	The change in value of an option relative to a small change in the price of the underlying asset or portfolio.
Delta hedging	Ongoing management of replicating options. Continuous readjustment of portfolio weightings according to estimated delta of replicated option.
Discount factor	The interest rate that comprises the denominator in a discounted cash flow calculation.
Discount security	A debt instrument paying no coupons, where interest is subtracted (discounted) from the purchase price and the face value is paid at maturity.
Distressed debt	Securities of companies or government entities that are either already in default, under bankruptcy protection, or in distress and heading toward such a condition.
Dodd–Frank	The Dodd–Frank Wall Street Reform and Consumer Protection Act. Passed as a response to the Great Recession, it brought the most significant changes to financial regulation in the United States since the

	regulatory reform that followed the Great Depression. It made changes in the American financial regulatory environment that affect all Federal financial regulatory agencies and almost every part of the nation's financial services industry.
Duration	A measure of the maturity and timing of cash flows of a fixed interest instrument.
DVA	Debt Value Adjustment.
EBA	European Banking Authority.
Economic capital	The amount of risk capital, assessed on a realistic basis, needed to support a firm's ongoing risk-taking activities, such as market risk, credit risk, legal risk and operational risk to ensure that it stays solvent over a certain time period with a pre-specified probability in a worst-case scenario. It is often calculated as Value-at-Risk.
Efficient frontier	A concept in modern portfolio theory introduced by Harry Markowitz and others in 1952. A combination of assets, i.e. a portfolio, is referred to as "efficient" if it has the best possible expected level of return for its level of risk, which is usually represented by the standard deviation of the portfolio's return.
Efficient portfolio	A portfolio with the lowest possible risk for a given expected return, or the highest expected return for a given level of risk.
Eigenvectors	A non-zero vector that, when multiplied with A, yields a scalar multiple of itself; the scalar multiplier is often denoted by lambda. In principal components analysis, an eigenvector is a statistically independent factor that results from the analysis.
Equity risk premium	The difference in return between equities and long-term bonds that reflects the difference in risk.
ESMA	European Securities and Markets Authority, a European Union financial regulatory institution and European Supervisory Authority.
ETF	Exchange Traded Fund.
ETL	Expected Tail Loss.
ETN	Exchange Traded Note.

Expected shortfall	A measure of extreme loss that describes the shape of the loss distribution in the tail, to the left of VaR, thus indicating how long the tail could be, rather than simply a point outcome. See also Expected Tail Loss (ETL), Conditional Value-at-Risk (CVaR).
Extel	The Exchange Telegraph company was founded in 1872 initially to lay the first telegraphic cable on the Atlantic seabed to connect electronically London and New York. Over the next 100+ years Extel (the name coming into common use for the company in the 1950s) grew into one of the leading news agencies, provider of financial information and associated businesses. Among the many notable achievements were "Extel Cards", the very first corporate snapshots/tear-sheets with brief data on profit and loss, employees, business activities and executive management. Extel Cards, naturally in hard copy, were first produced in 1922.
Extreme risk	Asset price and factor volatility in extreme or stressed market conditions.
Extreme tail loss	A measure of extreme loss that describes the shape of the loss distribution in the tail, to the left of VaR, thus indicating how long the tail could be, rather than simply a point outcome. See also Conditional Value-at-Risk (CVaR), Expected Shortfall (ES).
Fair price	The price at which the expected return to an asset exactly reflects its expected riskiness.
Fair value accounting	A method of objective valuation derived from the most recent security prices quoted and traded in the relevant market. Also known as Mark-to-market.
Fama French three factor model	A framework for valuing equities and modelling equity risk, similar to CAPM, but with three factors instead of the single market factor.
FATCA	US Foreign Account Tax Compliance Act.
FCA	Financial Conduct Authority.
FDIC	Federal Deposit Insurance Corporation.

Fed	US Federal Reserve.
Fed funds rate	The interest rate at which depository institutions actively trade balances held at the Federal Reserve, called Federal funds, with each other, usually overnight, on an uncollateralised basis. Institutions with surplus balances in their accounts lend those balances to institutions in need of larger balances. The fed funds rate is an important benchmark in financial markets.
FINRA	US Financial Industry Regulatory Authority.
FOREX	A forward contract in foreign exchange.
Forward rate agreement	An over-the-counter contract between parties that determines the rate of interest, or the currency exchange rate, to be paid or received on an obligation beginning at a future start date. The contract will determine the rates to be used along with the termination date and notional value. On this type of agreement, it is only the differential that is paid on the notional amount of the contract.
FPC	Financial Policy Committee.
Frictional liquidity	Cash held in a portfolio as a result of income received, awaiting investment or required to meet small redemptions and other requirements for cash, such as rights issues.
Front office/ Front end	The transactions and implementation functions of an investment management firm.
Front-running	A practice whereby a broker, having been informed of a large incoming order, trades the security first on his or her own account, subsequently crystallising a profit by transacting the securities concerned at a price that is made more attractive by the market impact of the trade itself.
FSA	Financial Services Authority.
FVA	Fair Value Adjustment.
FX	Foreign Exchange.
G7	Group of Seven Countries, comprises USA, UK, France, Germany, Italy, Canada and Japan, which meet to discuss mainly economic issues.

G10	Group of Ten Countries, comprises USA, UK, France, Germany, Italy, Canada, Japan, Belgium, the Netherlands and Sweden, which meet to discuss mainly economic issues. Switzerland was added later as an eleventh country, but the group retained its name.
G20	Group of Twenty Countries, comprises Argentina, Australia, Brazil, Canada, China, France, Germany, India, Indonesia, Italy, Japan, Mexico, Russia, Saudi Arabia, South Africa, South Korea, Turkey, the United Kingdom and the United States – along with the European Union (EU). The EU is represented by the European Commission and by the European Central Bank. The G20 meets to discuss mainly economic issues.
GAAP	Generally Accepted Accounting Principles are a standard framework of guidelines for financial accounting used in any given jurisdiction including standards, conventions and rules that accountants follow in recording and summarising and in the preparation of financial statements.
GARCH	Autoregressive conditional heteroskedasticity (ARCH) models are used to characterise and model observed time series, from which Generalised ARCH models.
GARP	Global Association of Risk Professionals.
Gaussian Copula	A family of models used to estimate the probability distribution of losses on a pool of loans or bonds.
GFC	Global Financial Crisis of 2007–2009.
GIPS	Global Investment Performance Standards.
Glass–Steagall	The US Banking Act of 1933.
Global Systemically Important Banks	A group of global systemically important banks identified by the Financial Stability Board.
Government curve	The yields of bonds issued by governments over different maturities.

Greeks	Partial derivative measures that describe the sensitivities of investments to changes in underlying factors such as interest rates and the passage of time.
Haircut	In finance, a haircut is the difference between the market value of an asset used as loan collateral and the amount of the loan. The amount of the haircut reflects the lender's perceived risk of loss from the asset falling in value or being sold in a fire sale. The lender will, however, still hold a lien for the entire value of the asset. In the event the collateral is sold to repay the loan, the lender will have a higher chance of being made whole. Expressed as a percentage of the collateral's market value, the haircut is the complement of the Loan-to-value ratio: together they equal 100% of the value.
Herstatt risk	Foreign exchange settlement risk due to time zone disparities, in particular that a counterparty will fail after having settled one side of a foreign exchange transaction, but before settling the other side.
Heuristics	Experience-based techniques for problem solving, learning and discovery that find a solution that is not guaranteed to be optimal, but good enough for a given set of goals.
HR	Human Resources.
Hybrids	Instruments combining a bond and a call option, a bond, a call and a put option, or a bond and a forward agreement on an equity. See also Convertible notes, Converting bonds.
IFRS	International Financial Reporting Standards.
IMA	UK Investment Managers' Association.
IMF	International Monetary Fund.
IMM	International Monetary Market.
IMM date	Quarterly dates of each year that serve as scheduled maturity or termination dates for most futures and option contracts. They are typically the third Wednesday of March, June, September and December. Also refers to the conventional quarterly termination

	dates of credit default swaps, which fall on 20 March, 20 June, 20 September and 20 December.
IMM swap	An IMM swap is a swap that terminates on the IMM dates.
Implied volatility	The standard deviation of the movement of the price of an asset that is indicated by the price of an option on that asset.
IMRO	UK Investment Management Regulatory Organisation. A predecessor of the Financial Services Authority in the UK.
Index credit default swaps	Exchange-traded derivatives instruments linked to the default on an index of basket of debt instruments.
Inflation linked bonds	Bonds where the principal is linked to a defined index of inflation.
Initial margin	A sum paid on opening a derivative position to provide collateral for adverse price movements in the contract.
Investment risk	The risk of failing to meet investment objectives.
Investment universe	The set of assets from which portfolios and benchmarks are selected.
IOSCO	International Organisation of Securities Commissions.
ISDA	International Swap Dealers' Association.
JGB	Japanese Government Bonds.
Jump diffusion	A computational method that helps model instances where asset prices gap up or down, that are otherwise not easily dealt with by most asset pricing methodologies. Jump diffusion processes were introduced by Robert C. Merton as an extension of jump models that are computationally tractable.
Jump risk	The risk of significant, discrete changes in the market value of an asset or portfolio.
Kurtosis	A measure of the fat-ness of the tails of a distribution.
KYC	Know Your Customer is a provision of European regulations aimed at preventing money laundering.

LCR   Liquidity Coverage Ratio – refers to highly liquid assets
                held by financial institutions in order to meet
                short-term obligations. The Liquidity Coverage Ratio is
                designed to ensure that financial institutions have the
                necessary assets on hand to ride out short-term liquidity
                disruptions.

LIBOR   London Inter-Bank Offered Rate. A benchmark
                interest rate calculated as the average interest rate which
                leading banks in London estimate would be charged if
                borrowing from other banks. LIBOR rates are
                calculated for 10 currencies and 15 borrowing periods
                ranging from overnight to one year and are published
                daily at 11:30 am (London time).

LIBOR   The yields payable by banks to other banks over
curve   different maturities.

Liquid   Short-term low yield instruments.
assets

Liquidity   The amount of liquid assets held by a bank or bank-like
(1)   organisation to meet demand deposit withdrawals.

Liquidity   A description of the volume of transactions in an asset
(2)   or market. Very liquid indicates many or frequent
                transactions, illiquid indicates few transactions.

Liquidity   Theory of interest rates that says that longer maturities
spread   entail greater risks for investors who demand a risk
                premium to compensate for the fact that at longer
                durations there is more uncertainty and a greater chance
                of a rise in inflation or an extreme event that causes the
                value of the bond to fall.

Long   Net bought. See also Short.

Loss given   When a borrower or bond issuer defaults, the loss to the
default   lender or bond holders is usually less than 100% of the
                amount lent or invested, resulting in some recoverable
                amount. The difference between the market value of
                the loan or bond and the recoverable amount is the loss
                given default. This means that modelling the risk of
                loans and other credit investments entails estimation,
                not only of the likelihood of default, but also of the

recovery rate in the event of default – and thus the magnitude of the losses that would result.

Macaulay duration	The name given to the weighted average time until bond cash flows are received, and is measured in years.
Mahalanobis Numbers Distance	A measure of the distance between a point P and a distribution D, introduced by P. C. Mahalanobis in 1936. It is a multi-dimensional generalisation of the idea of measuring how many standard deviations away P is from the mean of D.
Margin trading	The practice of borrowing money to invest whereby the investments form the collateral for the loan.
Mark-to-market	A method of objective valuation derived from the most recent security prices quoted and traded in the relevant market. Also known as Fair Value Accounting.
Market efficiency	Asset prices that reflect all information available about the asset.
Market impact	The change in the price of an asset due to the market's reaction to a transaction or the expectation of a transaction.
Market makers	Individuals or firms designated by stock and derivatives exchanges to provide liquidity in nominated instruments by quoting buy and sell prices.
Market neutral	An investment strategy whereby the net exposure to the market is zero.
Markowitz Portfolio Theory	A theory of finance that attempts to maximise portfolio expected return for a given amount of portfolio risk, or equivalently minimise risk for a given level of expected return, by carefully choosing the proportions of various assets. MPT is widely used in practice in the financial industry.
Maximum drawdown	The magnitude of the decline from a historical peak to a trough in the value of the fund.
MBS	Mortgage-Backed Security, a type of asset-backed security that is secured by a mortgage, or more commonly a collection, or pool, of sometimes hundreds of mortgages.

Mean reversion	The tendency of values in series of data to converge to their long-term average.
Mean-variance efficiency	The optimal combination of expected return and risk. Lying on the Efficient Frontier.
ML	Merrill Lynch.
Monte Carlo simulation	A broad class of computational algorithms that rely on repeated random sampling to obtain numerical results.
Moral hazard	When one party takes more risks because another party bears the burden of those risks.
MPC	UK Monetary Policy Committee.
MSCI	Morgan Stanley Capital International, a provider of international equity indices.
NSFR	Net Stable Funding Requirement is a new ratio introduced by the Basel III framework to measure a bank's structural funding profile. The NSFR standard is designed to ensure sustainable and stress-resistant funding of a bank's asset business as well as its off balance sheet activities.
Off the shelf	Products developed commercially. Usually refers to software products.
Opportunity cost	The return forgone.
Option volatility	The movement in the price of the option corresponding to a movement in the price of the underlying asset or contract.
Orthogonal	Correlations equal to zero. Changes in asset prices that are unconnected with each other. See also Statistically independent.
Panel	The practice of obtaining an indicative benchmark price or rate by conducting a "survey" whereby selected market practitioners are asked to quote a price or rate for a given, hypothetical transaction.
Parametric	Defined by parameters.
Participation rate	The ratio, in the context of portfolio protection, of option face value to risky assets in the underlying portfolio.

Passive investment	An investment strategy that uses no judgement at all, but relies solely on predefined decision rules for all ongoing investment decisions.
Payment Protection Insurance	Also known as credit insurance, credit protection insurance or loan repayment insurance, this is an insurance product (especially in the UK) that enables consumers to insure repayment of loans if the borrower dies, becomes ill or disabled, loses a job or faces other circumstances that may prevent them from earning income to service the debt.
Power Utility Function	Used to express utility in terms of consumption or some other economic variable that a decision maker is concerned with.
Prime broker	The generic name for a bundled package of services offered by investment banks and securities firms to hedge funds and other professional investors needing the ability to borrow securities and cash to be able to invest on a netted basis and achieve an absolute return. The prime broker provides a centralised securities clearing facility for the hedge fund so the hedge fund's collateral requirements are netted across all deals handled by the prime broker.
Principal components	The technique of applying regression analysis to quantify factors relating to historical returns to an asset or portfolio. The factors are identified subsequently by inspection.
Principal components analysis	Statistical analysis that assigns undetermined factors to historical return data to explain as much as possible of the estimated portfolio variance.
Principal trading	The practice of purchase and sale of securities for the benefit of the person or entity carrying out the trade.
Private equity	Investment in unlisted equity assets.
PRMIA	Professional Risk Managers International Association.
Protection strategies	Investments that are designed to limit the extent of adverse outcomes in a given investment period.

Put option	The right, but not the obligation, to sell an asset or futures contract at an agreed price at an agreed time. See also Call option.
Quant	Quantitative analyst, someone who applies mathematical techniques to financial investment.
RAROC	Risk-Adjusted Return on Capital.
Ratings triggers	A clause in a loan or bond contract that makes the loan due in full if the company's credit rating is lowered beyond a certain point, usually to a "speculative" or "junk bond" rating.
Real time	Continuously. Usually refers to transmission of market information.
Recovery rate	The percentage of the value of a loan that can be repaid following default or partial default by a borrower.
Reference price	An asset or commodity price quoted by an independent, official or semi-official source.
Regulatory capital	The capital needed to meet prescribed regulatory requirements.
Reinvestment risk	The risk of interest rates changing between bond coupon payments and following the maturity of a bond.
Relative value	The market or fair value of a security relative to the market or fair value of another security. A hedge fund strategy that, in theory, carries no net exposure to the market in which it invests.
Repo	Repurchase agreement, whereby a bond is sold with a contract to repurchase it at a given date and price in the future. In effect, short-term borrowing.
Risk model	A collection of stock betas to risk factors and the factor covariance matrix.
Risk parity	An approach to investment portfolio management that focuses on allocation of risk, usually defined as volatility, rather than allocation of capital. The risk parity approach asserts that when asset allocations are adjusted (leveraged or de-leveraged) to the same risk level, the risk parity portfolio can achieve a higher

	Sharpe ratio and can be more resistant to market downturns than the traditional portfolio.
Risk preference	Appetite for risk, or tolerance of losses.
Risk-adjusted return	Portfolio return minus the product of the benchmark return and the portfolio beta to benchmark.
Roll	A special case of a spread trade, where a derivatives position in a near settlement month is exchanged for an identical position in a more distant month.
Roll down	The effect observed in a positively sloped yield curve, where lenders profit from the passage of time since yields decrease as bonds get closer to maturity.
RPI	Retail Price Index.
SDR	Statutory Depository Receipts – an instrument listed on a US exchange, backed by securities listed on a non-US exchange. See also ADR.
SEC	US Securities and Exchange Commission.
Securitisation	The packaging of many individual holdings into a single security for re-sale.
Security market line	A representation of the capital asset pricing model that displays the expected rate of return of an individual security as a function of systematic, non-diversifiable risk.
Sensitivity analysis	A measure of the impact on a portfolio of small changes from one period to the next in the values of assets and factors to which it is exposed.
Serial correlation	Correlations between observations in consecutive periods.
Shock factor	The variable to be tested as part of a stress test.
Short	Net sold. See also Long.
Short selling	Selling securities or instruments that are not currently owned.
Short squeeze	The necessity to repurchase quickly, in an appreciating market, securities that have been sold short.
Simulation	A broad class of computational algorithms that rely on repeated random sampling to obtain numerical results.

SIV	Structured Investment Vehicle.
Skew	A measure of the asymmetry of a distribution, defined as the difference between the mean and the median.
Solvency II	An EU Directive that codifies and harmonises the EU insurance regulation. Primarily this concerns the amount of capital that EU insurance companies must hold to reduce the risk of insolvency.
SPAN	Standardised Portfolio ANalysis of risk.
Special purpose entity	A legal entity, separate from its parent firm with its own assets, which issues bonds in its own name.
Spread trade	A transaction comprising the simultaneous buying and selling of very similar instruments, such as futures that vary only in their settlement month.
Standard deviation	The distance from average describing 32% probability. One standard deviation either side of the mean captures 68% of all eventualities. Two standard deviations either side capture 95%.
Statistically independent	Correlations equal to zero. Changes in asset prices that are unconnected with each other. See also Orthogonal.
Stress test	Testing the effect of a defined economic shock to quantify what impact it would have.
Stressed investments	Investment in securities of companies or government entities that are either already in default, under bankruptcy protection, or in distress and heading toward such a condition.
Strike price	The price at which an option is exercised. See also Exercise price.
Structured Investment Vehicle	A non-bank financial entity established to earn a credit spread between the longer-term assets held in its portfolio and the shorter-term liabilities it issues with significantly less leverage (10–15 times) than traditional banks (25–50 times).
Subsidiarisation	Operating the foreign banking activities of global banks as separate subsidiaries of the parent bank rather than as branches.

Survivorship bias	A bias sometimes found in time series analyses, which stems from the omission of stocks that failed at some time between the start of the data sample and the time of the analysis. It biases results because the errors thus introduced cannot be assumed to average out over large sample sizes.
Swap curve	The yields of bonds issued by corporate borrowers of a given credit quality over different maturities.
Swaps push-out rule	Part of the Dodd–Frank legislation of 2010. It prohibits the provision of certain types of "Federal assistance" to certain swap dealers and major swap participants referred to as "swaps entities" and requires certain entities that rely on Federal assistance and have significant swaps business to move aspects of that business into non-bank affiliates, subject to additional rules, or in certain cases divest or cease to engage in that business.
Synthetic cash	The economic position resulting from simultaneously buying a physical asset and selling its exact face value in futures, forward contracts or swaps.
Synthetic options	Options created using a combination of options and the underlying asset or contract.
Synthetic swap	A swap that is replicated by a suite of bought and sold physical securities and futures.
Tail	The "tail" of the return distribution that quantifies the likelihood that an asset or a portfolio will deliver extreme losses over a given period of time.
Term structure	A curve that shows the relation between the (level of) interest rate (or cost of borrowing) and the time to maturity, known as the "term", of a debt for a given borrower in a given currency.
Thin market	A very illiquid market.
Tickets	Transactions.
Time value	That part of the option price that is a function of the asset volatility, time to maturity and interest rate. Total option price less intrinsic value.

Time-series analysis	The analysis of past returns.
Tobin's Separation Theorem	The proposition that the composition of the super-efficient portfolio is independent of the investor's appetite for risk. The two decisions: the composition of the risky portion of the investor's portfolio, and the amount of leverage to use, are entirely independent of each other.
Tracking error	A measure of the amount by which a portfolio's performance is likely to differ from some known benchmark portfolio. The standard deviation of the sum of differences between portfolio and benchmark returns. Also the square root of the variance.
Undertakings for Collective Investment in Transferable Securities (UCITS)	A type of fund subject to European regulation that permits it to be marketed to retail investors throughout the EU.
USS	Universities Superannuation Scheme.
VaR	Value-at-Risk – a measure of extreme, but not total, loss at a selected confidence level, given assumptions about the probabilities of all possible outcomes for a given asset or portfolio.
Variance	A measure of the amount by which a portfolio's performance is likely to differ from some known benchmark portfolio. The sum of differences between portfolio and benchmark returns over a defined period. Also the square of the standard deviation.
Variation margin	A sum paid subsequent to opening a derivative position to cover existing unrealised losses and to provide collateral for adverse price movements in the contract.
Volatility	The standard deviation of returns. The range within which returns are expected to occur 68% of the time.

Volatility trading	A trading strategy designed to benefit from forecast rises and falls in option implied volatility.
Wrong way risk	Where credit exposure increases when the credit quality of the counterparty deteriorates.
XVA	Collective term for derivative value adjustments.
Yield curve	The relationship between interest rates and time to maturity for bonds of a given credit quality.
Yield to maturity	The interest rate implied by the settlement price of a bond.
Zero coupon curve	A theoretical yield curve describing pure interest rates of a given quality for a range of maturities, excluding the effects of coupon payments and reinvestment risk.

Glossary of People

Ackerman	Joseph	A Swiss banker and former chief executive officer of Deutsche Bank. He has also been the Chairman of the International Institute of Finance, an influential Washington-based financial advisory body.
Antoncic	Madelyn	Vice President and Treasurer of the World Bank.
Bagehot	Walter	1826–1877. A British journalist, businessman and essayist, who wrote extensively about government, economics and literature.
Bair	Sheila	President of Washington College from 1 August 2015, previously Chairperson of the US Federal Deposit Insurance Corporation (FDIC) from 2006 to 2011.
Barnier	Michel	Vice President of the European People's Party (EPP) and European Commissioner for Internal Market and Services under Barroso.
Bean	Charlie	Deputy Governor for Monetary Policy at the Bank of England.
Binmore	Ken	A British mathematician, economist and game theorist. He is one of the founders of the modern economic theory of bargaining (along with Nash and Rubinstein), and has made important contributions to the foundations of game theory, experimental economics and evolutionary game theory, as well as to analytical philosophy.
Black	Fischer	An American economist, best known as one of the authors of the famous Black–Scholes equation.
Brown	Gordon	A British Labour Party politician who was the Prime Minister of the United Kingdom and Leader of the Labour Party from 2007 until 2010.
Buiter	Willem	A Dutch-born American-British economist. He is currently the Chief Economist at Citigroup.

Caruana	Jaime	General Manager of the Bank for International Settlements (BIS) and Governor of the Bank of Spain from July 2000 to July 2006.
Castleman	Christopher	Chief Executive of Hill Samuel, and subsequently as a director of Standard Chartered and a senior adviser to UBS Investment Bank, Castleman was widely admired in the financial world for his straightforwardness, his ability to motivate those who worked with him and his formidable intellect and stamina.
Cole	Tony	An Australian World Bank official from 1979 to 1981 and principal private secretary to Treasurer Paul Keating from 1983 to 1985. From 1991 to 1993, Cole was Secretary of the Department of the Treasury and then Secretary of the Department of Health, Housing, Local Government and Community Services.
Darling	Alistair	A British Labour Party politician who has been a Member of Parliament (MP) since 1987, and Chancellor of the Exchequer in the Labour Government from 2007 to 2010.
Darrell Duffie	James	A Canadian financial economist; is Dean Witter Distinguished Professor of Finance at Stanford Graduate School of Business.
Davies	Mervyn	A former banker and was a UK government minister until May 2010. His role as Minister of State for Trade, Investment and Small Business involved oversight of UK Trade and Investment – the United Kingdom's export support and inward investment agency – and he had dual accountability to the Department for Business, Innovation and Skills and the Foreign and Commonwealth Office. Davies was Chairman of Standard Chartered PLC between November 2006 and January 2009, and Chief Executive between 2001 and 2006. He was appointed a Director in 1997.
Diamond	Jamie	Current Chairman, President and Chief Executive Officer of JPMorgan Chase.
Dougan	Brady	An American business executive. Since 2007 Chief Executive Officer of Credit Suisse and previously CEO of Investment Banking and acting CEO Credit Suisse Americas.
Dunn	Richard	A member of Merrill Lynch's Executive Committee and Head of Market and Credit Risk. He was instrumental in the Wall Street "bail out" of hedge fund LTCM. Prior to this, Mr Dunn was Co-Head of Merrill's Equity Division, Head of European Debt and Head of Asian Debt and Equity.

Durbin	James	A British statistician and econometrician, known particularly for his work on time series analysis and serial correlation.
Engle	Robert	An American economist and the winner of the 2003 Sveriges Riksbank Prize in Economic Sciences in Memory of Alfred Nobel, sharing the award with Clive Granger, "for methods of analysing economic time series with time-varying volatility (ARCH)".
Feynman	Richard	An American theoretical physicist known for his work in the path integral formulation of quantum mechanics, the theory of quantum electrodynamics, and the physics of the superfluidity of supercooled liquid helium, as well as in particle physics. For his contributions to the development of quantum electrodynamics, Feynman, jointly with Julian Schwinger and Sin-Itiro Tomonaga, received the Nobel Prize in Physics in 1965.
Glauber	Robert	A Senior Advisor and the former CEO and Chairman of the Board at Morgan Stanley.
Grantham	Jeremy	A British investor and co-founder and chief investment strategist of Grantham Mayo van Otterloo (GMO), a Boston-based asset management firm.
Haldane	Andy	The Chief Economist and the Executive Director of Monetary Analysis and Statistics at the Bank of England.
Harvey	Andrew	A Fellow of the Econometric Society and a Fellow of the British Academy.
Hoenig	Thomas	Vice Chairman of the Federal Deposit Insurance Corporation, director since 16 April 2012.
Howard	Alan	Co-founder of Brevan Howard Asset Management LLP, and a former director of the Conservative Friends of Israel.
Hull	John	A Professor of Derivatives and Risk Management at the Rotman School of Management at the University of Toronto, a respected researcher in the academic field of quantitative finance (Hull–White model) and the author of two widely used texts on financial derivatives.
King	Mervyn	Was the Governor of the Bank of England and Chairman of its Monetary Policy Committee from 2003 to 2013.
Koenig	David	Previously Chair of the Board of Directors, Executive Director and President of the PRMIA Institute.
Köhler	Horst	A German politician of the Christian Democratic Union. He was President of Germany from 2004 to 2010. He was President of the European Bank for Reconstruction and Development from 1998 to 2000 and head of the International Monetary Fund (IMF) from 2000 to 2004.
Kritzman	Mark	Founding Partner and Chief Executive Officer of Windham Capital Management responsible for managing

		research activities and investment advisory services. Founding partner and board member of State Street Associates and faculty member at the MIT Sloan School of Management.
Layard	Richard	A British labour economist, currently working as programme director of the Centre for Economic Performance at the London School of Economics.
Ledermann	Walter	1911–2009. A German and British mathematician who worked on matrix theory, group theory, homological algebra, number theory, statistics and stochastic processes. He was elected to the Royal Society of Edinburgh in 1944.
Leibowitz	Martin	A financial researcher, business leader and a managing director of Morgan Stanley. His most well-known work (co-authored with Sidney Homer) is *Inside the Yield Book*, first published in 1972 and reissued in 2004, a work that, according to Frank Fabozzi, "transformed the markets' understanding of bonds". He was instrumental in developing the Dedicated Portfolio theory in the 1980s.
Lenstra	Hendik	A Dutch mathematician who worked principally in computational number theory and is well known as the discoverer of the elliptic curve factorisation method and a co-discoverer of the Lenstra–Lenstra–Lovász lattice basis reduction algorithm.
Mahalanobis	Prasanta Chandra	1893–1972. An Indian scientist and applied statistician, best remembered for work that produced the Mahalanobis Distance, who also conducted pioneering studies in anthropometry in India, founded the Indian Statistical Institute and contributed to the design of large-scale sample surveys.
Marks	Howard	An American investor and writer. After working in senior positions at Citibank, Marks joined TCW, an investment management company, in 1985 and created and led the High Yield, Convertible Securities and Distressed Debt groups. In 1995 he left TCW and co-founded Oaktree Capital Management.
Merton	Robert	An American economist, Nobel laureate in Economics, and professor at the MIT Sloan School of Management, known for his pioneering contributions to continuous-time finance, especially the first continuous-time option pricing model, the Black–Scholes formula.
Miskovic	Maureen	Served as Group Chief Risk Officer

		and Member of the Group Executive Board at UBS AG from January 2011 to December 2011.
Nickell	Stephen	A British economist and former Warden of Nuffield College, Oxford, noted for his work in labour economics with Richard Layard and Richard Jackman.
O'Neal	Stan	An American business executive who was formerly Chief Executive Officer and Chairman of the Board of Merrill Lynch & Co. Inc., having served in numerous senior management positions at the company prior to this appointment.
Patrick	Tom	Served as an Executive Vice Chairman of Finance and Executive Vice Chairman of Administration at BofA Merrill Lynch (Merrill Lynch & Co., Inc.) from November 2002 to July 2003. He now serves as Head of Equity for North America at Deutsche Bank AG, is a co-founder and co-owner of New Vernon Capital, LLC and serves as its Chairman and Principal.
Prince	Chuck	An American former Chairman and Chief Executive of Citigroup.
Rahn	Olev	BEc, ASIA, served as a Director of Constellation Capital Management Limited since 2003, and a founding Director of Bentley International Limited, then known as BT Global Asset Management Limited and is a Member of Advisory Board at Business Spectator Pty Ltd.
Ranieri	Lewis	A former bond trader and former Vice Chairman of Salomon Brothers, now of Ranieri Partners. He was a pioneer of securitisation and mortgage-backed securities.
Rice	Robert	Chief Executive of OCCAM Financial Technology. From 1987 to 1989 he was Managing Director of Baring Quantitative Management.
Rogoff	Ken	The Thomas D. Cabot Professor of Public Policy and Professor of Economics at Harvard University.
Roubini	Nouriel	An American economist. He teaches at New York University's Stern School of Business and is the chairman of Roubini Global Economics, an economic consultancy firm.
Rubin	Robert	American economist and banking executive who served as Secretary of the Treasury during the Clinton administration.
Shaked	Avner	A Visiting Professor at CERGE-EI since 1998. From May 2000 a member of the Executive and Supervisory Committee of CERGE-EI. State Street Distinguished Visiting Professor at CERGE-EI from Autumn 2001 to Spring 2009.

Stewart	John	Chairman of Legal & General Group since March 2010, a member of the Court of the Bank of England, a non-executive director of the Financial Reporting Council and Chairman of Guide Dogs for the Blind. Previous roles include a director of the Telstra Corporation, a member of the Australian Federal Attorney General's Business Government Advisory Group on National Security, a member of the Australian Prime Minister's Task Group on Emissions Trading, Chief Executive of Woolwich (1996–2000), deputy CEO of Barclays (2000–2003) and Chief Executive of National Australia Bank (2004–2008).
Sutton	John	The Sir John Hicks Professor of Economics at the London School of Economics.
Tarullo	Daniel	A member of the Board of Governors of the United States Federal Reserve Board since 28 January 2009, in which capacity he also serves as the Vice Chairman of the Federal Financial Institutions Examination Council. He is also a professor at the Georgetown University Law Center, specialising in international economic regulation, banking law and international law.
Tucker	Paul	A retired British economist and central banker. He was formerly the Deputy Governor of the Bank of England, with responsibility for financial stability, and served on the Bank's Monetary Policy Committee from June 2002 until October 2013 and its interim and then full Financial Policy Committee from June 2011.
Turner	Jonathan Adair	A British businessman, academic, a member of the UK's Financial Policy Committee, and was Chairman of the Financial Services Authority until its abolition in March 2013.
Weill	Sandy	An American banker, financier and philanthropist. He is a former Chief Executive and Chairman of Citigroup.
Woolley	Paul	A British economist who worked for the fund management firm GMO, retiring as Chairman of GMO Europe in 2006. He then founded the Paul Woolley Centre for the Study of Capital Market Dysfunctionality at the London School of Economics in 2007.

Further Reading

In researching this book, we came across material that readers may find as interesting and thought-provoking as we did. Here is a sample of what we consider the best, in alphabetical order by author:

- Ahamed, L., *Lords of Finance: The Bankers who Broke the World* (New York: Penguin, 2009).

    This *New York Times* Best Seller is a must-read for anyone interested in the history of financial crises. It recounts the events and circumstances leading up to the Wall Street Crash of 1929 and subsequent Great Depression. Readers may find the parallels with the Global Financial Crisis of 2007–08 to be eerie.

    He tells the story of 1929 from the perspective of the central bankers concerned: Britain, the US, France and Germany. This makes the book especially readable for non-financial readers. It also makes it a page-turner.

    Follow this link to see a 50-minute video of a talk he gave to the CFA Annual Conference on 8 May 2011: http://vimeo.com/27874662.

- Ailon, G., *The Discursive Management of Financial Risks Scandals: The Case of* Wall Street Journal *Commentaries on LTCM and Enron, Qualitative Sociology* (2012) 35: 251–270.

    This paper explores the influence on popular perceptions of financial crises and scandals of reporting in the medium of print. Citing 25 articles in the *Wall Street Journal* from 1998 to 2002 about the Long-Term Capital Management and Enron collapses, it finds a popular tendency to moralise about the outcomes, rather than any real attempt to understand the causes. In both cases, the authors find that press reports imply that the collapses could have been avoided, an argument they find to be based on dubious assumptions about what could (and by implication, should) have been known before the crises hit.

This is a valuable counter-balance to some of the populist arguments that sometimes seem to dominate debate about risk management in financial organisations.

- Blundell-Wignall, A., OECD, The Problem with Banking on the Future, Institute of Chartered Accountants, Australia, August 2013.

In this paper, Mr Blundell-Wignall puts forward some controversial observations and arguments about what can be learned from the financial crisis of 2008–09. He believes that the banking world has failed to learn the right lessons from the crisis. Regulation now coming into force, he believes, will prove to be ineffective.

For example, he observes that, contrary to prior expectations, it was not the unregulated part of the financial sector that caused problems, but the regulated sector, which begs the question of how effective regulation has been in the past.

He is unconvinced by the argument that tighter capital and liquidity controls will hinder bank lending to businesses: "The biggest banks do very little lending to real businesses anyway, and besides, Wells Fargo, a big US bank, is only 13 times leveraged yet still lending and profitable."

Readers with an appetite for lateral thinking and blunt expression will find this short paper a stimulating part of their reading on this subject.

- Brunnermeier, M. et al., The Fundamental Principles of Financial Regulation. ICMB International Centre for Monetary and Banking Studies, 2009.

In this well-argued paper, Markus Brunnermeier, Charles Goodhart, Andrew Crockett, Avinash Persaud and Hyun Song Shin elaborate on the views they share with Adrian Blundell-Wignall, that the wrong lessons are being learned from the financial crisis – the solution does not lie simply with more or tighter regulation. Rather, they believe the crisis presents a rare opportunity "to remedy fundamental market failures that have been ignored or improperly dealt with in our regulation so far".

- Cochrane, J.H., Toward a Run-Free Financial System, University of Chicago Booth School of Business, NBER, Cater Institute, April 2014.

  John Cochrane argues that the riskiness of bank assets is not the problem, but their liabilities. He argues that this is where efforts to ensure the future stability of the financial system should be directed.

- Danielsson, J. et al., Pro-cyclical Leverage and Endogenous Risk, LSE, October 2012.

  Jon Danielsson, Hyun Song Shin and Jean-Pierre Zigrand give a detailed account of how bank leverage is inherently pro-cyclical, affects economic activity and, by implication, aggravates crises when they happen.

- DiBartolomeo, D., Madoff Mayhem, Presentation to the London Quant Group, Cambridge, 2009.

  This is a modern-day version of *The Emperor's New Clothes* that H.C. Andersen would surely approve of.

  It chronicles the lead-up to the exposure of the massive fraud that bears the name of its perpetrators. Not only was the fraud easy to spot, it was both spotted and reported – repeatedly – to the Securities and Exchange Commission (SEC) as early as 10 years before Mr Madoff presented himself to the FBI.

  The SEC and others did not – or would not – believe what they were told because they were either blinded by the status and esteem in which Madoff was held in US financial markets, or they were fearful of being made to look silly, or some combination of the two.

  It reminds us how even the most thorough regulations and oversight can still fail in the face of human perception and vanity.

- Greenspan, A., Remarks to the Federal Reserve of Chicago's Forty-first Annual Conference on Bank Structure, 5 May 2005.

  Mr Greenspan observes that the combination of more complex and varied financial instruments, together with increased sophistication of risk measurement technology to complement them, has contributed greatly to the stability of the world's financial system.

But he also notes that concentrations of derivatives-related risk in non-financial organisations are generally not recorded, and cites a study that finds that the scale of such risks is small relative to that *within financial organisations*. The same study found no evidence of "hidden concentrations" of credit risk in non-banks.

Mr Greenspan sees some issues stemming from the CDO market, namely that simple credit ratings cannot reflect the risks stemming from default correlations across tranches. He also observes that many organisations' back offices are struggling to accommodate increasing volumes and complexity of financial instruments.

With respect to exposures to hedge funds, he notes: "Banks' due diligence procedures and hedge funds' disclosures have improved sufficiently that banks now can qualitatively assess the risk-management capabilities and overall risk profiles of the funds."

- Kane, E., Good Intentions and Unintended Evil, *Journal of Money, Credit and Banking* (1977) 9: 55–69.

  Edward Kane examines the history of US Federal Reserve (Fed) market interventions and its decision-making processes to argue his case that, through its role in influencing interest rates, the Fed is "a policy scapegoat for incumbent politicians", which he believes explains "the perennial incompleteness of Fed control strategies and the Fed's bureaucratic features".

- MacKenzie, D. and Spears, T., *The Formula that Killed Wall Street? The Gaussian Copula and the Material Cultures of Modelling* (University of Edinburgh, 2012).

  Picking up on the theme of financial models as black boxes, MacKenzie and Spears explore the fortunes of a particular model for pricing credit derivatives. In what unfolds, something akin to a game of Chinese whispers, they show clearly how a sensible, but computationally complex model can be misused with very unfortunate results. This happens because a computational simplification introduced for one legitimate use of the model becomes generalised for subsequent applications. Because few analysts understood the model well enough to spot the potentially corrupting effect of the early simplification, it became embedded so that the model was no longer fit for the purposes for which it is put.

- Mikes, A., From Counting Risk to Making Risk Count – Boundary Work in Risk Management, *Accounting, Organizations and Society* (2011) 36: 226–245.

Mikes investigates the behavioural aspects of risk management in seven large banks, including two detailed case studies.

She identifies two patterns of risk management. The first stresses the quantitative aspect of risk measurement and the second the importance of judgement in risk management.

The first approach relies on extensive risk measurement, and the implied assumption that if you measure enough things, all risks will be accounted for – including hard to quantify risks such as operations risk. This method reduces risk to a measure of Economic Capital, which has the advantage that it can be aggregated to the level of the organisation – and beyond. Mikes notes that the validity of the resulting risk management is heavily dependent on the veracity of the risk measurements. The risk manager's job therefore is concerned largely with ensuring that this is not open to question, which can, at the limit, encourage a "black box" view of the risk models.

The second approach demands a broad understanding of the organisation and its processes by the risk manager. It therefore suffers a number of practical limitations, not the least of which is that individuals with the necessary accumulated knowledge can be hard to find. Risk assessment based on judgement and experience are also hard to aggregate, and can be tricky even to report to senior management and external parties, such as regulators.

Mikes also shows how risk managers erect "boundaries" to their domains of responsibility. These serve two purposes: to establish their zone of influence and to limit the responsibility they bear in the case of things going wrong.

She notes the highly political nature of risk management in other aspects too: many organisations reward their staff on the basis of risk-adjusted performance, so the risk associated with their achievements has a direct bearing on how much they are paid. This provides the incentive for each individual to deflect risk from themselves rather than to seek to mitigate risk for the organisation.

- Shin, H.S., *Risk and Liquidity* (New York: Oxford University Press, 2010).

This book devotes a number of chapters to explaining some of the implications for systemic risk of widespread use of Value at Risk (VaR) as a primary measure of risk for banks and long-short hedge funds – regardless of the actual model used to estimate VaR. In clear prose that is supported by some simple maths and intuitive diagrams, he identifies at least three mechanisms whereby VaR can exacerbate systemic risk.

The first is that the combination of the test for a binary state of solvent-or-non-solvent and the tendency of VaR to ignore the possible costs of insolvency exacerbates the "agency" problem, whereby the interests of managers are at odds with those who bear the true costs of failure, which, in the case of banks, are borne by creditors and other stakeholders such as taxpayers.

The second mechanism is that risk appetite is pro-cyclical because VaR, on which it is based, is calculated as a function of the bank's capital, which is in a sense fixed. This ensures that risk appetite increases as the prices of risky assets increase, causing the bank – and other market participants – to chase return by buying more and pushing up prices. Mr Shin shows that this positive feedback loop works also in reverse: assets are sold as prices decline, which, when many participants are doing the same thing, results in a market rout. Reliance on VaR as an effective capital floor thus has a similar effect on incentives to take risk as leverage does. This pattern is redolent of Hyman Minsky's Market Instability Hypothesis. Mr Shin's contribution is to show that VaR can exaggerate the effect.

The third mechanism applies to long-short hedge funds, where VaR is often used in conjunction with variance-covariance modelling to estimate risk. Mr Shin describes how the assumption of known covariances between assets more often than not causes risk to be underestimated, because in times of market turbulence, covariances tend to be higher than in stable markets, when the covariance readings tend to be taken. This means that, in unstable markets, the fund's estimate of risk turns out to be too low, exaggerating the leverage effect of VaR and accelerating the fund's need to de-risk.

- Wall, L., Basel III and Stress Tests, www.frbatlanta.org, December 2013.

  Mr Wall observes that the effectiveness of stress tests depends entirely on their design, which is necessarily subjective and informed by the recent past. He points out that because of the subjectivity of risk measurement design, it can become hostage to the financial incentives of the individuals responsible for design and choice of parameters in risk measurement – and hence the measures actually generated.

- Wall, L., Simple Concept, Complex Regulation, www.frbatlanta.org, January 2014.

  In this blog, Mr Wall builds a strong case for addressing the causes of financial imbalances rather than simplistically attacking the symptoms by devising ever more complex regulations. He argues that, so long as there are financial incentives to circumvent regulations, large financial institutions will find legal ways to do so. Adding to the complexity and profusion of regulations merely adds scope for confusion.

Bibliography

Acker, D. and Duck, N., Reference-day Risk and the Use of Monthly Returns Data: a Warning Note. *University of Bristol, Department of Economics*, Discussion Paper No 04/557, April 2006.

Adams, M.B. and Tower, G.D., Theories of Regulation: Some Reflections on the Statutory Supervision of Insurance Companies in Anglo-American Countries, *The Geneva Papers on Risk and Insurance* (1994) 19: 156–177.

Adler, T. and Kritzman, M., Mean-variance versus Full-scale Optimisation: In and Out of Sample, *Journal of Asset Management* (2007) 7(5): 302–311.

Ahamed, L., *Lords of Finance: The Bankers who Broke the World* (New York: Penguin, 2009).

Aikman, D. et al, Taking Uncertainty Seriously – Simplicity versus Complexity in Financial Regulation. *Bank of England Financial Stability Paper* No 28, May 2014.

Ailon, G., The Discursive Management of Financial Risks Scandals: The Case of *Wall Street Journal* Commentaries on LTCM and Enron, *Qualitative Sociology* (2012) 35: 251–270.

Allen, F. and Carletti, E., New Theories to Underpin Financial Reform, Institute for New Economic Thinking, Cambridge, 8–11 April 2010.

Allen, W.A. and Meassner, R., The International Propagation of the Financial Crisis of 2008 and a Comparison with 1931, Cass Business School, London, May 2011.

Barwell, R., Taming the Wild Gyrations of Credit Flows, Debt Stocks and Asset Prices, *The Palgrave Macmillan Macroprudential Policy* (London: Palgrave Macmillan, 2013).

Basel Committee on Banking Supervision, Reducing Excessive Variability in Banks' Regulatory Capital Ratios – Report to the G20, November 2014.

Basel Committee on Banking Supervision, Guidelines – Corporate Governance Principles for Banks, Basel, 9 January 2015.

Bazot, G., *Financial Consumption and the Cost of Finance: Measuring Financial Stability in Europe (1950–2007)* (Paris School of Economics, 2014).

Blundell-Wignall, A., OECD, Chartered Accountants Presentation, Institute of Chartered Accountants, Australia, May 2013.

Blundell-Wignall, A., OECD, The Problem with Banking on the Future, Institute of Chartered Accountants, Australia, August 2013.

Boucher, C.M. et al., *Risk Models-at-Risk*, LSE Research Online, December 2013.

Breit, J., Science v Art in Risk Management, *Information Week*, 4 April 2013.

Brunnermeier, M. et al., The Fundamental Principles of Financial Regulation, International Centre for Monetary and Banking Studies, 2009.

Brunnermeier, M. et al., Model Risk of Risk Models, US Federal Reserve, July 2014.

361

Byres, W., Global Consistency in Financial Regulation – Is the Glass Half Full, Half Empty, or Just More Transparent? BIS Risk Minds and Regulation Forum, 10 September 2013.

Byres, W., Perspectives on the Global Regulatory Agenda, RMA Australia CRO Forum, Sydney, 16 September 2014.

Cochrane, J.H., Toward a Run-Free Financial System, University of Chicago Booth School of Business, NBER, Cater Institute, April 2014.

Connor, G. and O'Kelly, B., A Coasian Approach to Bank Resolution Policy in the Eurozone. LSE Financial Group Special Paper 214, 2012.

Danielsson, J. et al., Pro-cyclical Leverage and Endogenous Risk, LSE, October 2012.

Danielsson, J. et al., Does Risk Forecasting Help Macroprudential Policy Makers? Systemic Risk Centre, LSE, March 2013.

Danielsson, J. et al., *Model Risk of Risk Models*, Finance and Economics Discussion Series Divisions of Research & Statistics and Monetary Affairs Federal Reserve Board, Washington, DC, July 2014.

DiBartolomeo, D., Madoff Mayhem, London Quant Group, Cambridge, 2009.

Dodd, R., The Economic Rationale for Financial Market Regulation, Financial Policy Forum, Special Policy Report 12, Washington, 2012.

Dowd, K., Moral Hazard and the Financial Crisis, *Cato Journal* (2009) 29(1): 141–166.

Dowd, K., Math Gone Mad – Regulatory Risk Modelling by the Federal Reserve, CFA Institute, Policy Analysis Number 754, 3 September 2014.

Dudley, W.C., Opening Remarks at the Workshop on Reforming Culture and Behavior in the Financial Services Industry, Federal Reserve Bank of New York, 20 October 2014.

Dudley, W.C., Testimony on Improving Financial Institution Supervision: Examining and Addressing Regulatory Capture, Federal Reserve Bank of New York, 21 November 2014.

The Economist, Balkanisation of Banking – Putting Humpty together Again. 23 November 2013.

Financial Stability Board, Guidance on Supervisory Interaction with Financial Institutions on Risk Culture – A Framework for Assessing Risk Culture, 7 April 2014.

Gai, P. and Vause, N., Measuring Investors' Risk Appetite, *Bank of England International Journal of Central Banking* (2006) 2(1): 167–188.

Gorton, G., Slapped in the Face by the Invisible Hand: Banking and the Panic of 2007, Federal Reserve Bank of Atlanta's 2009 Financial Markets Conference: Financial Innovation and Crisis, May 2009.

Gorton, G., *Misunderstanding Financial Crises: Why We Don't See Them Coming* (Oxford: Oxford University Press, 2012).

Greenspan, A., Risk Transfer and Financial Stability, Federal Reserve Bank of Chicago Annual Conference on Bank Structure, 5 May 2005.

Greenspan, A., *The Map and the Territory* (New York: Penguin, 2013).

Grind, K., *The Lost Bank: The Story of Washington Mutual – The Biggest Bank Failure in American History* (New York: Simon & Schuster, 2012).

Haldane, A., Risk Off, Bank of England, 18 August 2011.

Haldane, A., The Dog and the Frisbee, Federal Reserve Bank of Kansas City 36th Symposium, Jackson Hole, 31 August 2012.

Hanson, S.G., Kashyap, A.K. and Stein, J.C., A Macroprudential Approach to Financial Regulation, *Journal of Economic Perspectives* (2011) 25(1): 3–28.

Herring, R.H. and Einbeis, R.A., Making Bank Capital Requirements Simpler, More Comparable and More Transparent, Shadow Financial Regulatory Committee, September 2013.

High-Level Group on Financial Supervision in the EU, The Regulatory Framework: Balancing Risk Sensitivity, Simplicity and Comparability, Basel Committee on Banking Supervision Discussion Paper, July 2013, Report, 25 February 2009.

Hoenig, T.M., Back to Basics: A Better Alternative to Basel Capital Rules, American Banker Regulatory Symposium, Washington DC, 14 September 2012.

IFI Global Research Survey, Risk Management in the AIFMD Era, May 2014.

Igan, D. and Mishra, P., Three's Company: Wall Street, Capitol Hill and K Street, IMF Centre for International Finance and Regulation, 2012.

IIF, Final Report, *Committee on Market Best Practices*, July 2008.

IIF, Implementing Robust Risk Appetite Frameworks to Strengthen Financial Institutions, June 2011.

IIF, Promoting Sound Risk Culture, IIF Issues Paper, 2013.

IIF Steering Committee on Implementation, Reform in the Financial Services Industry: Strengthening Practices for a More Stable System, Report, December 2009.

Ingves, S., Restoring Confidence in Banks, BIS Basel Committee on Banking Supervision 15th Annual Convention of the Global Association of Risk Professionals, New York, 4 March 2014.

Kane, E., Good Intentions and Unintended Evil, *Journal of Money, Credit and Banking* (1977) 9: 55–69.

Kane, E., Politics and Policymaking, *Journal of Monetary Economics* (1980) 6: 199–211.

Kaplan, R.S. and Mikes, A., The Big Idea: Managing Risks – a New Framework, *Harvard Business Review* (2012) June: 48–60.

Keynes, J.M., *The General Theory of Employment, Interest and Money* (New York: Harcourt Brace, 1936).

Kinlaw, W.B., Kritzman, M. and Turkington, D., The Divergence of High- and Low-Frequency Estimation: Causes and Consequences, QWAFAFEW, July 2014.

Kinlaw, W.B., Kritzman, M. and Turkington, D., The Divergence of High- and Low-Frequency Estimation: Causes and Consequences, *Journal of Portfolio Management* (2014) Fortieth Year Special Anniversary Issue.

Kinlaw, W.B., Kritzman, M. and Turkington, D., Liquidity and Portfolio Choice – A Unified Approach, *MIT Sloan School Working Paper 4959-12*, 2012.

Klamer, A., *Conversations with Economists* (Maryland: Rowman & Littlefield, 1988).

Knight, F.H. *Risk, Uncertainty and Profit* (New York: Mineola, 1921).

Kritzman, M., Optimal Rebalancing for Institutional Portfolios – Mean-Variance v Full-Scale Optimisation, Society of Actuaries Investment Symposium, March 2008.

Kritzman, M., *Puzzles of Finance: Six Practical Problems and Their Remarkable Solutions* (New York: John Wiley & Sons, 2000).

Kritzman, M., Risk Disparity, *MIT Sloan School Working Paper 5001-13*, 2013.

Kritzman, M. and Yanzhen, L., Skulls, Financial Turbulence and Risk Management, *Financial Analysts' Journal* (2010) 66(5): 30–41.

Kritzman, M., Yanzhen, L., Page, S. and Rigobon, R., Principal Components as a Measure of Systemic Risk, *Journal of Portfolio Management* (2011) 37(4): 112.

Krugman, P., *The Theory of Interstellar Trade* (Princeton University, July 1978).

Lambsch, A., Adaptive Stress Testing, FNA, PRMIA, November 2013.

Lawrence, M., Risk Management – Where to from Here? First Enterprise Risk Management Seminar, September 2009.

Leeming, A., *The Super Analysts – Conversations with the World's Leading Stock Market Investors and Analysts* (Singapore: John Wiley & Sons, 2000).

Levy, C., Lamarre, E. and Twining, J., Taking Control of Organizational Risk Culture, *McKinsey Working Papers on Risk*, February 2010.

Lewis, M., *Flash Boys – A Wall Street Revolt* (New York: Norton, 2014).

Lingel, A. and Sheedy, E., The Influence of Risk Governance on Risk Outcomes – International Evidence, *Macquarie University Applied Finance Centre Research Paper No 37*, 2012.

Lowenstein, R., *When Genius Failed: The Rise and Fall of Long-Term Capital Management* (New York: Random House, 2000).

Mackenzie, D., *Opening the Black Boxes of Global Finance* (University of Edinburgh, 2012).

Mackenzie, D. and Spears, T., *The Formula that Killed Wall Street? The Gaussian Copula and the Material Cultures of Modelling* (University of Edinburgh, 2012).

Marks, H., Risk Revisited, *Oaktree Capital*, 3 September 2014.

Mikes, A., From Counting Risk to Making Risk Count – Boundary Work in Risk Management, *Accounting, Organizations and Society* (2011) 36: 226–245.

Minsky, H., *Stabilizing an Unstable Economy* (New York: McGraw Hill, 1986).

Ohana, S., Financial Rogue Waves, CFA UK, November 2010.

Ormerod, P., *Why Most Things Fail: And How to Avoid It* (London: Faber and Faber, 2006).

Ormerod, P., *Positive Linking: How Networks can Revolutionise the World* (London: Faber and Faber, 2012).

Persad, N., Risk Culture and Managing It, *The Actuarial Profession*, October 2010.

Posner, R.A., Theories of Economic Regulation, *NBER Working Paper No 41*, 1974.

Power, M., *The Risk Management of Everything – Rethinking the Politics of Uncertainty* (London: Demos, 2004).

Principles for Sound Compensation Practices, Financial Stability Forum, 2 April 2009.

Resolving Globally Active, Systemically Important, Financial Institutions, Bank of England, London, 10 December 2012.

Senior Supervisors Group, Observations on Risk Management Practices during the Recent Market Turbulence, 2008.

Senior Supervisors Group, Risk Management Lessons from the Global Banking Crisis of 2008, 2009.

Shin, H.S., *Risk and Liquidity* (New York: Oxford University Press, 2010).

Snow, C.P, *The Two Cultures* (Cambridge: Cambridge University Press, 1959).

Stigler, G.J., *The Theory of Economic Regulation* (University of Chicago, 1971).

Stulz, R.M., Six Ways Companies Mismanage Risk, *Harvard Business Review* (2009) March: 86–94.

Taylor, J.B., The Financial Crisis and the Policy Responses – an Empirical Analysis of What Went Wrong, *NBER Working Paper 14631*, November 2008.

Training Workshop Report, *Enhancing Supervision of Financial Institutions' Risk Appetite Frameworks*, The Australian APEC Study Centre, Shanghai, 20–23 May 2013.

US Financial Crisis Inquiry Commission, *Press Release Official Transcript*, Washington, DC, 27 January 2010.

Wall, L., Simple Concept, Complex Regulation, www.frbatlanta.org. January 2014.

Wall, L., Basel III and Stress Tests, www.frbatlanta.org, December 2013.

Waring, A., *Corporate Risk and Governance: An End to Mismanagement, Tunnel Vision and Quackery* (Farnham: Gower, 2013).

Wei, X., Bubbles, Crises and Heterogeneous Beliefs, in J.-P. Fouque and Lang, J. (eds), *Handbook for Systemic Risk* (New York: Cambridge University Press, 2013).

White, W.R., The Prudential Regulation of Financial Institutions: Why Regulatory Responses to the Crisis Might Not Prove Sufficient. *University of Calgary, SPP Research Papers* 6(33), October 2013.

Williams-Walsh, M., Risky Moves in the Game of Life Insurance, *New York Times*, 11 April 2015.

Wolf, M., *The Shifts and the Shocks: What We've Learned – and Still Have to Learn – from the Financial Crisis* (London: Penguin, 2014).

Index